NOT JUST SCHOOLWORK

REVISED EDITION
2002 COPYRIGHT PENDING

BY AMY MAID BURKE AND NATHAN LEVY

An NL Associates, Inc. Book

N.L. Associates, Inc., Revised Edition 2004
Original Copyright © 1976 by Mandala

ISBN 1-878347-55-1
Formerly ISBN 1-878347-47-0, 0-8290-0354-1, 0-916250-15-6

Printed in the United States of America

Not Just Schoolwork in the original form has been used in classrooms all over the United States and in several foreign countries. The revision, done in collaboration with Nathan Levy and Amy Maid Burke, is meant to take out those few things that no longer apply to the twenty-first century and add some things to enrich the already superior content. We hope that future generations of learners can continue to profit from our efforts.

-Nathan Levy and Amy Maid Burke

Permissions

table of contents...

INTRODUCTION

In the fifties it was Sputnick that set the stage for America's push toward scientific excellence. The sixties and early seventies spawned the humanistic education movements. This return to the more Dewey progressive-open education was reinforced by the impact of the British primary schools. The middle and later seventies see the slogan "back to the basics" as educationally in. While all three movements are contingent upon political, economical and social attitudes none is sufficient as a sole educational thrust.

Not Just Schoolwork arose out of our needs to provide students with experiences which take into consideration basic needs, human needs, and critical thinking needs. We wanted our students to be able to create expressions that arose out of their experiences in their world. We wanted them to be critical, creative and have the skills to express themselves.

After students are in control of basic writing skills, i.e. sentence structure, paragraphing skills, and creative story writing, it is essential to provide subject matter to write about. Students constantly remark, "I want to write, but what should I write about?" That is when we realized that some relevant curriculum was needed. *Not Just Schoolwork* exists because we value creative thinking, creative writing, social and self awareness.

Not Just Schoolwork is divided into four major sections that focus on the many possibilities of creative thinking.

> I. Perceptions of the World
>
>> Perceiving through the Senses (Do you sense what I sense?)
>> Perceiving the Self (Do you feel what I feel?)
>> Perceiving Others (Do you think what I think?)
>> Perceiving Ideas (Do you see what I see?)
>
> II. Creative Story Writing
>
> III. Units
>
>> Spell and Write
>> Writing the News
>> Holidays
>> Moods
>> Science Fiction
>> Music
>
> IV. Tools of the Trade—helps for student and teacher

HOW TO USE THIS BOOK

Some teachers like to have resources available for students in centers, others organize writing instruction times. Some are informal, others formal in their approach to written expression. It doesn't seem to matter as long as the ultimate goal is to assist the student to mature along the continuum of skill building and expression.

We gave our students weekly writing assignments. The "creative writing" section lends itself to weekly activities. Sections one and three are useable for long or short term assignments. We found that if we did the assignments with our students that their motivation increased. They were interested in our opinions and values and were willing to share theirs as we did ours.

The lessons included here can either be used by teachers as a resource for additional ideas, or can be reproduced as student activity sheets. The activities are not dependent upon each other even though units do exist and can be built upon. As they covered more activities we could begin to blend their expressions with the other subjects we taught. Social Studies and English have many concepts which can be expressed in written form.

TEACHER INPUT

The teacher's role in this program is to assist the student in developing fluency in thinking and writing skills. As facilitator, s/he will provide a student with the opportunity to become open to the world and its complexities. Students will air their values, challenge their stands and make decisions after experimentation. The classroom will become a language arts—social and self awareness laboratory.

We also tried to tie together the cognitive and affective learning processes. We wanted students to differentiate between fact and opinion. We helped them develop options for problem solving. We wanted them to become involved in the process of clarifying their thinking, because they began to think more abstractly. At that point they were able to be involved in the process of thinking about thinking. When students begin to experience their thoughts they are beginning to live this process.

We stressed the mechanics of writing also. However, we tried to nurture our students so that they would not be intimidated by the writing process and perhaps give up. We proceeded slowly and carefully, first allowing the students to become comfortable with their thoughts, then guiding them to begin the technical aspects of correcting and proofreading.

We cannot stress enough that there are no right or wrong answers to our activities. When our students got to the point of believing this, their expression became freer, more fluent and more personally their own.

The final section "Tools of the Trade" is provided so that you can concentrate on skill building. The checklists help students with their verbal expression. The other activities focus on paragraphing, creative story expression and other skills necessary in written expression.

CONCLUSION

When we looked for curriculum materials to help us do what we wanted to do with our students, we found none. This was the first impetus to write this book. Having this book will not solve all your students' creative writing problems. What it will do is to give you and your students a place to start. As your students get past the self consciousness stage, you'll find them using their intuition and imagination. We encourage you in your task of facilitating your students in social and self awareness through written expression, which is **NOT JUST SCHOOLWORK.**

I. perceptions of the world...

Perceiving Through the Senses...

PERCEIVING THROUGH THE SENSES

Have you ever tried to describe some event, object, feeling, or person and found something lacking in your description? We have, and know most people have. Transferring your mental image to written form is difficult. With all your experience, think how difficult that situation would be for your students who are going to write all types of descriptions. You can well imagine that they'll need assistance.

This first section of *Not Just Schoolwork* is designed to ask students to explore and respond to the world with their senses. Each exercise acts as a catalyst to challenge the students to make comparisons, to describe and to identify contrasts. They are then asked to organize, interpret, examine and apply their personal sensory experiences to a written assignment. The exercise lead students to a world they may not have perceived before. Through class discussion and individual conferences with the teacher the students are able to share these observations. By combining these discussions with writing skills, students are growing cognitively and affectively.

Your role in these activities will be to choose appropriate exercises according to the needs of your class. We have not tried to make them developmental in any way. The activities in the beginning are more descriptive while the later ones are more extensive in drawing on the feelings of the students. As discussions and discoveries occur, you can assist the students in the refinement of your thinking. The classroom will become a language-arts sensory awareness laboratory!

The Tools of the Trade section includes the description checklist and feeling checklist. They are tools to be used by the students to give order, to describe characteristics of people, places, objects and feelings. The checklists act as road-maps which will aid the students in describing phenomena as completely as possible. The checklists can be used again and again according to the needs of your students and the assignments.

As you go through these activities: *ENJOY THEM*. There is a special quality that makes these exercises personal. You will get involved in the lives of your students as they share their excitement in being able to clearly express themselves. You will find that they enjoy hearing from you and the way you perceive with your senses.

this is like homework...

Complete <u>half</u> of the following comparisons. Say whatever comes into your mind.

Spaghetti is like...
My skin is like...
Blue ink is like...
A breeze is like...
A marshmallow is like...
Soda is like...
A tear is like...
A globe is like...
A diamond is like...
Veins are like...
Fire is like

The letter Z is like...
A violin is like...
A submarine is like...
Sneakers are like...
Fear is like...
A clock is like...
A football is like...
Rubber bands are like...
Chocolate cake is like...
A supermarket is like...
A mirror is like...

<u>Hint</u>: Compare each item to something else..."Falling leaves are like silver dollars," "Snow is like vanilla ice cream..."

Somewhere over the rainbow...

Complete <u>ten</u> of the following comparisons...the dictionary will help if you are not sure of the colors!

Chartreuse is like...   Scarlet is like...
Amber is like...   Aqua is like...
Alabaster is like...   Lavender is like...
Magenta is like...   Ochre is like...
Sienna is like...   Violet is like...
Turquoise is like...   Beige is like...

Sepia is like...

<u>Hint</u>: Compare each color to something... "Black is like King Kong in an underground cave at midnight," "Red is like a volcano blowing itself apart."

dishwasher descriptions...

Choose either #1, #2, or #3.

 Describe a fork in <u>one</u> paragraph. Use your description checklist. Use as many of the five senses as you can. Include <u>DETAILS</u>.

or

 Describe a spoon in <u>one</u> paragraph. Use your description checklist. Use as many of the five senses as you can. Include <u>DETAILS</u>.

or

 Describe a knife in <u>one</u> paragraph. Use your description checklist. Use as many of the five senses as you can. Include <u>DETAILS</u>.

<u>Hint</u>: Put the object you are describing in <u>front</u> <u>of</u> <u>you</u>. You may use comparisons to describe your object.

Food for thought...

This is a <u>two</u> paragraph assignment.

1 Describe <u>one</u> of your most <u>favorite</u> foods, in <u>detail</u>. Make it sound incredibly delicious... mouth-watering!

2 Describe <u>one</u> food you really <u>dislike</u>, in <u>detail</u>. Make it sound awful!

<u>Hint</u>: Try to have both foods in front of you while you are writing. Remember to include: sight, smell, sound, texture, and taste.

Mmm...

keep on eating...

Sometimes the best part about a meal is in the <u>contrasts</u>...
the colors of the foods, textures, the temperatures, and
the tastes - sweet, sour, salty...

1) Plan a <u>full</u> meal using contrasting foods. Example:
steaming tomato soup, rare roast beef, mashed potatoes
with melted butter, hard rolls, crisp green lettuce,
and frosty chocolate ice cream with hot fudge.

2) <u>Describe</u> a food that you consider "happy" and give
your reasons <u>WHY</u>.

3) Describe a food that you consider "depressing" and
give your reasons <u>WHY</u>.

4) Is caviar a snobbish food? <u>Is chili hot-tempered?</u>
Can foods have <u>personalities</u>? Write <u>why</u> or <u>why not</u>
and give specific examples to make your point.

know-it-all...

Choose <u>one</u> <u>simple</u> activity (like tying your shoelaces, making a peanut butter sandwich, working a yo-yo, etc.) and <u>describe</u>, in detail, <u>HOW</u> <u>TO</u> <u>DO</u> <u>IT</u>. Your instructions need to be completely accurate so anyone could repeat the activity.

Do the activity yourself - before and during your writing of the instructions - include all steps. Explain even the simplest action.

After completing this assignment give your instructions to someone. Have this person perform the activity by <u>exactly</u> following your instructions.

Did your instructions work? <u>Why</u> or <u>why</u> <u>not</u>?

color wheel...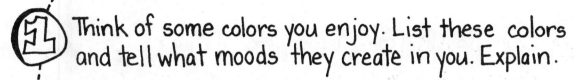

There are colors which reflect the mood of a person. Colors can make a person feel icy cold or lusciously warm. Colors can make people terribly tense, extremely sad, or gleefully happy. A smile can be captured in a gaily colored background and a frown, in a dimly colored room. Color is everywhere!

Answer these questions in <u>three</u> paragraphs:

1 Think of some colors you enjoy. List these colors and tell what moods they create in you. Explain.

2 Write about your <u>angry</u> color. Tell why you feel this way. Write about your <u>snobbish</u> color. Tell why you feel this way. Write about your <u>mysterious</u> color. Tell why you feel this way.

3 With paper and crayons <u>blend</u> some colors (your choice.) How are blended colors different from "plain" colors? Find words to describe how blended colors make you feel.

house beautiful...

Imagine your kitchen pictured in full color in a magazine. Is it the same place without the noises, smells, memories of last night's dinner, and your knowledge of what's in the refrigerator or behind the cupboard doors? In a paragraph (or more) write a description of your kitchen. Make it DETAILED. Include your five senses...sight, sound, smell, touch, and taste. Your description checklist will help you.

Hint: Don't do this from memory. Go into your kitchen, sit down, and write. The reader should have a clear picture in his or her mind of your kitchen from what you write. Rather than naming the sink, stove, and refrigerator, describe them along with the other not as common kitchen equipment or props.

12

No one ever said it was going to be easy...

Do number one _or_ number two.

(1) Describe an apple. (Be sure you have an apple in front of you before you begin.) Try to find other words for <u>red</u> or <u>round</u> in your description. Include your five senses (touch, smell, taste, sight, and sound.) The description checklist is useful here.

(2) Describe an egg. (Be sure you have an egg in front of you before you begin.) Try to find other words for <u>white</u>, <u>brown</u>, or <u>oval</u> in your description. Include your five senses (touch, smell, taste, sight, and sound.) The description checklist is useful here.

<u>Hint</u>: This will not be easy to do. You will <u>really</u> have to "look" at your object. Talk about texture, weight, etc. Describe <u>EVERYTHING</u> you see. For example, some apples are not entirely one color. You can compare the object to different things...it smells like, it looks like, etc.

describe...what?

Have you ever tasted a plan? Or touched a memory? Or seen love? In this activity you will be asked to describe something as difficult.

Choose either #1 or #2. Make your answer one or more paragraphs.

 1 Describe the <u>taste</u> of <u>water</u>.

or

2 Describe the <u>color</u> of your choice to a person who <u>cannot</u> see.

<u>Hint</u>: You will really need to examine your topic...drink a glass of water, look at something that is the color you have chosen. Make your description specific. Use adjectives. You may need to use similes and metaphors.

<u>Teacher</u>: Make lists of similes and metaphors to help your students with them.

the fort river department store...

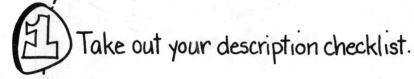

1 Take out your description checklist.

2 For your writing assignment today, you will choose <u>one</u> object, found anywhere in the school, to <u>describe</u>, IN DETAIL. Describe the <u>one item you would most like to take home with you</u>! (Maybe you've always dreamed of owning a pay telephone, an electric pencil sharpener, or a coke machine. <u>Before</u> you write - <u>think</u> about all the different things here at school.)

3 Make your description detailed. Go to where the object is and write. Now, in a shorter paragraph, explain <u>WHY</u> you would like to own this thing...what would you do with it, where would you keep it, would you let anyone else use it?

WOW!

listen ooo

What does getting up in the morning <u>SOUND</u> like?
This will be a description paper - but <u>only</u> sounds.
Make the reader hear the same sounds you do when
you get up. You can include as much time as you want,
up to the time you leave for school. Describe the
sounds IN DETAIL. In this description paper, <u>leave
out</u> all opinions. This is to be an exact record of the
SOUNDS you hear. This should be done in one or more
paragraphs. Describe as <u>many</u> sounds as you can.

it's here, somewhere...

Have you ever wondered what a star looks like close up? Do you know what the back of your eyeball feels like? Today we are going to try to find things we

can't see or touch or taste.

Now, make a list of as many things you can think of and answer these questions for _each_ thing you list:

1 If you can't see, touch, or taste this thing, how do you know it exists? (="I just know" isn't enough.)

2 When was the first time (think back) that you "discovered" this thing? What were you doing? What kind of mood were you in?

BUT WHERE IS IT ???

a puzzle to ponder...

Which takes up more space...a pickle or a pain?

Paragraph #1...discuss the amount of space a pickle takes up.

Paragraph #2...discuss the amount of space a pain takes up. (You can choose a specific pain, or talk about pain, in general.

Paragraph #3... answer the original question and defend your answer. Explain <u>why</u>. Draw some conclusions.

another puzzle...

Which weighs more...a scream or a sack of potatoes?

Paragraph #1... discuss how much a scream weighs.

Paragraph #2... discuss how much a sack of potatoes weighs.

Paragraph #3... answer the original question and defend your answer. Explain <u>why</u>. Draw some conclusions.

cold feet...

*Choose <u>one</u> kind of floor!

① Take off your shoes and socks and feel the floor with your feet. Make a list of <u>eight</u> words (or more) that describe the way the floor feels. (You can stand on carpeting, a wooden floor, linoleum, tile...there are many possibilities.) Be sure to include this list with the rest of the assignment.

② **NOW,** <u>use</u> <u>your</u> <u>list</u> <u>of</u> <u>words</u> to describe an object that can be found on Venus. Be sure to <u>name</u> your object and tell what it is used for.

<u>Hint</u>: You can close your eyes to imagine what Venus is like and what objects you'd find there.

beauty is in the eye of the beholder...

In this writing assignment you will write about the most beautiful things <u>you</u> can think of. These can be particular things, actions, feelings, or moods. Your essay will be <u>five</u> paragraphs long:

Paragraph #1... <u>define</u> beauty. What does it mean to <u>you</u>?

Paragraph #2... describe something that you think is beautiful. (IN DETAIL). Why do you think this thing is beautiful?

Paragraph #3... describe a second thing that you think is beautiful. (IN DETAIL). Why do you think this thing is beautiful?

Paragraph #4... describe a third thing that you think is beautiful. (IN DETAIL). Why do you think this thing is beautiful?

Paragraph #5... it is often said that "Beauty is in the eye of the beholder." What do <u>you</u> think this means?

<u>Hint</u>: Describe beauty by using colorful adjectives, detailed descriptions, metaphors, and similes.

Perceiving the Self...

(Do you feel what I feel ?)

PERCEIVING THE SELF

"I celebrate myself and sing myself . . . ."
—Walt Whitman

Students need an opportunity to define and explain themselves. This section was developed to allow your students that opportunity. In it they gather information from their own experience, bodies and feelings.

Each exercise provides a frame of reference to initiate thought. From that point the students must define, translate and interpret a relationship between the concepts in the assignment and themselves. The students are responsible for analyzing and evaluating their own values and opinions. The final product may be a thought provoking paragraph, thoughtfully answered questions, stimulating discussion or an autobiography.

In order for your students to reach higher thought levels it is necessary to provoke precise responses from them. We found that most students gave general answers. We had to say things like "Why" or "How come" in order to get them to be more specific. The more we pushed for preciseness the more they reached for higher levels of expression.

Part of the self is examining the choices one makes. In most of the assignments in this section students make choices or decide on points of view. Once students decide where they stand on an issue they need to be fluent in the description which demonstrates their choice. The defense of the position is important as well as the point of view.

Ultimately we are concerned that students internalize their values, have a positive sense of self and experience their sense of competence. As we saw them and listened to them share their work we become more convinced that our goals for self awareness and growth were happening to them and us.

forget it ...remember it

Spend some time thinking and making a list of the things you'd like to forget or remember.

Then describe one thing you'd most like to forget or remember. Write <u>WHY</u> you would like to forget it or remember it.

(This can be a person, a bad experience, a good experience... ANYTHING!)

i seem to be a verb...

Think about the different parts of speech: nouns, verbs, adjectives, pronouns, adverbs, prepositions, conjunctions, and interjections. Which part of speech are <u>you</u> most like...and <u>WHY</u>? First, think about what each part of speech <u>is</u> and <u>does</u>. Then, think about what <u>you</u> are like. Make some comparisons. Write your answer in a paragraph.

who, me ?

You're like many __things__. You look like things and you act like things. Pick __one__ of these things and compare yourself to it.

In one paragraph (or more) write __how__ you are like the thing you have chosen. Try to be specific: if you are comparing yourself to a car, make sure you mention what kind of car you are like...Porsche, Cadillac, Toyota, etc. If you are comparing yourself to a tree, mention the kind of tree...birch, elm, Christmas, redwood, etc.

__Ideas__: to compare yourself to...food, furniture, clothing, appliances, tools...

Self-portraits...

1 Draw a picture representing your:
id, ego, and super ego. (Three pictures, one for each.)

Things to consider: What is each one - define id, ego, and super ego. What does your id, ego, and super ego do for you?

2 Now, write several paragraphs to explain what you have drawn. Try to explain everything in your pictures.

Teacher: This assignment was done after a class discussion of id, ego, and super ego.

and, for only $49.95...

Companies are always coming out with new and improved versions of their products. Some have new flavors or new scents, or more power and zip. If you could be redesigned and repackaged, how would you be new and improved? Consider your looks and/or your personality. Write a paragraph and draw a picture of your NEW YOU.

... and who are you?

"i—i hardly know, just at present — at least i know who i was when i got up this morning, but i think i must have been changed several times since then."

— Lewis Carroll

Write a paragraph about how <u>you</u> have changed since morning - this morning or any other morning... Have someone else write a paragraph on how you have changed since this morning.

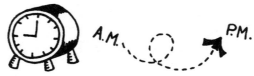

madison avenue...

BOLD, EXCITING, REFRESHING...

Advertisements are everywhere...television, radio, magazines, billboards, stores, newspapers, subways... People also advertise themselves! Look at the people around you - the way they look tells you something about them. Blue jeans, a policeman's uniform, and a suit and tie suggest a difference in what people are doing, and perhaps, in their personalities.

1) List as many ways you can think of on how you advertise yourself. <u>Why</u> have you chosen to present this information about you to other people?

2) What's hard to tell about a person from the way he or she looks?

3) Why do <u>you</u> think people form opinions about a person from the way he or she looks? Think of when you have done this. Try to form an opinion without "trying the product."

4) What do you think people hope to gain by advertising themselves in a certain way? Explain.

the 10-most wanted list...

YOU have been missing for three months. A member of the Missing Persons Bureau is looking for you. (Agent 006.) <u>Describe</u> the person Agent 006 is looking for:

Paragraph #1... Invent a reason why you are missing.

Paragraph #2... Describe your <u>physical</u> appearance in detail. (Use your description checklist.) Do you have any unusual or identifying features? If so, describe. What clothes are you most likely to be wearing? Describe.

Paragraph #3... What <u>habits</u> do you have that might help Agent 006 recognize you? Describe three or four habits.

Paragraph #4... To what places (specific <u>or</u> general) are you likely to go? Describe.

Paragraph #5... What <u>things</u> are you likely to do while you are missing? Describe.

Paragraph #6... What people (be specific) are you likely to get in touch with while you are missing? <u>Why</u> these particular people?

Remember, while you are "on the road" you will have to eat and sleep. You will be doing something, somewhere, each day. Where are you <u>most</u> <u>likely</u> to be, eat, sleep, etc?

My Way...

Inside myself I feel feelings like everyone else. When I stand in front of a mirror I look like no one else. My fingerprints are different. My face is different. I walk differently. I talk differently.

While all of us can do things that are similar - like sports, writing, hobbies, being a son or daughter, there are special things that are unique. Consider how you laugh, what you feel, the way you treat others. What's your special touch that makes you different?

① In what ways are <u>you</u> different?

② <u>Why</u> are you different in these ways?

③ When is being different a help and when is it a handicap?

take pride...

Everyone has at least <u>one</u> thing that they do well. In a paragraph broadcast to the world about your talent. Be sure to include <u>what</u> you do well, <u>how</u> you learned to do it, if you practice, and <u>why</u> you think you do it well. In your paragraph include the feelings you have about possessing this talent.

dreams or nightmares...

It has been said that... "Yesterday's dreams are a small pile of ashes."

1. What do <u>you</u> think this quotation means? Explain and analyze.

2. Explain some of your dreams that didn't work out <u>or</u> really don't mean too much anymore.

3. <u>When</u> does a dream become a nightmare? Explain.

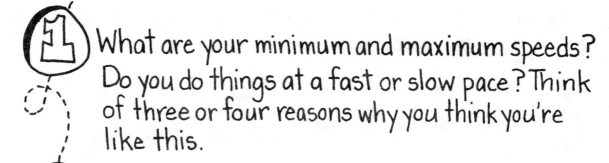

maximum speed: 55 miles per hour

1 What are your minimum and maximum speeds? Do you do things at a fast or slow pace? Think of three or four reasons why you think you're like this.

2 Write how doing things <u>fast</u> can help you <u>and</u> hurt you.

3 Write how doing things <u>slowly</u> can help <u>and</u> hurt you.

<u>Hint</u>: When writing how going fast can help or hurt you consider things like: taking risks, being responsible, being a leader or follower, being vulnerable...

day dream...

Plan **two** perfect days for yourself. Start with the time you get up until the time you go to sleep. What will you do, where will you go, will you be with anybody, what and where will you eat, will you buy anything (if so, what), will you see anything "special?" **Why** do you want to do these things? Plan each day in a separate paragraph. Don't worry about money or transportation, but be realistic in terms of what you can do in one day.

WOW! PERFECTION!!! WOW!

inside out...

Many times when you feel things getting on your nerves, you aren't reacting to those things—instead, you are reacting to something <u>inside</u> of you. Many times these reactions "inside" are worse than the situation itself.

1. Think of the words <u>you</u> <u>say</u> <u>to</u> <u>yourself</u> when you are unhappy about the way people are treating you? Why do you think you say these things?

2. What are the sentences <u>you</u> <u>hear</u> in <u>your</u> <u>head</u> when you try to overcome a difficult problem? Why do you think these sentences are there?

3. What do <u>you</u> <u>see</u> <u>yourself</u> <u>doing</u> when people around you are angry and are acting mean? Why do you think you do what you do?

4. What are the <u>thoughts</u> <u>you</u> <u>have</u> when you feel tired but have <u>not</u> yet reached your goal? Why do you think what you do?

5. What do <u>you</u> <u>say</u> <u>to</u> <u>yourself</u> when people around you are treating others unfairly? Why do you think you say these things?

Interview ten people to find out what they would like to be sure to accomplish before they die. From that list or from ideas of your own, what would _you_ like to do before you die? Think of _why_ you want to do this thing so badly. Write a paragraph explaining your choice.

Me, myself, and i...

This is a project for the week... an <u>AUTOBIOGRAPHY</u>.

Paragraph #1... <u>Birth</u> <u>Facts</u>: Time, where, date, name of hospital. Were you named after anyone - who? Why did your parents name you what they did? Include your middle name. Birth weight, height. Include any other interesting facts about your birth. What is your birth sign?

Paragraph #2... <u>Family</u> & <u>Home</u>: Describe <u>each</u> member of your family so people will know what they are like - looks, personality, occupation, age. Where do you fit - oldest, middle, youngest? Any famous relatives? What ethnic group is your family? Do you have any pets - if so, what kind, names, how long have you had them? Describe the house you live in now. Where else have you lived - other cities, other houses? How old were you when you moved? What do you remember about these places? Include anything else that is interesting about your family or your background. (Hobbies, family projects, etc.)

Me, myself, and i ...

Paragraph #3... <u>Early</u> <u>Life</u> (ages 1-6) and

Paragraph #4... <u>Later</u> <u>Life</u> (ages 7- present): Describe things you remember that happened to you in your life during these two time periods. Do this <u>in order</u> — people you met, things you did, places you went to, events both sad and happy. You can also use stories that your parents have told you, especially ages 1-6.

Paragraph #5... <u>Memorable</u> <u>Events</u>: Talk about important things that have happened to you in your life... birthdays, beginning school, getting a pet, moving- ANYTHING you consider important in your life. (Your feeling checklist will help you.) Be sure to include one of the <u>best</u> things that ever happened to you and one of the <u>worst</u> things that ever happened to you, and explain <u>WHY</u>.

Me, myself, and i ...

I LIKE...

Paragraph #6... <u>Description</u> of <u>You</u> <u>as</u> <u>You</u> <u>are</u> <u>Now</u>: What do you look like (describe in detail), what is your personality like (shy, out-going, athletic, sensitive, etc.?) What are your faults? What are your interests, hobbies, habits? Do you belong to any clubs or organizations? Have you ever won an award? How have you changed in the last year? <u>WHAT</u> <u>MAKES</u> <u>YOU</u>, <u>YOU</u>? You can include what others say about you. (One way to complete this part of your project is to have some of your friends interview you. Have a tape recorder running so you can transcribe what you say. Topics for the interview could include your views on: politics, religion, money, work, sex roles, etc.)

Paragraph #7... <u>Likes</u> <u>and</u> <u>Dislikes</u>: What are some of your favorites—color, food, T.V. show, song, book that you've read, season, etc? Who do you admire, famous and non-famous people? What is your idea of having a good time? What do you find boring? What do you dislike? Include any other likes and dislikes

Me, myself, and i...

you can think of. What are your pet peeves? What is something you get angry about?

Paragraph #8... <u>Feelings</u>: What are some things you feel strongly about? What is <u>important</u> to you? Why are these things important to you? Explain. Choose some words from the feeling checklist to help you describe feelings which are descriptions of you.

Paragraph #9... <u>Others</u>: How do you think <u>other</u> people see <u>you</u>? Describe and explain why you think people see you the way they do. What do you think people think of you?

Paragraph #10... <u>Future Plans</u>: Discuss your hopes for the future — career, education, accomplishments, possessions you hope to have, family plans, where you hope to live, what you would like to be doing, travel, etc. Include anything else you are planning for the future — dreams, wishes, ambitions...

<u>Teacher</u>: Students were told that any information they considered too sensitive to discuss could be omitted from their autobiographies. They were also encouraged to make this a multi media project.

money, the minute you want it...

What <u>two</u> things would you <u>most</u> like money for:

    to do things for other people ?

    to fulfill a dream of yours?

    to be able to go wherever you want ?

    to feel "grown-up ? "

    to buy your own food and clothing ?

why ? Be specific. Write a paragraph explaining your choices.

Save it for a rainy day...

Imagine that you are going to pack <u>three</u> of your possessions away in a trunk that you will <u>not</u> open for fifty years...

What three things will you put away and <u>WHY</u>?

Consider what you will want to see from your childhood things. Also, think about <u>why</u> people save things...memories, because they will become valuable with time, etc. The items you choose must be in your possession <u>now</u>.

Write three paragraphs. In each one, <u>name</u> the item you will save, <u>describe</u> it, and give your reasons <u>why</u> it is important to you to save it.

...**50** years pass...

So Longooo

If you were forced to leave your home and pack all your possessions in only <u>one</u> suitcase (medium size), <u>what</u> things would you take along, and <u>why</u> would you take them? These must be things you can pack in a suitcase. Think about things that really mean a lot to you, things that you wouldn't want to lose. Make your answer a paragraph long.

I'D TAKE MY...

i'd rather be...

Which would you rather be...

an only child ?

the youngest child ?

the oldest child ?

why ?

Write a paragraph explaining your choice.

MINE ooo What do you mean when you say that an object "belongs to you..?" There are obvious answers such as: "I paid for it," "Someone gave it to me," or "I have a piece of paper that says it's mine." Try to think of others.

What is the RELATIONSHIP between you and the thing? What does it mean to you, and what do you mean to it?

A thing might be valued because it performs a useful service, like a warm coat, or a pair of ice skates. It might have value because it is a symbol of success, like a trophy, or a diploma. Or it might have value because of the memories it represents, like a childhood toy, or a photograph.

1 Choose one of your most valued possessions (make it an object.) Write a paragraph, or more, about how much this possession means to you. Describe the object. Explain how you acquired it. Why is it so valuable to you?

2 Now, write another paragraph which expresses the opposite feeling. Pretend that you dislike this possession (the same object you wrote about in the first paragraph) and try to be convincing, so it seems you really don't like it. Do not make up things about the object that are not true. Find things which would make you feel opposite toward the object.

Luck or Skill ...

Some things in life happen because of <u>luck</u>, and other things happen because of <u>skill</u>.

 **Write** a paragraph about something that has happened to you because of some <u>skill</u> you possess. This can be something you got to do, something you are able to do, or something that happened to you... but only because of some special talent or skill that you have.

 **Write** a paragraph about something that has happened to you, something you got to do, or something you are able to do because you are <u>lucky</u>. Remember, this example must be due to luck, only.

 Life is made up of skill and luck. Try to explain the different importance of each. Point out how both can be used to your advantage. Make several lists of times when luck and skill works.

back when...

Look around the room at different people or things until you see something that reminds you of something from your past — a place, person, an object, or event. Write that memory. That memory can now help you think of other things. Once you get started, keep going. Don't worry about the order of things. Let your thoughts flow through your head. It may help to close your eyes when you do this.
Now answer these questions:

 1) What is a memory? Explain.

 2) How do your memories make you feel? Discuss.

 3) Why do you think that you remember only certain things and forget other things?

 4) What does it mean to "live on memories alone?"

 5) Find five or six reasons why memories are good things.

do you believe...

I THINK... ? ?

1. List about five things you believe in strongly. Explain your feelings about these things. Did you consider things like family, religion, and money?

2. What are some issues on which you have <u>not</u> yet formed a definite opinion? Tell why you haven't made your mind up and the pro's and con's of the issue. Consider things like drugs, life and friendship.

3. Have you ever made a choice that surprised everyone? What was it and <u>why</u>? If not, why do you think your decisions are so predictable?

GEE, I DON'T KNOW...

a pot of gold...?

It is said that at the end of every rainbow there is a pot of gold which will bring the person who finds it good luck and wealth. You now have your own personal rainbow...

1. What is at the end of it? (Think in terms of your GOALS and AMBITIONS.)

2. How will you get to it? (How will you reach your goals, what will you have to do?)

3. What obstacles might you encounter along the way?

4. What are some things you might have to do without, or sacrifice, because of your rainbow?

5. Will anyone else benefit from your "pot of gold?" Why or why not?

6. Why is your "pot of gold" so important to you?

This essay is a look at the goals you have set for yourself. They can change. You may use short-term goals (one or two days away), or long-term goals set far in the future.

Write one paragraph for each question.

growing up...

Time Flies...

What is the difference between <u>you</u> and <u>adulthood</u>?
Do this assignment in <u>two</u> paragraphs — one paragraph explaining the differences, and one paragraph stating your conclusions about the differences.

WELL, I'M...

yes and no...

Try to list the times you say "yes" and the times you say "no". Do you find anything in common in your lists.

How would your life be different (or would it be) if you said "no" instead of "yes" much more often? Answer this question in a paragraph. Be sure to use specific examples, and talk about the consequences of this action — saying "no" to most things.

NO!

YES!

the cold shoulder...

"People always turned their backs on me. Nobody ever bothered to speak to me kindly. While groups of people would play together, I would always play alone or stand in a corner, watching them. It wasn't that I was afraid of them, I just didn't know what to say.

As I grew older, being alone became a bigger problem. I had no one to go to baseball games with. Every time I went to the movies, I went alone. It's a lonely feeling when you live like that.

I figured out that I couldn't live that way. So I went out and tried to meet people. I found out that I could talk to someone if I tried to be honest. I decided that I wasted too much time being alone. If I had made an effort to reach people, they would have reached out and greeted me..."

1) What do **you** think was this person's problem? Explain.

2) How would **you** handle this problem? Explain.

3) Think of times you have a problem speaking to people. Do any of those times have anything in common?

4) When do **you** turn your back on people? Describe what **honesty** has to do with communicating with people.

to have or not to have...

These are qualities that a person may have. Number the list below (1-15) in order of their importance to you.

popularity   uniqueness

sophistication   athletic ability

sensitivity   sense of humor

being trusted   pride

honesty   intelligence

helpfulness   being brave

creativity   talent

level-headed

Now, write a paragraph on why your #1 choice is the most important to you, __and__ write a paragraph on why your #15 choice is last on your list. Take some time to compare your choices and reasons with each other.

<u>Teacher</u>: Process this lesson by asking your students to fill in the blanks:

I learned...   I wish...   I hope...

I was surprised...   I want...

55

who do you trust?

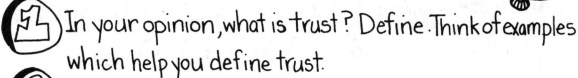

1. In your opinion, what is trust? Define. Think of examples which help you define trust.

2. Why do _you_ trust someone? Explain. Think of the characteristics of people you trust.

3. Who do you trust? Make a list. (Family, friends, teachers, etc.)

4. People are either born with distrust or they learn it. Which do you think happens? Do you have anything to prove your answer?

5. In your opinion, how important is it to be able to trust someone? Explain.

6. How long does it take you to know if you can trust someone or not - 20 minutes, 2 hours, 2 days - which one is most like you?

7. What are the things about you that convince others you can be trusted?

8. In your opinion, at what stage in a person's life does trust develop?

PROTECT YOURSELF...

During the course of a day, you sometimes find yourself in situations where you can be hurt physically - many times those type of accidents can be avoided. But how do you protect yourself from the __personal__ hurts you feel inside - hurt feelings, hurting others, feeling impatient, left-out, etc? Answer these questions in several paragraphs.

TO PROTECT YOURSELF FROM PERSONAL HURTS:

 How do you act? Explain.

 What do you say to yourself? Explain.

 What do you do about the situation? Explain.

 How is the future different because of your actions?

57

Calling outer space...

If life does exist on another planet or in space, I wonder why they haven't bothered to make contact with humans. I have a couple of good reasons why they might <u>never</u> try to reach us. People of different nations go to war. Different races and religions don't agree about their rights. Some people don't get along. Given a choice, would you want to make contact?

In a paragraph (or more) explain why you think we haven't heard from anyone on another planet <u>and</u> why you think people on earth act the way they do.

HELLO?

happy birthday...

Which would <u>you</u> rather have your friend give you for your birthday...

... a gift your friend picks out?

... money to buy yourself something?

... a gift that your friend makes for you?

... nothing but good wishes?

In a paragraph, explain your choice. Now, rank order the four items. Which would you choose second, third, and fourth? Share your list with another person. How are your choices similar or different?

alone in a crowd...

"Friends are really strange – well, at least mine are! We do the regular things, tell secrets, play together, and fight for each other. The problem is that my friends expect me to do all the things that they do. They say, 'If you are our friend, you'll do such and such.' How do I make them understand that there are things I just <u>WON'T</u> do?"

1) Why do <u>you</u> think this problem sometimes occurs? Explain.

2) What would <u>your</u> solution to this problem be? Explain.

3) What do you think "being alone in a crowd" means? Discuss. Do you agree this can happen? Why or why not?

me and you and a dog named blue...

Imagine that you are shipwrecked on a deserted island. You may pick any <u>three</u> people (or animals) that you would like with you on the island. Write a paragraph for each person or animal that you picked. Include: who, why, what you expect from them, what you can provide for them.

The people you choose may be friends, acquaintances, famous people, etc.

Friendship...

1. What two qualities do you <u>most</u> want in a friend?

2. Name <u>three</u> ways in which a present friendship of yours would be better, if only the other person would...

3. What did <u>you</u> do and/or say to yourself the last time a friend disappointed you? <u>Why</u> did you react that way?

4. Which do you think is harder for you - to <u>make</u> a friend or <u>keep</u> a friend? Why?

Answer each question in a paragraph.

Thank you, mr. edison...

"I'm always trying to do something outstanding. Every time that I do something I find out that it has already been done."

Write a paragraph that explains something <u>new</u> you could do. Explain this activity in detail. Now answer these questions:

1. Describe the importance of doing something that has <u>never</u> been done before.

2. How can <u>you</u> benefit from doing things that have been done before?

3. Describe the creative person. Then describe yourself. See how your two descriptions are similar.

4. People who are extremely creative and inventive are sometimes <u>not</u> recognized, and are even persecuted by the society in which they live. They are often labeled "quacks". Their genius is not recognized until many years later – many times after the person has died. What would <u>you</u> do if you did something truely brilliant and no one would listen to you? What would be the things that would keep you at work in spite of public ridicule? What would make you want to quit and conform to society?

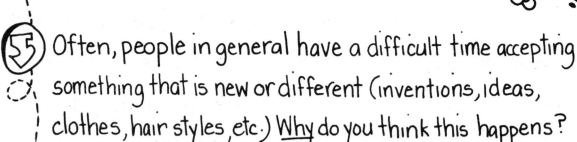

thank you, mr. edison...?

5) Often, people in general have a difficult time accepting something that is new or different (inventions, ideas, clothes, hair styles, etc.) <u>Why</u> do you think this happens?

6) What is the last "different" thing you wanted to do that you were <u>serious</u> about, and you met with disapproval from your parents, teachers, friends or anyone else? <u>Why</u> do you think this happened?

Perceiving Others...

(Do you think what I think?)

PERCEIVING OTHERS

Students are affected by peers, teachers, custodial and transportation staff. They reshape their views of life as others surround them. This section focuses students on the people around them. It is designed for them to interpret, analyze and evaluate the way they view relationships. It is a look at human interaction and the people process.

When our students began to think of others they realized that their lives were filled with information about others. Personal relationships, trust and peer pressure were some of the things which arose. We've used these concepts in our activities. These topics stimulated discussion of the actual events in their lives.

One student who was promoted to Junior High returned to explain that although she had not taken the assignments seriously, she could now see how they applied to her life. We talked about changes in her social environment and how those changes really affect the way she felt about those around her.

The students developed their own Hall of Fame. They were gracious with their honors. They named mothers, fathers, friends, relatives and a variety of others, whom they perceived as famous. Their reason for choosing particular people was quite clear. They identified people who made some significant contribution in their lives.

film...

"I am a camera. You are a camera. Perhaps I am in your movie. Perhaps you are in mine. Perhaps a film festival is in order. We could all share our scenes..."

Develop _your_ film. Who do you share your scenes with and _how_ do you share them? Answer this questions in several paragraphs.

---

president for a day...

If _you_ were the President of the United States, which would you spend the _most_ money on... and why?

... the Space Program   ...the National Defense Program
... the Poverty Program   ...Reconstruction of Inner Cities
... Foreign Aid   ... Educational Reform

Which would you spend the _least_ on? why?

pro or con...

With another person take <u>one</u> side of argument.
Persuade your audience that:

1. Girls should (or should not) be allowed to play Little League Baseball.
   <u>or</u>
2. All students should (or should not) be allowed to use calculators while doing math.

Choose #1 or #2. Decide if you are for (pro) or against (con) the statement. Have good, solid reasons to back up your point of view. "Because" is inadequate. Think of <u>all</u> the reasons you can. (This may be easier to do if you pretend you are having an argument with someone.) You will both have a chance to present your point of view.

68

fame...

Who would you place in your _own_ personal Hall of Fame? Think of _five_ people (famous _and_ non-famous) to induct into your Hall of Fame. Explain _why_ these people deserve to be recognized (what they have done.) Try not to pick more than one person from the same occupation. This is a five-paragraph assignment.

---

you and me...

"There is no one who knows everything; there is no one who knows nothing."

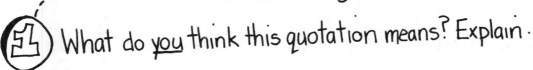

1. What do _you_ think this quotation means? Explain.

2. Do you agree with it? Why or why not?

3. What is something _you_ would like to learn from someone else?

4. What is something _you_ would like to teach?

tea for two...

Choose <u>seven</u> <u>famous</u> people with whom you would like to have dinner. Start with Sunday and write <u>one</u> paragraph for <u>each</u> day of the week... write <u>who</u> you would like to have to dinner and <u>why</u> <u>you</u> <u>would</u> <u>like</u> <u>to</u> <u>have</u> <u>dinner</u> <u>with</u> <u>that</u> <u>person</u>. Write why you think that person is interesting. What do you expect to learn <u>about</u> that person? What do you want to learn <u>from</u> that person? What will that person learn from <u>you</u>? What will you talk about?

Try <u>not</u> to choose people in the same occupation. Be sure to include where you would eat and what you would order.

the choice of a lifetime...

If it was possible to choose <u>one</u> thing for <u>all</u> the people living in this country, would you choose to:

1 - make <u>all</u> the people <u>rich</u> (millionaires)?

2 - make <u>all</u> the people <u>honest</u>?

3 - make <u>all</u> the people <u>healthy</u>?

4 - make <u>all</u> the people <u>young</u>?

Answer this question and write <u>why</u> you feel the way you do. Do this assignment in several paragraphs.

do unto others...

"There is a destiny that makes us brothers...none goes his way alone. All that we send into the lives of others...comes back into our own."   —E. Markham

1) Describe what this quote means to you.

2) With what do you agree or disagree? Write a paragraph discussing your feelings and ideas about this statement. The feeling checklist will help you.

---

heavy...

"I do my thing, and you do your thing.
I am not in this world to live up to your expectations.
And you are not in this world to live up to mine.
You are you and I am I.
And if by chance we find each other, it's beautiful.
If not, it can't be helped."
                    —Frederick Perls

1) What is Frederick Perls saying to you in this quote. Explain in a paragraph.

2) React to the meaning of the last line. Check the feeling checklist to express your feelings fully.

72

the grass is always greener...

"...i cried because i had no shoes until i met a man who had no feet..."

Your writing assignment is to analyze this statement.

A Guideline

Paragraph #1... What do you think this proverb means?

Paragraph #2... Why do you think people are sometimes dissatisfied with themselves, their lives, and what they have?

Paragraph #3... Does this proverb have any meaning in your life? Give some examples of how it does or doesn't.

Paragraph #4... Is being dissatisfied the same as being selfish? Is it the same as being greedy? What words would you use in place of "dissatisfied?"

Paragraph #5... How does a person choose between what they really need and what they want? What kinds of things do you really need, and what things do you just think you need, but could live without? Be specific.

Paragraph #6... What is the general attitude or message this proverb communicates? How does it make you feel?

Perceiving Ideas...

(Do you see what I see?)

PERCEIVING IDEAS

All that exists in the world is identified through ideas. The tree that stands outside your home, the quiet person in a noisy crowd, the picking of proper clothes, all deal with perceiving ideas we have about them. The exercises in this section ask the students to examine, react, analyze and evaluate the many ideas of the world. Some of the exercises focus on areas such as: origins of particular assumptions, capital punishment and the inevitability of change. The objective of this section is to have the students open up to the world's ideas.

This section led to many discussions and much thoughtful writing. Our students' conversations were self-examining, and thorough in that they encompassed identification and evaluation of the issues. The writing levels were expanded because the subject matter forced the students to use examples or give proof of why certain ideas exist as they do.

The exercises, like the previous ones, allow the students opportunities to shape and reshape different ideas. The quotations in this section were included to guide the student to some basic concepts that are a part of our world. Through the use of the quotations, poems, and general statements, we hope you look beyond the assignments to the values the students must exhibit through their answers.

think about it...

1. What is an idea? Explain.

2. What makes people have <u>different</u> ideas?

3. How do people get <u>NEW</u> ideas?

4. How do <u>you</u> get an idea?

5. When and where do <u>you</u> get ideas? (Most often.)

6. What kind of <u>mood</u> do you have to be in to get an idea?

7. Write one idea that <u>you</u> have had (about anything.)

8. Some people think that there is nothing new in the world - everything has already been done and invented. React.

Write some ideas about:

soundproof...

If a tree falls in a forest and there is <u>no one</u> there, does the tree make a sound? <u>THINK</u> - try to reason this out.

Answer the question and explain <u>why</u> you came to your decision.

a story without words...

Several years ago there was a well-known advertisement for a camera company which featured the slogan: "One picture is worth a thousand words."

1 What do you think this slogan means?

2 Do you think pictures or words tell a story better? Find some pictures which tell stories. Write the story.

3 If words tell stories better, <u>why</u> do <u>you</u> people paint or take photographs? What are the benefits of doing something <u>visually</u>? What are the disadvantages?

4 If pictures tell stories better, <u>why</u> do <u>you</u> think people write books, poetry, drama? What are the advantages of doing something in <u>printed</u> form? What are the disadvantages?

Answer <u>each</u> question in a paragraph.

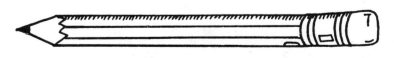

why ?

Write <u>one</u> question beginning with the word "<u>WHY</u>" and then answer it in <u>one</u> paragraph or more.

<u>Ideas</u>: Why is the sky blue?

Why do people hurt each other?

Why is Hank Aaron such a good home-run hitter?

Why does McDonalds make so much money?

etc.

* Be sure to write the question you are answering!

<u>Teacher</u>: This assignment can be expanded to include:

Write one question beginning with the word "<u>WHO</u>."
Write one question beginning with the word "<u>HOW</u>."
Write one question beginning with the word "<u>WHAT</u>."
Write one question beginning with the word "<u>WHERE</u>."
Write one question beginning with the word "<u>WHEN</u>."

the payment: pro or con...

Adults get paid for the work they do. So it seems only fair that kids should get paid for the work they do – going to school!

1. First, argue <u>for</u> this statement. Give <u>all</u> your reasons why kids should be paid for the work they do in school. Be convincing!

2. Now, take the <u>opposite</u> point of view and argue <u>against</u> this statement. Give <u>all</u> your reasons why kids should <u>not</u> be paid for the work they do in school. Again, be convincing.

Answer these questions fully with examples.

---

junk...

1. Make a list of <u>ten</u> or more things that <u>you</u> think are junk.

2. Where do you find junk?

3. Some people collect junk. Write a paragraph or more about a piece of junk you have collected and can't bear to get rid of.

4. "The mind is really a junkyard." What do <u>you</u> think that means? Do you agree with it? Why or why not?

JUNK?

do you see what i see ?

1 Do you think you see the world differently than your parents, or your teachers, or your friends? Explain.

2 Pick <u>one</u> thing or idea that you think you look at differently than other people. In your <u>first</u> paragraph, write about how <u>you</u> look at the thing or idea you picked. Now, try to put yourself in someone else's place...one of your teachers, parents, or friends, and write a <u>second</u> paragraph about how you think that person sees the <u>same</u> <u>thing</u> you do.

<u>Ideas</u> <u>you</u> <u>might</u> <u>want</u> <u>to</u> <u>consider</u>: a T.V. show, honesty, politics, a book, spending money, the time you go to sleep, eating a certain food...

3 Add a paragraph which describes your feelings about these differences. Your feeling checklist will help you.

life...

"Too much sanity may be madness and the maddest of all, is to see life as it is and not as it should be."

-Man of La Mancha

Do you agree with this statement... that it is <u>better</u> to have dreams of what <u>could</u> be, than to see life as it really <u>is</u> today? Answer this question and write why or why not. Do this in a paragraph.

Make a list of feelings this quote causes in you. Pick some of these feelings to be described in a paragraph.

---

an impossible assignment...

Write several paragraphs about an impossible relationship that you would like to have happen. For example: you and Robert Redford, snow on a 95° day, the Boston Red Sox winning the Super Bowl.

In your paragraphs answer these questions:

1- <u>What</u> is the impossible relationship?

2- <u>Why</u> would you like the relationship to happen?

3- <u>Why</u> will this relationship <u>NEVER</u> take place?

THIS is iMPOSSIBLE!

One Person's Treasure is another person's junk...

Think of something you own that you value highly and that someone else might consider "junk." <u>Or</u>, think about something that someone else owns that they think is valuable and that you consider "junk." <u>Name</u> <u>the</u> <u>object</u> and write:

Paragraph #1... <u>Why</u> do you think of the object the way in which you do? In other words, why do you consider it either valuable or junk?

Paragraph #2... <u>Why</u> do you think that the other person (be specific, <u>name</u> a person) considers the object valuable or junk?

a fish story...

"If you <u>give</u> me a fish, I will eat tonight. If you <u>teach</u> me how to fish, I will eat for a lifetime." - CHINESE PROVERB

1. What do <u>you</u> think this quotation means? Explain.
2. How does it apply to you?
3. What is operating in this quote - id, ego, or super ego? Why? Defend your point.

<u>Teacher</u>: This lesson was done after a discussion of id, ego, and super ego.

---

the winning answer...

1. How do you feel about a person who <u>always</u> plays to win? Why do you feel this way?
2. When, if ever, is winning <u>NOT</u> important?
3. Why do <u>you</u> think people want to win? How do <u>you</u> deal with winning and losing - what do you say, what do you do?
4. Is losing ever good? Why or why not?

Answer all these questions - a paragraph for each. Use examples.

Social Climbing...

"Some people reach the top of the ladder only to find that it is leaning against the wrong wall."

1. What do you think this quotation means?

2. What do you think it means to "reach the top of the ladder?"

3. Why do you think there is so much importance in this country placed on achievement, social climbing, getting up the ladder of success, and "keeping up with the Joneses?"

4. How are "getting ahead" and "achievement" important? If you think success is important, explain why. If you think it is unimportant, explain why.

5. Is success always a good thing? Why or why not?

6. Why do you think "failure" is considered a bad thing? Is it bad? Why or why not?

7. How do you handle failure? What do you do, say to yourself, how do you act?

in the beginning...

Imagine that when a baby is born s/he is able to understand whatever you say. In several paragraphs, write what you feel the baby should know about dealing with life. In other words, give your <u>best</u> advice to an infant on how to survive in <u>this</u> <u>world</u>.

Consider sharing things like: how to make money, how to get along with others, how to be part of a family, how to get what you want, how to be happy...

wandering...

"If sometimes you don't get lost, there's a chance you may <u>never</u> find your way."

1° In your opinion, what do you think the quote means?

2° Do you agree with this quote? Why or why not?

Answer each question in a paragraph.

Our world and welcome to it...

"It was the best of times, it was the worst of times,
It was the age of wisdom, it was the age of foolishness,
It was the epoch of belief, it was the epoch of incredulity,
It was the season of Light, it was the season of Darkness,
It was the spring of hope, it was the winter of despair,
We had everything before us, we had nothing before us,
We were all going direct to Heaven, we were all going direct the other way —
In short, it was like the world we live in."   -Charles Dickens

Choose __three__ of the above "opposite-type" statements and think about them in terms of our world __today__. In __six__ paragraphs, using SPECIFIC EXAMPLES, show how the statement you have chosen holds true for __today's__ world.

__Example__: If you pick "It was the age of wisdom, it was the age of foolishness," write a paragraph to discuss how __this__ is an age of wisdom (in your opinion), and give __examples__ to prove your point. In a second paragraph, show how this is __also__ an age of foolishness. Again, give __examples__.

listen...

WHAT?

1 Have you ever heard someone say, "Almost doesn't count." What do you think, does it or doesn't it? Why or why not? If "almost" counts, when does it count? If "almost" doesn't count, when doesn't it count? Give specific examples for both.

and

2 "Somewhere, a book once said, all the talk ever talked, all the songs ever sung, still lived and had vibrated way out in space and if you could travel far enough you could hear George Washington talking in his sleep or Caesar surprised at the knife in his back. So much for sounds. What about light then? All things once seen, they didn't just die, that couldn't be. It must be then that somewhere you might find all the colors and sights of the world in any one year."   - Ray Bradbury

Can you put this quote into your own words? Do you agree? Why or why not? What sounds and sights are you glad are immortal? What sounds and sights would you rather have forgotten?

and

3 "Too many people don't know what they think until they hear someone else say it."

What does this quote mean? Do you agree with it? Why or why not? Does this ever happen to you? Why and when does this happen?

88

Visions...

An essay is a short, personal literary composition dealing with a single subject. Analyze the statements below and then follow this format for your essays.

Paragraph #1...Tell what the statement means. How does the meaning apply to <u>you</u>? Use specific examples.

Paragraph #2...Do you think the statement is true? In your opinion, is it an important statement? Answer both questions and tell why or why not.

You are to do this <u>twice</u>, once for each statement.

1. "It's better to have loved and lost, than to have hated and won."

2. "Some people see things that are, and ask why. Other people see things that are, and ask why <u>not</u>."

to teach or not to teach...

"The object of teaching a child is to enable him to get along without a teacher."

1. What do _you_ think this quotation means?
2. Do you agree with it? Why or why not?
3. What does education mean to _you_?
4. Does independence have anything to do with education? Why or why not?
5. What do _you_ think "teaching" means?

---

if...

if coke is the real thing and lifesavers are a part of living, do you deserve a break today?

In several paragraphs answer this question yes or no, and write _WHY_. Before you write this assignment plug in your imagination. Then respond.

baseballs, hot dogs, apple pies & chevrolets...

A spaceman just landed in your town and knocks on your door...

Paragraph #1... What ten things that best represent American life would you show the spaceman, and <u>WHY</u>? Make them things you have in your house <u>now</u>.

Paragraph #2... What five foods would you serve the spaceman, and <u>WHY</u>? Try to choose foods that are representative of what Americans eat.

Paragraph #3... What two places would you take the spaceman to visit in <u>your</u> town, and <u>WHY</u>? Try to pick places that are in some way representative of America.

ANYWHERE U.S.A.

music and art...

CREATING...

For your assignment this week you will write on all <u>four</u> quotations in either the music section <u>or</u> the art section. You may <u>not</u> do some from both categories. Choose one or the other. You will write <u>one</u> paragraph for <u>each</u> quotation. Answer the following questions for each quotation: What does the quote mean? Do you agree with it? Why or why not? Be as specific as you can, use "real-life" examples to prove your point...paintings or artists you know about, songs or musicians you know about. <u>Everyone</u> will write about the quotation on creativity - what it means, do you agree or disagree with it, and why? Use examples from your <u>personal</u> <u>experience</u>.

MUSIC:

1- "Music is essentially useless, as life is." -GEORGE SANTAYANA

2- "Music is a way to give form to our inner feelings without attaching them to events or objects in the world." -GEORGE SANTAYANA

3- "Music was invented to confirm human lonliness." -LAWRENCE DURRELL

4- "A nation creates music-the composer only arranges it."
-MIKHAIL GLINKA

music and art...

art:

1- "Every artist paints his own autobiography." — HAVELOCK ELLIS

2- "Art is meant to disturb." — GEORGES BRAQUE

3- "Art, like life, should be free, since both are experimental." — G. SANTAYANA

4- "Art does not <u>reproduce</u> the visible, rather, it <u>makes</u> visible." — PAUL KLEE

creativity:

1- "In creating, the only hard thing is to begin; a grass blade is no easier to make than an oak tree." — JAMES RUSSELL LOWELL

an eye for an eye...?

Answer these questions:

1 What is justice? Write your <u>own</u> definition. You may look up "justice" in the dictionary, but put the definition into <u>your</u> <u>own</u> <u>words</u>.

2 It is often said, "There is no justice in this world." If you agree with this statement, write <u>WHY</u> and give at least <u>two</u> specific examples to prove your point. If you disagree with this statement, write <u>WHY</u> and give at least <u>two</u> specific examples to prove your point.

3 Write one or two laws that <u>you</u> think should be written to protect kids. Write <u>why</u> you think there is a need for the law.

---

changes...
"things do not change, we do." —THOREAU

Paragraph #1... Discuss how <u>things</u> do or do not change. Use specific examples.

Paragraph #2... Discuss how <u>people</u> do or do not change. Use specific examples.

Paragraph #3... Draw some conclusions - do you agree with this statement? Why or why not?

missed... ooo

"Some things you miss forever... some things you don't miss at all."

1 Discuss something you will miss forever. Tell what it is and what it means to you. Why will you miss it.

2 Discuss something you <u>don't</u> miss. Tell what it is and why you don't miss it.

3 Discuss something you are <u>surprised</u> you miss. Tell what it is and why you are surprised you miss it.

don't assume anything...

These are some common assumptions in our culture. They might be true or they might be false. You must decide what is true or false for you. Be careful - you really need to think about each one and its IMPLICATIONS - what it suggests for people and their lives.

For each number decide whether you think it is TRUE or FALSE. Explain your answer. Back up your reasons with specific facts or examples. How do you know what you know and what makes you know if it is true or false? Also, where do you think the assumption comes from, or how do you think it got started?

1- People need cars.

2- People need to eat three meals a day.

3- People who go to college are smarter than people who don't.

4- Adults know more than children.

5- The most important thing a person can be is popular.

6- Men aren't good cooks.

7- Women take care of children better than men do.

8- Boys are better at sports than girls are.

9- Teachers know everything.

10- Pink is a girl's color.

don't assume anything...

11- The older a person gets the more responsible he or she gets.

12- The United States is a democratic country.

13- It's cheaper to eat at McDonalds than it is to eat at home.

14- Everything's better with Blue Bonnet on it.

15- Handicapped people are unhappy.

16- You can tell what a person is like by the way he or she looks.

17- At age eighteen you become an adult.

18- Grey hair is a sign of old age.

19- Coke is the real thing.

20- George Washington was our first president.

FACTOR FICTION?

II. creative writing...

to begin with...?

For your writing assignment this week you will write _two_ separate paragraphs.

1) My <u>Block</u> (a description of the street you live on and how you feel about it.)

2) <u>If</u> <u>I</u> Had <u>One</u> <u>Million</u> <u>Dollars</u> (what would you do with it, exactly?)

---

two more...

For your writing assignment this week you will write _two_ separate paragraphs.

1) <u>The</u> <u>Best</u> <u>Meal</u> <u>I</u> Ever Had (describe it, where did you eat it, who served it to you?)

2) <u>If</u> <u>I</u> Could <u>Be</u> Any <u>Age</u> (what age would you be and why?)

YUMMY   I'd be...

absence makes the heart grow fonder...

You have just been absent from school for three weeks...write an imaginary note with an imaginary excuse for your imaginary absence. Write it like a letter – make it at least a paragraph long.

---

paint...

If you could paint your town or city **any** color, what color would you paint it and **why**? Answer this question in a paragraph or more. Imagine how...

Strange...

Imagine that you found this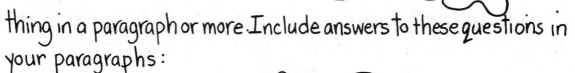

in your room. Write about this

thing in a paragraph or more. Include answers to these questions in your paragraphs:

1 = What is it?

2 = What can it do?

3 = What color is it?

4 = What is it made of?

5 = Where can you find another one like it?

6 = How did it end up in your room?

7 = Why is it in your room?

8 = How does it make you feel?

9 = What are you going to do with it?

10 = How much do you think it is worth?

Hint: Let your imagination run wild. The out of the ordinary is fun to read.

directions...

Write <u>ten</u> sentences that begin with the words :

above me...

or

Write <u>ten</u> sentences that begin with the words:

below me...

or

Write <u>ten</u> sentences that begin with the words:

600 miles to the west of me...

or

Write <u>ten</u> sentences that begin with the words:

1000 light-years away from me, out in space...

Use your imagination to think of real <u>or</u> imaginary things... when you complete ten sentences, write one or two sentences summing up how the things you wrote about make you <u>feel</u>. The feeling checklist will help you.

Martians...

Imagine that you are a Martian scientist who has come to observe Earthlings at work and play. This is your first time on Earth and life on Mars is very different, so you have to make wild guesses about what is going on. What's more... you (as well as all other Martians) have NO HEARING. Choose three of the following things to explain to your Martian friends back home. Do this assignment in three paragraphs or more. Remember, you will have to describe these things as they appear to be - you don't know what they are, and you can't hear, either!

- your classroom.
- a supermarket.
- a baseball game.
- twelve midnight on New Year's Eve.
- McDonalds restaurant.
- a pajama party.
- a shopping center.
- a telephone.
- a trash compacter.
- someone shaving with an electric razor.
- a circus.
- a rock concert.
- a toothpick.
- a movie.
- someone yawning.
- a garden hose.

the door... ?

For your writing assignment this week you will write a story about <u>a door</u>.

Paragraph #1... Describe the door <u>in detail</u>. Your description checklist will help.

Paragraph #2... To what is the door attached? (House, bank, closet, castle, etc.) Explain and describe.

Paragraph #3... <u>What</u> is on the other side of the door? What is going on, <u>who</u> <u>or</u> <u>what</u> is there, <u>how</u> did it get there, <u>why</u> is it there?

Paragraph #4... What will happen when <u>you</u> open the door? Explain and describe.

Paragraph #5... Close your eyes and touch the door. Describe the feelings that touching the door gives you. The feeling checklist is helpful. Write a conclusion.

a captive audience

HELP! I'm trapped in a ..... supermarket
..... toy store
..... bakery
..... museum
..... a spaghetti factory
..... you choose one of your own

Choose <u>one</u> of the above places to be trapped in after hours. Now, write a story about your adventures after dark.

Paragraph #1... <u>Describe</u> where you are and how you happened to get locked in. <u>What</u> were you doing - <u>why</u> did it happen, <u>who</u> were you with?

Paragraph #2... Once you've discovered you're locked in and have some time to fool around, what will you do? Describe.

Paragraph #3... Plan your escape. How will you use what's in the store, factory, or museum to get out? What is your plan? Describe in detail.

Paragraph #4... How do you finally get out? Does your plan work? If not, why not, and what will you do? What happens when you get out? Describe. Write a conclusion to your story.

THE ADVENTURES of SUPER-KID

POW

faster than a speeding bullet...more powerful than a locomotive...

For your writing assignment this week, you will write a five paragraph story about an adventure of Super Kid.

Paragraph #1... Describe Super Kid. Use your description and feeling checklists. Be sure to include the kinds of powers he or she possesses.

Paragraph #2... Describe the <u>setting</u> of the story-exactly where and when does it take place.

Paragraph #3... In these two paragraphs you will develop the plot and
and   tell the actual story. Include at least <u>one problem</u>
Paragraph #4... Super Kid must face and solve.

Paragraph #5... This paragraph should be the conclusion, or ending to your story. Solve all problems, resolve all conflicts and tie up any loose ends. Try to write an interesting ending.

ZAP

The Wizard of Weird

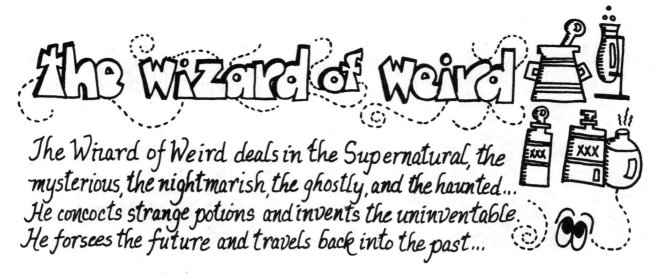

The Wizard of Weird deals in the Supernatural, the mysterious, the nightmarish, the ghostly, and the haunted... He concocts strange potions and invents the uninventable. He forsees the future and travels back into the past...

WRITE A STORY ABOUT THE WIZARD OF WEIRD...

Paragraph #1... Describe the Wizard. Use your description and feeling checklists. What kinds of things can he do? Use examples.

Paragraph #2... Describe the setting. Where and when does this story take place? Describe the Wizards laboratory.

Paragraph #3... Use these two paragraphs to develop the plot of your story. and What happens? What does the Wizard do? Who does he do it
Paragraph #4... to, for, or with? How does he do it? Why does he do it?

Paragraph #5... Write a conclusion to your story.

the great _____ robbery
(fill in blank)

VAN

Robber

Choose <u>one</u> of the following to fill in the blank:

a) peanut butter   c) pencil

b) pickle   d) rubber band

You are going to write a story about the Great _____ Robbery.
(fill in)

Paragraph #1... Describe <u>where</u> and <u>when</u> the robbery takes place.

Paragraph #2... Describe the robbers. There are at least <u>three</u>. What are they like -looks, actions, personalities...

Paragraph #3... <u>Why</u> did the robbery take place? What did the robbers want to do with the loot?

Paragraph #4... <u>What</u> happened during the robbery? Describe the plan. <u>How</u> did it happen? <u>How</u> much did they take?

Paragraph #5... Did the robbers succeed? If so, how? What did they do with the loot, where did they go? If not, <u>why</u> not? What went wrong? Write a <u>conclusion</u> to your story.

CARTON

NYC

BROKEN LOCK

LOOT

raw steak rides again... ☆

The town is Dodge City... the date is January 5th, 1890. Raw Steak is a cowboy in the wild, wild west. His best friends are Wyatt Earp and The Lone Ranger. He has a pet cactus named Tex. Raw Steak is a deputy sheriff. He rides a trail-to-who-knows-where...

Write a story about Raw Steak using <u>one</u> of the following titles:

- Raw Steak Meets Godzilla.
- Raw Steak Discovers the Lost <u>(you fill in)</u>.
- Raw Steak & the Silver Bullet.
- Raw Steak Captures The Good, The Bad, & The Ugly.

This will be a <u>5</u> paragraph story. Begin with an interesting <u>first line</u>. Try to use dialogue that fits the old west. Remember, this is the time of stagecoaches, the Pony Express, cattle drives, etc. Use the outline below. You may write the paragraphs in any order you want. (In other words, you can start with the action, or the setting, or whatever...)

A. Description of Raw Steak & Tex. Use description checklist. Include appearance, personality, hobbies, etc.

B. Description of setting. Where and when does the story take place?

C. Plot, or actual story - <u>two</u> paragraphs. What happens? Who else is involved in the story? How does it happen? Why does it happen?

D. Conclusion. Try to write an interesting ending.

Oh, give me a home...

110

a detective I.M. Sharp Mystery

Presenting Detective I.M. Sharp in... The Case of the Hidden Diamond.

For your writing assignment this week, you will make up a mystery story. You may develop "the case" any way you want, but make it revolve around a hidden diamond.

Paragraph #1... Describe the setting of your story - where does it take place? When does it happen? Write an exciting first line. ← diamond

Paragraph #2... Describe Detective I.M. Sharp. Use your description and feeling checklists. How long has he been a detective? What does the "I.M." stand for? For whom does he work? How did he get involved in this case? Who hired him? ← clue GULP ← fear ! ← suspense

Paragraph #3... Discuss the diamond. How many carats; how large; what does it look like; to whom does it belong; does it have a legend or story behind it, like the Hope Diamond; what is its history; does it have a curse that goes along with it; what is it worth? HELP! ← drama

Paragraph #4... These 2 paragraphs will tell your story. Be sure to include: and who hid the diamond, why was it hidden, where was it hidden,

Paragraph #5... how was it hidden, when was it hidden? ← mystery

Paragraph #6... Conclusion to your story. Try to build up suspense. How does I.M. Sharp recover the diamond (or does he?) Your ending should be as exciting and interesting as your first line. ← mysterious footprints

Write a story about a city that pollutes itself to extinction (ALMOST!)

Paragraph #1... Where and when does this story take place? Describe the city in detail. This can be a real city or an imaginary city.

Paragraph #2... Describe <u>three</u> people who live in this city-who are they; what do they do; how do they act? Use your description checklist.

Paragraph #3... <u>How</u> does the pollution overtake the city? <u>What</u> happens; <u>how</u> long does it take; <u>why</u> does it happen?

Paragraph #4... <u>Who</u> saves the city? <u>How</u> is it saved? <u>Why</u> is it saved?

Paragraph #5... <u>What</u> does the city do to make sure that this problem <u>won't</u> happen again? What is the long range plan? Write a conclusion to your story.

foward into the past...

Time Flies Backwards!

Imagine that you have gone into a time machine that transports you back to a <u>primitive</u> world in which creatures that are <u>now</u> <u>small</u>, are very big and powerful, and creatures that are <u>now</u> <u>large</u>, are very small and weak. Also imagine that you are by yourself and that you have not found any signs of human civilization.

Write a five-paragraph story about what you see (describe) and what you have to do to survive. Be sure to include: an interesting opening line; how big or small things are; what they look like; what experiences you have; how you solve problems as they occur; and how you feel while you are there. You can write the entire story about <u>one</u> creature, or about several different ones.

Buzz zzz...

GULP!

10 feet

KEEP OUT!

MAIL

WELCOME

it all happened when...

You are going to write a story about:

1 How people learned the meaning of friendship

or

2 How people learned the meaning of loneliness

This assignment will be at least five paragraphs long. This is to be a <u>fable</u> and should be imaginary, although you can base your story on facts. Before you begin, decide what friendship or lonliness means to <u>you</u>.

Be sure to include: setting (where and when), description of any characters in your story, what happens, how it happens, and why it happens. Write an interesting first line.

rock around the clock...

Imagine yourself in the 1950's. Young people were interested in motorcycles, gangs, hot rods, sock hops, and beach parties. The stars of the day were James Dean, Elvis Presley, Chubby Checker, and the Marines. Girls wore full skirts, straight skirts, and bobby socks, and were always trying to snag the most popular boys in school to go on a date to the malt shop or a drive-in movie. Guys walked around in their letter sweaters or black leather jackets, loafers, peggers, or pointy shoes, trying to make time with a good-looking "chick."

Imagine yourself in the 1950's. You may be anyone you wish. Write a story about one experience you had in the 1950's. Your story should be approximately six paragraphs long. Have at least three characters in your story. Describe and develop their personalities and appearances. Describe your setting. Include: <u>what</u> happened, <u>how</u> it happened, <u>why</u> it happened, <u>when</u> it happened, <u>where</u> it happened, and w<u>ho</u> it happened to.

Here are some words that were used in the 1950's. To create the proper atmosphere, use at least <u>fifteen</u> of them in your story. Ask your parents and "older" friends for ideas too. Do some research to find out what times were really like then...

rock around the clock...

sheen = car
crazy = wild
bohemian = hippie
beatnik = hippie
keen = terrific
malted = milkshake
fuzz = police
fink = to tell on someone
rat = to tell on someone
boss = cool
platter = record
hip = cool
hot rod = souped up car
ducktail = slicked back hair

drag = car race
hang-a-Louie = take a left
hang-a-Ralph = take a right
sock hop = a prom-type dance
pad = house
kooky = out of the ordinary
bopping = type of dance
chick = girl
peggers = tapered pants
down = feeling low
D.J. = disc jockey
New Yorker = a type of dance
Lindy = a type of dance
suedes = shoes

daddy 'o / hey, man...

Like crazy!

See You in September

For your writing assignment this week, you are going to write a four paragraph story about what you want to be doing on the afternoon of September 22, 2019. (Figure out how old you will be in 2019.)

Paragraph #1...<u>WHERE</u> will you be?

Paragraph #2...<u>WHAT</u> will you be doing?

Paragraph #3...<u>WHO</u> will you be with that afternoon? Why will they be there? If you will be alone, why will you be alone? How will you feel?

Paragraph #4...<u>WHY</u> do you want to be doing this? What will it accomplish in your life? Will you have to prepare for doing this? How?

Time Flies...

Once Upon a Time...

Write a story about:

1ˢᵗ How People Learned to Laugh ... <u>or</u>

2ⁿᵈ How People Learned to Care for Other People ...<u>or</u>

3ʳᵈ How People Learned to Cry.

Once upon a time...

This assignment will be done in five paragraphs. Be as descriptive as you can. This is to be a <u>fable</u> and should be "made-up," although you can base your story on facts. Be sure to include: <u>WHERE</u> it happened, <u>WHEN</u> it happened, <u>WHO</u> was involved, <u>WHAT</u> happened, <u>WHY</u> it happened, and <u>HOW</u> it happened.

<u>Hint</u>: Before you begin, try to remember the first time you started caring for others, thought something was really funny, or cried...

how it came to be...

For your writing assignment this week, you will write a myth or legend about how <u>one</u> of the following came to be:

1- How Mountains Came To Be
2- How the Hamburger Came To Be
3- How Music Came To Be
4- How Football Came To Be
5- How Washing Machines Came To Be
6- How the Alphabet Came To Be

This is to be a six paragraph story. Be sure to include:

<u>WHAT</u> happened.   <u>WHO</u> was involved.

<u>WHERE</u> it happened.   <u>HOW</u> it happened.

<u>WHEN</u> it happened.   <u>WHY</u> it happened.

Describe in detail. Explain everything. Have a great opening sentence. Write an interesting ending.

You may use this outline in any order:

• Introduction and Setting (Where and When)

• Who was involved

• What happened, how did it happen, why did it happen? (approximately three paragraphs.)

• Conclusion (ending.)

III. units...

INTRODUCTION

Several times during the course of the school year, we found it both necessary and worthwhile to depart from the Basal-Reading System to implement week-long units that gave the students the opportunity to put their "reading knowledge" to use as well as to increase their awareness of the world through diverse contemporary pieces. These units came to be because we both believed that reading should not be taught as a sacred and unapproachable skill exclusive of life, and more importantly, we wanted our reading material to reflect and investigate human values that would support critical thinking, decision-making, and the idea of survival. In the absence of any "packaged system" that met our goals, we turned to creating our own materials.

The units included here fall into two basic categories: reading comprehension strategies and perceptual interpretations, and investigations of various literary forms. One essential idea behind these units was to make these reading and writing exercises enjoyable and interesting for the student. In keeping with this objective, we structured the units in the following manner. Each unit covered one week and was substituted in place of the regular reading program, for an hour and a half each day. Writing and Spelling assignments were handed out and explained first thing on Monday. The Spelling assignment was done individually and was handed in when completed by the student, to be checked by a teacher and returned promptly. Spelling words were reviewed in groups, some time during the Thursday period, with a Spelling test given at the beginning of the Friday period. (Spelling tests corresponded to the spelling assignment. We asked one question for each word and tested for synonyms, usage in a sentence, definition, part of speech, and matching the definition with the word, in addition to spelling the word.) Students had until Thursday to complete their writing assignments. We required each student to write a rough draft as well as a final copy (in ink with a minimum of mistakes). Rough drafts were due by Thursday, at the beginning of the reading period. Before handing them in to a teacher, each student was responsible for proof-reading his or her paper. Rough drafts were then checked for content and structural mistakes. Correcting the rough draft took the form of "conferences" with each student. Final copies were due at the end of the day on Friday. (As the year went on, the students learned how to budget their time according to their capabilities and comfort level. Some students handed in their rough drafts on Tuesday, while others waited until Thursday. However, for each unit, we made certain that most required work could be completed in the allotted classroom time).

The actual reading material was handed out each day; usually one assignment per day. We re-distributed the students into "new" reading groups (mixing high and low ability students) and aimed for groups which we felt would be compatible for stimulating discussions. Students read individual copies of the song or poem or story, and were encouraged to interpret and answer the questions with a minimum of teacher explanation. Students requiring explanations were given individual help. We stressed the need for *quality* in their answers, and emphasized that they would be responsible for defending their answers. (Our philosophy was that there were few, if any, "right" or "wrong" answers and that the quality of their work depended on how well they could reason and defend what they had to say.) When completing the initial assignment for the day, the students were given the rest of the time to work on their spelling and writing assignments. (During this time, the teachers corrected rough drafts and spelling and generally helped students with any problems relating to the assignments, and made sure everyone was progressing toward completion.) Approximately thirty minutes before the end of each reading period, everyone stopped what they were doing and broke up into their "discussion groups". During this time the reading assignment and questions for the day were reviewed. This was a time for explanation and interpretation, going over questions, asking new ones, sharing feelings and in general, "going wherever the conversation led." More often than not, the students became quite involved in exploring their personalities, their lives, and the world around them.

spell and write...

Spelling Stories... DICTIONARY

For your writing assignment this week, you will write a story using __ALL__ of your spelling words in it. Do your spelling words first. Get the definition, the part of speech, and a synonym for each word. Then, look at all your definitions and think of a story (any story) that would involve all the words. Let your imagination run wild. The story will be at least five paragraphs long.

the words:

fragile	annex	unkempt
rotund	fable	sinister
trivial	chaos	antique
murmur	lucrative	extravagant
meager	magenta	taut

__Teacher__: Change the words according to the spelling ability of the students.

124

Spelling Stories...

Words have a special power. With them you are able to create <u>images</u>. For the words below, look up the definition, part of speech, and find a synonym for each word. Then, write about what the word <u>really</u> means. Create an image of that word. Write a paragraph for <u>each</u> word. Make each paragraph <u>fit</u> the word.

1- forlorn

2- interdependence

3- heritage

4- melancholy

5- apparition

writing the news...

Each student receives one fairly current <u>Time</u> or <u>Newsweek</u> magazine and reads it from cover-to-cover. The magazines can be different for each student. During the allotted time period for this activity, each pupil is responsible for reading his or her magazine, answering the corresponding questions ("I Have a Question;") completing the writing assignment ("What's New?") and the spelling assignment.

what's new ?

--Today in --the news...

"Nowadays truth is the greatest news..." —THOMAS FULLER, M.D

" How many beautiful trees gave their lives so that today's scandel should, without delay, reach a million readers!..." — EDWIN WAY TEALE

" A good newspaper, I suppose, is a Nation talking to itself..." —ARTHUR MILLER

" People everywhere confuse what they read in newspapers with news..." —A.J. LIEBLING

" The window to the world can be covered by a newspaper..." —STANISLAW LEC

" The evil that Men do lives on the front pages of greedy newspapers, but the good they do is often buried with little concern inside..." —BROOKS ATKINSON

" News is popular, but it is popular mainly as fiction. Life is one world, and life seen in the news is another..." —G.K. CHESTERTON

Choose any __three__ quotations. For each quote you will write __two__ paragraphs. Use examples to help you express your thoughts and feelings.

Paragraph #1... Explain the quotation. Do you agree with it? Why or why not? What is the point (or purpose) of this quote?

Paragraph #2... How does this quote apply or relate to what you've been reading this week?

i have a question...

You will be responsible for answering all of these questions...use your magazine to find the answers.

1- In your opinion, what is the most newsworthy (valuable) story in your magazine? **Why** is it so important? **What** is it about?

2- What point does the <u>editorial</u> in your magazine make? What is it about? How well does the editor prove his or her point?

3- What type of letters to the editor are in your magazine? Are they mostly favorable or unfavorable? Can you tell what type of people seem to read these magazines from the letters?

4- What is the cover story about? Summarize it. How well is the story covered? Does it leave you asking any questions? If so, what?

5- What kinds of ads are found in your magazine? Do they fall into certain groups? Why do you suppose these <u>types</u> of ads are in the magazine?

6- It has been said, "One picture is worth a thousand words." What picture in your magazine applies to this statement? In other words, which picture is most expressive? Why? What is the story that goes along with the picture? Cut the picture out and attach it to your answers.

7- Do the stories in the Education Section apply to <u>your</u> education? Why or why not?

8- Of all the book <u>or</u> movie reviews in your magazine, which one is the most convincing? Why? If none were, why not?

128

i have a question...

9· Find one example of an <u>international</u> news story. What is it about? Find an example of a <u>national</u> news story. What is it about? What is the difference between an international and national news story?

10· In your opinion, what person in the news was most interesting to read about? Why? What did s/he do?

11· Rewrite any one news story (of your choice) as a <u>fictional</u> (imaginary) story.

12· What is the style or mood of a news story? How is a news story written to make it different from a fictional story?

13· Is there any humor in the news? Find an example of a humorous news story and tell what it is about and why you think it is funny.

14· Copy one headline you found in your magazine. Write about how it <u>fits</u> the story. Why or why not is this a good title for the story?

15· Choose one sports story and summarize it.

16· Find the Law Section. Do any of the stories concern <u>human rights</u>? If so, how? If not, what are the stories about?

Spelling...

Write the definition, part of speech, and a synonym. Use <u>each</u> word in a fifteen line poem (it doesn't have to rhyme) about the news. You may change the order of the words.

1. celebrity
2. economy
3. update
4. columnist
5. objectivity

6. analysis
7. policy
8. opinion
9. forum
10. editorial

11. correspondent
12. international
13. recession
14. newsworthy
15. transition

✳ Try to find the meaning that applies to the <u>NEWS</u>.

holidays...

These activities offer the student an opportunity to involve language arts with the holiday seasons. The student will be asked to write stories, create cards, use spelling words that have holiday connotations, and to give a personal interpretation to a holiday.

HAPPY...

which witch ?

WRITE ONE PARAGRAPH AND MAKE IT SCARY!

The <u>words</u> you choose will help create a mood of absolute terror. Use Halloween-type adjectives. Be careful, this is harder than it sounds. You only have <u>one</u> paragraph in which to frighten your reader. Try to create your mood by using descriptive words rather than by relying on your subject matter.

This is the season of the witch

Choose <u>one</u> of the following titles and write a scary story!

1~ The Vampire Dies at Midnight
2~ The Icy Fingers of Doom
3~ The Ghost of Count Dracula

boo!

This will be a five paragraph story. Be descriptive. Be sure to include: setting (where and when), descriptions of all the characters, an interesting opening line, and a conclusion. Answer these questions: <u>WHAT</u> happens, <u>WHY</u> does it happen, <u>WHO</u> does it happen to, and <u>HOW</u> does it happen?

Spelling horrors

HELP

1. frighten	6. appalling	11. eerie	16. corpse	21. alarming
2. panic	7. dreadful	12. gruesome	17. phantom	22. suspicious
3. haunted	8. tremble	13. macabre	18. sorcery	23. shadow
4. terror	9. hideous	14. sinister	19. doom	24. jittery
5. petrify	10. ghoulish	15. ominous	20. mysterious	25. apparition

Choose fifteen of these words to use in your creative writing story. <u>Underline</u> the words you use in your story.

gratitude... Thanksgiving is the time of year when people are especially aware of things for which they are thankful...

Write two thank you notes to two different people and thank them for something they have done for you during this past year.

1- You may thank anyone you know - a relative, friend, acquaintance, etc.

2- Write these as you would a "thank you note." Use two pieces of paper.

3- Be sure to include an explanation of what it was that this person did for you - where and when they have done it for you, why you are thankful for what this person has done (why does it mean something to you) and how you feel about it.

4- Make each note one paragraph in length.

FORM

DEAR _____ ,

DATE

THANK YOU

YOUR LETTER

_____ YOUR NAME

November 24, 1975

Example:

To All of You,

Somehow, in the course of a school day, many things that should get said, never do. We'd like to take this opportunity to say thank you to all of you for something we consider important. We think that one of the nicest things about teaching is the chance it presents for us to learn from you. Through you, and because of you, we are constantly learning things about ourselves as people, as adults, and teachers. Without all of you, this wouldn't be possible. So you are important to us for this reason, and others. Thank you for being you...

Mrs. Maid and Mr. Wallace

For your writing assignment this week, choose #1 or #2.

1) Write a Thanksgiving story from a turkey's point of view. Be sure to include the sights, sounds, smells, and tastes of the holiday. Describe things. Answer these questions: WHERE does the story take place, WHEN does it take place, WHAT happens, HOW does it happen, and WHY does it happen. This is to be a six paragraph story.

or

2) Write a Thanksgiving story that takes place in the year 3001 (in a futuristic society.) Be sure to include the sights, sounds, smells, and tastes of the holiday. What will Thanksgiving be like in the future... will everyone go out to eat at Kentucky Fried Turkey, will Plymouth Rock have fallen into the ocean, will people be taking rocket trips to their relative's houses? Describe things. Answer these questions: WHO is the story about, WHERE does the story take place, WHAT happens, WHY does it happen, and WHAT WILL PEOPLE IN THE YEAR 3001 BE THANKFUL ABOUT? This is to be a six paragraph story.

words for which to be thankful...

1. aroma
2. celebration
3. savory
4. gratitude
5. succulent
6. ritual
7. appetite
8. devour

9. edible
10. gastronomy
11. poultry
12. entrée
13. nourishment
14. gorge
15. pilgrimage
16. cornucopia

PILGRIM

✳ Pick the definition that best applies to Thanksgiving.
Use at least <u>six</u> of the words in your creative writing story and <u>underline</u> them in your story.

BOAT
MAYFLOWER

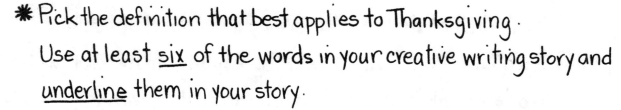
PLYMOUTH ROCK
1620

This is the season for giving. Many people give and receive gifts. You will write a short, three paragraph story about a gift you have received that you didn't want. This can be imaginary if this has never happened to you, but try to use a real-life example.

Paragraph #1... What is the gift. Describe it in detail. You can also describe the outside of the package — size, wrapping, etc.

Paragraph #2... Write about your feelings before you opened the package and how you felt after you saw the gift. Use the feeling checklist for help.

Paragraph #3... Okay, so you don't like the gift. Think of a person that could really use (or might want) this gift. Write who you would give this gift to and why. (It isn't enough to say a needy person, what kind of needy person — who, specifically?)

Now, answer this question in a few sentences:

Do you agree with this statement —

It's not the gift that counts, it's the thought behind it.

Write yes or no, and answer WHY.

when you care enough to send the very best...? 👀

Since this is the season when people's thoughts turn to peace and goodwill toward others, your writing assignment this week will be to design and compose a <u>card</u> expressing <u>your</u> feelings or beliefs about "PEACE." This is <u>not</u> to be a Christmas or Hanukah card.

You will be responsible for creating a coherent and meaningful design for the front of your card. This will be a design of your own choosing (drawing, collage, pen and ink, etc.) Be creative. Use your imagination. You may combine art techniques and use assorted mediums (charcoal, pastels, ink, scraps of material, wood, etc.) You may need to bring in some materials from home for this project. You will be responsible for collecting the things you need. <u>THE DESIGN IS TO BE RELATED TO YOUR MESSAGE</u>.

For the inside of the card, write a message conveying one or several of your ideas about "Peace on Earth." (Note that there is more than one kind of peace - there is "inner peace" as well as "<u>world</u> peace." Your message can take the form of <u>two</u> paragraphs, a poem, or prose. Carefully consider what you write. Trite descriptions or clichés (things that everybody says) may be worn out messages. This message will be <u>your</u> statement (feelings) you would like to share about peace.

Once your message is written, consider <u>placement</u> (layout) of the words on the paper. <u>Where</u> and <u>how</u> you place your words can be as important as the message itself.

The <u>inside</u> of your card can be as artistic as the <u>outside</u> ... which means beautiful printing or script.

Your rough draft can be sketched on the outside of your card, <u>plus</u> the <u>EXACT</u> message you plan to put on the inside.

New Year's Resolutions...

A resolution is a promise that says you will do something at a later date. People usually have a hard time keeping their resolutions. Let's _not_ worry about the future. What bothers _you_ about _you_, _NOW_? (Even if you can't do anything about it _this_ year.) In other words, what would you like to change about the way you _act_? Answer this question in one paragraph or more.

Spelling for the holidays

1. tranquillity
2. harmony
3. calm
4. yuletide
5. frigid

6. blizzard
7. icicle
8. glacier
9. snowbound
10. goodwill

11. prosperity
12. avalanche
13. boughs (of holly)
14. tinsel
15. brotherhood

Look up the definition, part of speech, and write a synonym for each word. Now, write a fifteen line poem (it _doesn't_ have to rhyme) using one of the spelling words in each line. You may change the order of the words if you want.

MOODS...

Each child will be responsible for completing the writing and spelling assignments as well as reading "Mood Paragraphs," "Moods in Poetry," a short story, and answering related questions.

We used the short story "After Twenty Years" by O. Henry, but any short story creating a specific mood will work.

Miscellaneous Moods...

Mood is a state of mind or feeling. Read these paragraphs and pay particular attention to the <u>moods</u> they try to develop. When you finish reading, go back over the paragraphs and <u>underline</u> those words which you think help create the mood of the paragraph. Also, check (✓) those paragraphs which you think most successfully create a certain mood or tone. Be prepared to defend your choices. Consider <u>how</u> the mood was created.

The sidewalks were haunted by dust ghosts all night as the furnace wind summoned them up, swung them about, and gentled them down in a warm spice on the lawns. Trees, shaken by the footsteps of late-night strollers, sifted avalanches of dust. From midnight on, it seemed a volcano beyond the town was showering red-hot ashes everywhere, crusting slumberless night watchmen and irritable dogs. Each house was a yellow attic smoldering with spontaneous combusion at three in the morning.

Dawn, then, was a time where things changed element for element. Air ran like hot spring waters nowhere, with no sound. The lake was a quantity of steam very still and deep over valleys of fish and sand held baking under its serene vapors. Tar was poured licorice in the streets, red bricks were brass and gold, roof tops were paved with bronze. The high-tension wires were lightening held forever, blazing, a threat above the unslept houses.

The cicadas sang louder and yet louder.

The sun did not rise, it overflowed.

Ray Bradbury, **Dandelion Wine**

She wore a dark striped dress reaching down to her shoe tops, and an equally long apron of bleached sugar sacks, with a full pocket: all neat and tidy, but every time she took a step she might have fallen over her shoelaces, which dragged from her unlaced shoes. She looked straight ahead. Her eyes were blue with age. Her skin had a pattern all its own of numberless branching wrinkles, and as though a whole little tree stood in the middle of her forehead, but a golden color ran underneath, and the two knobs of her cheeks were illumined by a yellow burning under the dark. Under the red rag her hair came down on her neck in the frailest of ringlets, still black, and with an odor like copper.

Eudora Welty, "A Worn Path"

Mother, in her pink apron with her hair in curlers, was leaning over the oven of the gas stove basting the turkey. Glenn was standing beside her with his mouth watering as he watched the little splashes of juice sizzle as they trickled off the kitchen spoon onto the brown tight skin of the turkey.

John Dos Passos, "Red, White, and
Blue Thanksgiving"

141

miscellaneous moods...

The garden grew as by a miracle, and the blackberry winter passed with the early April winds, doing no harm. Beans broke their waxen leaves out of hoe-turned furrows, bearing the husk of the seeds with them. Sweet corn unfurled tight young blades from weed mold, timid to night chill, growing slowly and darkly. Crows hung on blue air, surveying the patch, but the garden was too near the house. Our shouts and swift running through the tended ground kept them frightened and filled with wonder.

James Still, "Mole-Bane"

She hurried into a new spring evening dress of the frailest fairy blue. In the excitement of seeing herself in it, it seemed as if she had shed the old skin of winter and emerged a shining chrysalis with no stain; and going downstairs her feet fell softly just off the beat of the music from below. It was a tune from a play she had seen a week ago in New York, a tune with a future—ready for gayeties as yet unthought of, lovers not yet met. Dancing off, she was certain that life had innumerable beginnings. She had hardly gone ten steps when she was cut in upon by Donald Knowleton. She soared skyward on a rocket of surprise and delight.

F. Scott Fitzgerald, "A Woman with a Past"

The barn was blank as a blind face. The lantern was flickering, and in that witching light the stalls and the heap of sleighs, plows, old harness, at the back wall of the barn were immense and terrifying. The barn was larger than his whole house in Brooklyn, and ten times as large it seemed in the dimness. He could not see clear to the back wall, and he imagined abominable monsters lurking there. He dashed at the ladder up to the haymow, the lantern handle in his teeth and his imitation-leather satchel in one hand.

Sinclair Lewis, "Land"

In the assembling plant everyone works "on the belt." This is a big steel conveyor, a kind of moving sidewalk, waist-high. It is a great river running down through the plant. Various tributary streams come into the main stream, the main belt. They bring tires, they bring headlights, horns, bumpers for cars. They flow into the main stream. The main stream has its source at the freight cars, where the parts are unloaded, and it flows out to the other end of the factory and into other freight cars. The finished automobiles go into the freight cars at the delivery end of the belt. The assembly plant is a place of peculiar tension. You feel it when you go in. It never lets up. Men here work always on tension. There is no let-up to the tension. If you can't stand it, get out.

Sherwood Anderson, "Lift Up Thine Eyes"

More Moods...

Write one word that you feel expresses the mood for each paragraph. Now, re-write any two of the three paragraphs and write each one so that the paragraph will express the opposite mood.

The pass was high and wide and he jumped for it, feeling it slap flatly against his hands, as he shook his hips to throw off the halfback who was diving at him. The center floated by, his hands desperately brushing Darling's knee as Darling picked his feet up high and delicately ran over a blocker and an opposing linesman in a jumble on the ground near the scrimmage line. He had ten yards in the clear and picked up speed, breathing easily, feeling his thigh pad rising and falling against his legs, listening to the sound of cleats behind him, pulling away from them, watching the other backs heading him off toward the sideline, the whole picture, the men closing in on him, the blockers fighting for position, the ground he had to cross, all suddenly clear in his head, for the first time in his life not a meaningless confusion of men, sounds, speed. He smiled a little to himself as he ran, holding the ball lightly in front of him with his two hands, his knees pumping high, his hips twisting in the almost girlish run of a back in a broken field. The first halfback came at him and he fed him his leg, them swung at the last moment, took the shock of the man's shoulder without breaking stride, ran right through him, his cleats biting securely into the turf. There was only the safety man now, coming warily at him, his arms crooked, hands spread. Darling tucked the ball in, spurted at him, driving hard, hurling himself along, all two hundred pounds bunched into controlled attack. He was sure he was going to get past the safety man. Without thought, his arms and legs working beautifully together, he headed right for the safety man, stiff-armed him, feeling blood spurt instantaneously from the man's nose onto his hand, seeing his face go awry, head turned, mouth pulled to one side. He pivoted away, keeping the arm locked, dropping the safety man as he ran easily toward the goal line, with the drumming of cleats diminishing behind him.
Irwin Shaw, "The Eighty-Yard Run"

It was a magnificent July day, one of those days which come only when the weather has been fair for a long time. From the very earliest dawn the sky is clear; the morning glow does not flame like a conflagration: it pours itself forth in a gentle flush. The sun, not fiery, not red-hot, as in the season of sultry drought, not of a dull crimson, as before a tempest, but bright, and agreeably radiant, glides up peacefully under a long, narrow cloudlet, beams freshly, and plunges into its lilac mist. The thin upper edges of the outstretched cloudlet begins to flash like darting serpents; their gleam resembles the gleam of hammered silver . . .
Ivan Turgenev, "Byezhin Meadow"

more moods...

He stood for a moment looking about. Behind him the rain whirled at the door. Ahead of him, upon a low table, stood a silver pot of hot chocolate, steaming, and a cup, full, with a marshmallow in it. And beside that, on another tray, stood thick sandwiches of rich chicken meat and fresh-cut tomatoes and green onions. And on a rod just before his eyes was a great thick green Turkish towel, and a bin in which to throw wet clothes, and, to his right, a small cubicle in which heat rays might dry you instantly. And upon a chair, a fresh change of uniform, waiting for anyone—himself, or any lost one—to make use of it. And farther over, coffee in steaming copper urns, and a phonograph from which music was playing quietly, and books bound in red and brown leather. And near the books a cot, a soft deep cot upon which one might lie, exposed and bare, to drink in the rays of the one great bright thing which dominated the long room . . . He was looking at the sun.
Ray Bradbury, **The Illustrated Man**

The rain continued. It was a hard rain, a perpetual rain, a sweating and steaming rain; it was a drizzle, a downpour, a fountain, a whipping at the eyes, an undertow at the ankles; it was a rain to drown all rains and the memory of rains. It came by the pound and the ton, it hacked at the jungle and cut the trees like scissors and shaved the grass and tunneled the soil and molted the bushes. It shrank men's hands into the hands of wrinkled apes; it rained a solid glassy rain, and it never stopped . . . The lieutenant looked up. He had a face that once had been brown and now the rain has washed it pale, and the rain had washed the color from his eyes and they were white, as were his teeth, and as was his hair. He was all white. Even his uniform was beginning to turn white, and perhaps a little green with fungus.
Ray Bradbury, **The Illustrated Man**

moods in poetry...

What moods do you find in these poems? Write one or two words that express the mood of each poem. How does each poet create the mood in his or her poem? What differences are there in creating moods for poetry rather than prose?

Lucy in the Sky with Diamonds
John Lennon and Paul McCartney

Picture yourself in a boat on a river,
With tangerine trees and marmalade skies
Somebody calls you, you answer quite slowly,
A girl with kaleidoscope eyes.
Cellophane flowers of yellow and green,
Towering over your head.
Look for the girl with the sun in her eyes,
And she's gone.
Lucy in the sky with diamonds.

Follow her down to a bridge by a fountain
Where rocking horse people eat marshmallow pies,
Everyone smiles as you drift past the flowers,
That grow so incredibly high.
Newspaper taxis appear on the shore,
Waiting to take you away.
Climb in the back with your head in the clouds.
And you're gone.
Lucy in the sky with diamonds.

Picture yourself on a train in a station,
With plasticine porters with looking glass ties,
Suddenly someone is there at the turnstile,
The girl with kaleidoscope eyes.

moods in poetry...

The Word "Plum"
Helen Chasin

The word "plum" is delicious

pout and push, luxury of
self-love, and savoring murmur

full in the mouth and falling
like fruit

taut skin
pierced, bitten, provoked into
juice, and tart flesh

question
and reply, lip and tongue
of pleasure.

Ozymandias
Percy Bysshe Shelley

I met a traveler from an antique land
Who said: Two vast and trunkless legs of stone
Stand in the desert . . . Near them, on the sand,
Half sunk, a shattered visage lies, whose frown,
And wrinkled lip, and sneer of cold command,
Tell that its sculptor well those passions read
Which yet survive, stamped on these lifeless things,
The hand that mocked them, and the heart that fed:
And on the pedestal these words appear:
"My name is Ozymandias, King of Kings:
Look on my works, ye mighty, and despair!"
Nothing beside remains. Round the decay
Of that colossal wreck, boundless and bare
The lone and level sands stretch far away.

146

moods in poetry...

Foul Shot
Edwin A. Hoey

With two 60's stuck on the scoreboard
And two seconds hanging on the clock,
The solemn boy in the center of eyes,
Squeezed by silence,
Seeks out the line with his feet,
Soothes his hands along his uniform,
Gently drums the ball against the floor,
Then measures the waiting net,
Raises the ball on his right hand,
Balances it with his left,
Calms it with fingertips,
Breathes,
Crouches,
Waits,
And then through a stretching of stillness,
Nudges it upward.

The ball
Slides up and out,
Lands,
Leans,
Wobbles,
Wavers,
Hesitates,
Exasperates,
Plays it coy
Until every face begs with unsounding screams—
And then
                                        And then
                                        And then,

Right before ROAR-UP,
Dives down and through.

moods in poetry...

Edouard
Ogden Nash

A bugler named
Dougal MacDougal
Found ingenious ways
To be frugal.
He learned how to sneeze
In various keys,
Thus saving the price
Of a bugle.

Gone Forever
Barris Mills

Halfway through shaving, it came—
the word for a poem.
I should have scribbled it on the mirror with a soapy finger,
or shouted it to my wife in the kitchen,
or muttered it to myself till it ran
in my head like a tune.

But now it's gone with whiskers
down the drain. Gone forever,
like the girls I never kissed,
and the places I never visited—
the lost lives I never lived.

Spelling ooo Write the definition and part of

speech. Then write a twenty line poem using each of the spelling words.
You may change the order of the words. The poem does <u>not</u> have to rhyme.

1. morose
2. convoluted
3. dreary
4. whimsical
5. colossal

6. lethargic
7. tremulous
8. jaunty
9. effervescent
10. treacherous

11. mangy
12. permeate
13. gaudy
14. gelid
15. sultry

16. phantasmagoria
17. onomatopoeia
18. musty
19. mellow
20. illimitable

<u>Teacher</u>: Vary these words to your students' ability.

Creating Your Own Moods ooo
Examine the list below:

1. gloominess
2. loneliness
3. terror
4. depression
5. frustration
6. coldness
7. wealth

8. poverty
9. darkness
10. warmth
11. humorous
12. defeat
13. agony
14. joy

15. chaos
16. crowded
17. irony
18. uneasiness
19. despair
20. bitterness
21. helplessness

22. happiness
23. violence
24. sinister
25. mysterious
26. astonishment
27. dullness
28. laziness

You will choose <u>ten</u> words from this list and you will write ten separate
paragraphs expressing the "mood" of the word. The paragraphs are to be totally
<u>unrelated</u>. Each paragraph will have to fit the mood of the word. This can be done in
<u>two</u> ways: by descriptive words and situations, and the way in which your words are
placed on the paper. Use the descriptive checklists.

149

Science Fiction...

Each child will choose his or her own <u>SCIENCE FICTION</u> book. After reading the book, each child will write a two paragraph summary of the book as follows: Paragraph #1... Explain the plot.

Paragraph #2... What is the <u>science fiction</u> in your book?

The child will also be responsible for reading the short story, "EPICAC" by Kurt Vonnegut and answering the related questions, completing the writing assignment and the spelling assignment, and reading the two poems and answering the related questions. The student will also be responsible for taking part in group discussions on all of the above assignments.

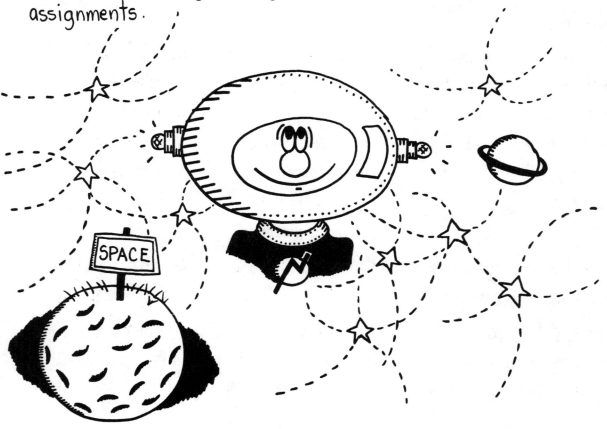

Questioning "EPICAC"...

1- Why didn't EPICAC work out the way he was supposed to?

2- Look up the word "vindicate." Why do you think the narrator of the story wants to <u>vindicate</u> EPICAC?

3- Can people ever be like machines in any way? Why or why not?

4- Originally, why didn't Pat want to marry the narrator of the story?

5- How was the narrator "using" EPICAC?

6- If machines are built by people to serve people, which is superior (or smarter)?... humans for creating the machines or the machines for performing the work better and faster?

7- What was EPICAC's unsolvable problem?

8- Who was more "human" in the end, EPICAC or the man? Define what you mean by "human."

9- For <u>EPICAC</u>, was it better to have loved and lost than to have <u>never</u> loved at all?

10- Was the narrator a murderer or did the machine commit suicide?

11- What kind of person was the narrator?

12- What does the last line mean -"Say nothing but good of the dead?" Why do you think the author ended the story this way? Did the narrator have any right to say anything bad about EPICAC?

13- How is this story <u>science fiction</u>? Explain.

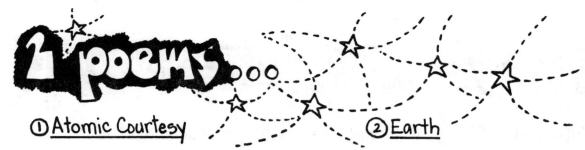

2 poems...

① Atomic Courtesy

To smash the simple atom
All mankind was intent
Now any day the atom...
May return the compliment!

— ETHEL JACOBSON

② Earth

"A planet doesn't explode of itself," said drily
The Martian astronomer, gazing off into the air —
"That they were able to do it is proof that highly
Intelligent beings must have been living there."

— JOHN HALL WHEELOCK

① How are these two poems being SARCASTIC? *LOOK UP THIS WORD*

② What is the author's prediction for mankind in poem #1?

③ How is poem #2 a CONTRADICTION? *LOOK UP THIS WORD*

④ Poem #2 implies that "intelligence" isn't always put to the best use. If you think this is true, prove it by using specific examples. If you think this is false, give your reasons why.

⑤ Are these poems "science fiction", or is there any truth in them? Why or why not?

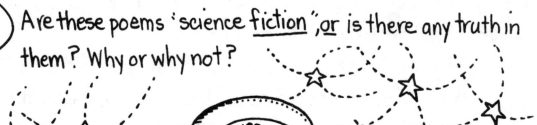

fiction ...or fact ?

KNOCK!

...a man sits in his chair after the total destruction of the world—he knows that all other humans have been destroyed. There is a knock at the door... who is it? Or, what is it?

...November 4, 2976. The first robot has been elected President of the World...

...Macy's Department Store announced a sale today on their huge stock of mechanical pets, rumored to be just like the "real thing." Of course, nobody has seen the "real thing" for over 2000 years...

...It is the year 2500. Government scientists are making their last desperate effort to save the only flower in the country...

Choose one of the above topics and develop it into a six paragraph story. Be sure to include setting, character development (human or non-human), events leading up to the story, the problem, the solution, what happened, how it happened, and why it happened. Allow your imagination to take over.

Space Spelling ooo

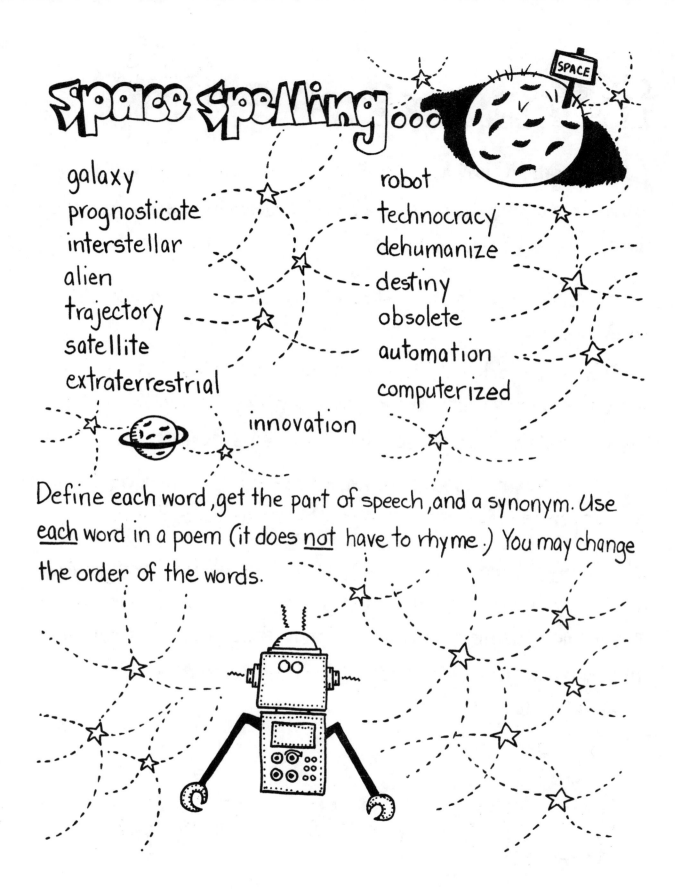

galaxy
prognosticate
interstellar
alien
trajectory
satellite
extraterrestrial

robot
technocracy
dehumanize
destiny
obsolete
automation
computerized

innovation

Define each word, get the part of speech, and a synonym. Use **each** word in a poem (it does **not** have to rhyme.) You may change the order of the words.

Loneliness:

Poem To Be Read at 3 a.m.
Eleanor Rigby
From Two Jazz Poems
A Coney Island Life

poem to be read at 3 a.m.

Donald Justice

Excepting the diner
On the outskirts
The town of Ladora
At 3 a.m.
Was dark but
For my headlights
And up in
One second-story room
A single light
Where someone
Was sick or
Perhaps reading
As I drove past
At seventy
Not thinking
This poem
Is for whoever
Had the light on.

1- What made the author notice the 2ND story room?

2- Was the author really <u>NOT</u> thinking when he drove past? Why or why not?

3- "To think that I'm not going to think of you, is to think of you." (Zen Saying) How does this saying apply to the poem?

4- Why do you think the author of the poem wrote it for someone he didn't know?

5- Why did the author want this poem to be read at 3 a.m.? Write another title for the poem.

6- Describe the most interesting person you've ever noticed but didn't get to meet. Include why you noticed this person and how s/he made you feel.

7- Write a poem for someone you don't know.

Eleanor Rigby

John Lennon & Paul McCartney

Ah—look at all the lonely people!
Eleanor Rigby, picks up the rice in the church where a wedding has been, lives in a dream.
Waits at the window, wearing the face that she keeps in a jar by the door, who is it for?
All the lonely people, where do they all come from?
All the lonely people, where do they all belong?

Father McKenzie, writing the words of a sermon that no one will hear, no one comes near.
Look at him working, darning his socks in the night when there's nobody there, what does he care?
All the lonely people, where do they all come from?
All the lonely people, where do they all belong?

Eleanor Rigby, died in the church and was buried along with her name, nobody came.
Father McKenzie, wiping the dirt from his hands as he walks from the grave, no one was saved.
All the lonely people, where do they all come from?
All the lonely people, where do they all belong?

1- What do Eleanor Rigby and Father McKenzie have in common?

2- Why do you think Eleanor Rigby has another face?

3- What "masks" do you wear? Be specific. Why do people need masks, or do they?

4- How important do you think communication is in any relationship?

5- How important is communication to life? Is not being able to communicate a kind of disease? Explain.

6- Is it possible that people could be in church but still not hear Father McKenzie's sermons? How could this happen?

7- Why was no one saved? Explain.

8- Can you ever be lonely in a room filled with people? Why or why not?

9- How does "loneliness" differ from "being alone?"

10- "All the lonely people, where do they all belong?"

from two jazz poems

Carl Wendell Hines, Jr.

yeah here am i
am standing
at the crest of a tallest
hill with a trumpet
in my hand & dark
glasses
on.

bearded & bereted i proudly stand!
but there are no eyes to see me.
i send down cool sounds!
but there are no ears to hear me.

1- Why is the man in the poem proud?

2- Why do you think the man is alone?

3- Why do you think the author wrote this poem using a lowercase "i"?

4- What do you wish someone had been around to <u>see</u> you <u>do</u>? Explain.

5- What do you wish someone had been around to <u>hear</u> you <u>say</u>? Explain.

6- "It's lonely at the top." What does this quote mean, and how does it apply to the poem?

a coney island life

James L. Weil

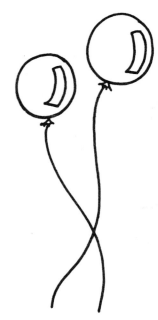

Having lived a Coney Island life
on rollercoaster ups and downs
and seen my helium hopes
break skyward without me,
now arms filled with dolls
I threw so much for
I take perhaps my last ride
on this planet-carousel
and ask
how many more times round
I have
to catch that brass-ring-sun
before the game is up.

1- Describe the kind of person talking in the poem.

2- What are some of the ups and downs in your life?

3- What is "the game" the poet is talking about in the last line?

4- How is life like a game?

5- How do you feel about the proverb: "If you don't succeed at first,
try, try again?" Should you always try again? Is there ever a
time when you should quit? Explain your answers.

6- Do you believe that everything in life happens for the best? Why
or why not?

Sometimes i wonder:

Tapestry
Garbage
What Am I Doing Here?
Old Friends
The Term

Tapestry

Don McLean

Every thread of creation is held in position
By still other strands of things living
In an earthly tapestry hung from the skyline of smoldering cities
So gray and so vulgar as not to be satisfied with their own negativity
But needing to touch all the living as well.

Every breeze that blows kindly is one crystal breath
We exhale on the blue diamond heaven
As gentle to touch as the hands of the healer
As soft as farewells whispered over the coffin
We're poisoned with venom with each breath we take
From the brown sulphur chimney
And the black highway snake.

Every dawn that breaks golden is held in suspension
Like the yolk of the egg in albumen
Where the birth and the death of unseen generations
Are interdependent in vast orchestration
And painted in colors of tapestry thread
When the dying are born and the living are dead.

Every pulse of your heartbeat is one liquid moment
That flows through the veins of your being
Like a river of life flowing on since creation
Approaching the sea with each new generation
You're now just a stagnant and rancid disgrace
That is rapidly drowning the whole human race.
Every fish that swims silent, every bird that flies freely
Every doe that steps softly
Every crisp leave that falls, all the flowers that grow
On this colorful tapestry, somehow they know
That if man is allowed to destroy all we need
He will soon have to pay with his life
For his greed.

162

tapestry

1- What is a tapestry?

2- Why do you think the title of this poem is "Tapestry?"

3- This poem talks about the chain of life - do you agree that everything in this world, the past, present, and future, is linked together by the thread of life? Why or why not?

4- <u>Who</u> and <u>what</u> are <u>you</u> dependent on?

5- What does the poet mean when he says that every dawn (or day) is "held in suspension?"

6- Why do you think the poet compared life to a vast orchestra?

7- What is happening to the world, according to the poet?

8- Why does the poet call human beings "greedy?"

9- What does this line mean: "When the dying are born and the living are dead?"

10- How do you think the poet feels about the <u>quality</u> of life on earth? How do <u>you</u> feel about it?

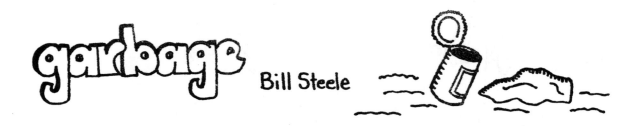

garbage

Bill Steele

Mister Thompson calls the waiter, orders steak and baked potato
But he leaves the bone and gristle and he never eats the skins;
Then the bus boy comes and takes it, with a cough contaminates it
As he puts it in a can with coffee grounds and sardine tins;
Then the truck comes by on Friday and carts it all away;
And a thousand trucks just like it are converging on the bay.
Garbage!!! Garbage!!! We're filling up the sea with garbage.
Garbage!!! Garbage!!!
What will we do when there's no place left to put all the garbage?

Mister Thompson starts his Cadillac and winds it up the freeway track
Leaving friends and neighbors in a hydrocarbon haze
He's joined by lots of smaller cars all sending gases to the stars
There to form a seething cloud that hangs for thirty days
While the sun licks down upon it with its ultraviolet tongues
'Til it turns to smog and settles down and ends up in our lungs.
Garbage!!! Garbage!!! We're filling up the sky with garbage.
Garbage!!! Garbage!!!
What will we do when there's nothing left to breathe but garbage?

Getting home and taking off his shoes he settles down with evening news
While the kids do homework with the T.V. in one ear
While Superman for thousandth time sells talking dolls and conquers crime
They dutifully learn the date of birth of Paul Revere
In the paper there's a piece about the mayor's middle name,
And he gets it done in time to watch the All-Star Bingo Game
Garbage!!! Garbage!!! We're filling up our minds with garbage!
Garbage!!! Garbage!!!
What will we do when there's nothing left to read
and there's nothing left to hear and there's nothing left to need
and there's nothing left to wear and there's nothing left to talk about
and nothing left to walk upon and nothing left to care about
and nothing left to ponder on and nothing left to touch
and there's nothing left to see and there's nothing left to do
and there's nothing left to be—but garbage?

164

garbage

1- This poem is about different types of garbage - what is garbage?

2- What is the message the poet is trying to get across?

3- It has been said that the mind is a junkyard - do you agree, why or why not?

4- What kinds of garbage do <u>you</u> fill your mind with?

5- What would life be like when there's "nothing left to walk upon, or care about, or see, or touch, or do?" How important are these things for life?

6- Can a person ever become "garbage?" Why or why not?

7- If there's nothing left to be (last line), what <u>options</u> are open to you? Do you have any options? Are options important in living?

what am i doin' here?

Ric Masten

When you're takin' that vacation
Out in the countryside
Don't stay too long there in the wilderness
'Cause a man seems kinda small
And a mountain awful tall
It could make you look inside yourself and ask . . .
Where did I come from
Where am I goin'
And what am I doin' here.

When you're drivin' in the country
Keep a-steppin' on the gas
Hurry, hurry, hurry on your way
If ya slow down to a walk
Ya might hear the country talk
You might hear the country laugh and say . . .
Where did you come from
Where are you goin'
And what are you doin' here.

Keep the radio playin'
And turn the volume up
Keep your transistor plugged into your ear
If you listen and you're still
In the silence of the hills
Ya might hear things you didn't want to hear . . .
Like: where did ya' come from
Where are ya goin'
And what are you doin' here.

166

what am i doin' here?

Leave your litter in the forest
And scattered by the road
So man can feel a little more at home
The telltale signs of man
His paper and his cans
We see 'em and we think we're not alone . . .
But where did we come from
Where are we goin'
And what are we doin' here.

Are we gonna keep a-runnin'
From the questions that we fear
Until we bring the whole thing crashin' down
And on the day we disappear
There'll be no one left to hear
The burnin' sky ask the barren ground
Where did they come from
And where were they goin'
And what . . .
Were they doin' here?

1- What kinds of things do you miss by rushing through life?

2- How is the poet being <u>sarcastic</u> in this poem?

3- What is the poet's prophecy for the future?

4- It has been said that sometimes you look at things and don't really see them, and that you listen to things but don't really hear them. Explain how this might be true.

5- Why is it important to ask yourself questions?

6- Why wouldn't you want to hear the questions asked in this poem? Or would you?

7- What kinds of things might <u>you not</u> want to hear about yourself and the world you are living in?

8- Where did <u>you</u> come from, where are <u>you</u> going, and what are you doing here?

Old Friends

Paul Simon

Old friends,
Old friends
Sat on their park bench
Like bookends.

A newspaper blown through the grass
Falls on the round toes
On the high shoes
Of the old friends.

Old friends,
Winter companions,
The old men
Lost in their overcoats,
Waiting for the sunset.
The sounds of the city,
Sifting through trees,
Settle like dust
On the shoulders
Of the old friends.

Can you imagine us
Years from today,
Sharing a park bench quietly?
How terribly strange
To be seventy.

Old friends,
Memory brushes the same years.
Silently sharing the same fear . . .

Old Friends

1- Why do you think the people were compared to bookends?

2- Why are the men waiting for the sunset?

3- Why do you think they were sitting on the bench all day?

4- What do you think are the patterns in these people's lives?

5- How do you feel about growing old?

6- What is the fear that these people share?

7- Why do you think some people fear getting old?

8- Is it ever possible to have too much time? Why or why not?

9- What do you think about the fact that when you finally have so much time to do whatever you want (due to retirement etc.), you have so little time left to live?

10- How should people "wait for the end" – or should they wait at all?

11- Compare the seasons of the year (spring, summer, fall, and winter) to growing old.

the term

William Carlos Williams

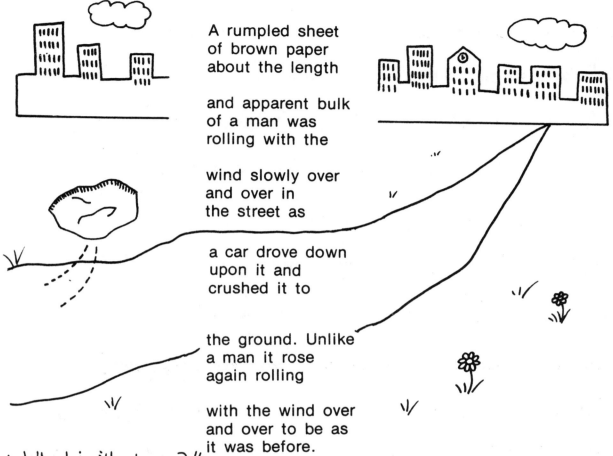

A rumpled sheet
of brown paper
about the length

and apparent bulk
of a man was
rolling with the

wind slowly over
and over in
the street as

a car drove down
upon it and
crushed it to

the ground. Unlike
a man it rose
again rolling

with the wind over
and over to be as
it was before.

1- What is "the term?"

2- The paper rose again after it was crushed, what does this suggest to you?

3- Things live forever (or a lot longer than people.) People die. Could this be a
   message as to what or who is really important in the scheme of life?

4- Humans have searched for ways to become <u>immortal</u> - is immortality important to <u>you</u>?

5- How important is the life of anyone or anything, if all things eventually die?

6- How are people <u>vulnerable</u> - are other living things more <u>or</u> less vulnerable than humans?

7- What are the <u>patterns</u> that are talked about in this poem?

how do i fit?

Southbound on the Freeway

May Swenson

A tourist came in from Orbitville,
parked in the air, and said: The creatures of this star
are made of metal and glass.
Through the transparent parts
you can see their guts.
Their feet are round and roll
on diagrams or long
measuring tapes, dark
with white lines.
They have four eyes
The two in back are red.
Sometimes you can see a five-eyed
one, with a red eye turning
on the top of his head.
He must be special—
the others respect him
and go slow
when he passes, winding
among them from behind.
They all hiss as they glide,
like inches, down the marked
tapes. Those soft shapes,
shadowy inside
the hard bodies—are they
their guts or their brains?

Southbound on the freeway

1- According to the tourist, who inhabits the earth?

2- What are the diagrams that the poet talks about?

3- What is the five-eyed creature with the red eye?

4- What are the soft shapes that are inside the hard bodies?

5- From what you have just read, how do you think this poet looks at life?

6- What does this poem say about <u>technology</u>?

7- Do you think this is an accurate picture of what life is like today? Why or why not?

8- Do you think there is any truth in what the tourist sees? Why or why not?

9- Why do you think the poet chose to call the poem "Southbound on the <u>Freeway</u>", rather than "Southbound on the Highway", or "Interstate," or "Thruway," or "Parkway".. ? (Hint: Look carefully at the word "Freeway.")

10- Answer the question at the end of the poem. In other words, do people control machines or do machines control people? <u>WHY</u>?

The Forecast

Dan Jaffe

Perhaps our age has driven us indoors.
We sprawl in the semi-darkness, dreaming sometimes
Of a vague world spinning in the wind.
But we have snapped our locks, pulled down our shades,
Taken all precautions. We shall not be disturbed.
If the earth shakes, it will be on a screen;
And if the prairie wind spills down our streets
And covers us with leaves, the weatherman will tell us.

1- Why do you think this poem is called "The Forecast?"

2- What does the poet predict will happen to humans in the future?

3- Considering life as it is now, and might be, why do you think people might be driven indoors?

4- According to the poet, how will people feel things, sense things, know things, and learn things?

5- Is this forecast optimistic? Why or why not?

6- Do you ever feel like shutting yourself off from the rest of the world? Why or why not?

7- One idea that can be gotten from the poem is that people are losing touch with the "real" world (reality.) Why and how could this happen?

8- What can you do to keep in touch with the "real" world?

9- Is looking at the world (life) through machines (television, movies, etc.) real or unreal? Why?

patterns

Paul Simon

The night set softly
With the hush of falling leaves
Casting shivering shadows
On the houses through the trees
And light from a street lamp
Paints a pattern on my wall
Like the pieces of a puzzle
Or a child's uneven scrawl.

Up a narrow flight of stairs
In a narrow little room
As I lie upon my bed
In the early evening gloom.
Impaled on my wall
My eyes can dimly see
The patterns of my life
And the puzzle that is me.

From the moment of my birth
To the instant of my death
There are patterns I must follow
Just as I must breathe each breath.
Like a rat in a maze
The path before me lies
And the pattern never alters
Until the rat dies

And the pattern still remains
On the wall where darkness fell
And it's fitting that it should
For in darkness I must dwell.
Like the color of my skin
Or the day that I grow old
My life is made of patterns
That can scarcely be controlled.

1· What is a pattern?

2· What are some of the patterns <u>you</u> <u>must</u> follow?

3· Why do you think the poet calls himself a puzzle?

4· How is a puzzle like a pattern?

5· What type of person do you think would write a poem like this?

6· What is the poet saying about life?

7· Describe a person who you know. Tell what patterns s/he fits into and <u>why</u> you think that person has chosen those patterns.

8· Do <u>you</u> always choose your patterns? Why or why not?

9· Can you do anything to alter (change) the pattern of your life? If so, what?

10· How do patterns determine your fate and fortune?

11· For what do we use patterns?

the circle game

Joni Mitchell

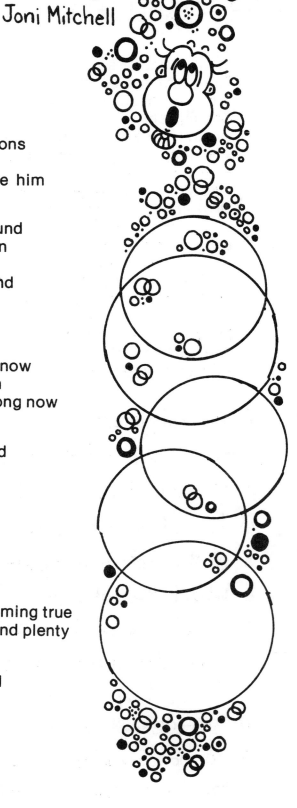

Yesterday a child came out to wonder
Caught a dragonfly inside a jar
Fearful when the sky was full of thunder
And tearful at the falling of a star
Then the child moved ten times round the seasons
Skated over ten clear frozen streams
Words like, when you're older, must appease him
And promises of someday make his dreams

    And the seasons they go round and round
    And the painted ponies go up and down
    We're captive on the carousel of time
    We can't return, we can only look behind
    From where we came
    And go round and round and round
    In the circle game

Sixteen springs and sixteen summers gone now
Cartwheels turn to car wheels thru the town
And they tell him, Take your time, it won't be long now
Till you drag your feet to slow the circles down

    And the seasons they go round and round
    And the painted ponies go up and down
    We're captive on the carousel of time
    We can't return, we can only look behind
    From where we came
    And go round and round and round
    In the circle game.

So the years spin by and now the boy is twenty
Though his dreams have lost some grandeur coming true
There'll be new dreams, maybe better dreams and plenty
Before the last revolving year is through.

    And the seasons they go round and round
    And the painted ponies go up and down
    We're captive on the carousel of time
    We can't return, we can only look behind
    From where we came
    And go round and round and round
    In the circle game.

the circle game

1- How is life like being on a carousel?

2- Why do you think this poem is called "The Circle Game?"

3- What can't you return to? (see line #12.)

4- How can <u>time</u> hold you captive?

5- How is the passing of time (the circle game) like a pattern?

6- How do you think the poet feels about the past?

7- Why do people want to "slow the circles down?"

8- What happens to people's <u>lives</u> and <u>feelings</u> once they start playing the circle game?

9- How do <u>you</u> play the circle game?

10- It has been said that we look at the present through a rear-view mirror (think of being in a car.) In other words, we are a nation that marches backwards into the future. Do <u>you</u> think the ideas in this poem agree or disagree with this statement? Why or why not?

11- Can you ever stop playing the circle game? If so, when? Or, why not?

12- How do <u>you</u> <u>feel</u> about the circle game?

little boxes

Malvina Reynolds

Little boxes on the hillside,
Little boxes made of ticky tacky,
Little boxes on the hillside,
Little boxes all the same.
There's a green one and a pink one
And a blue one and a yellow one
And they're all made out of ticky tacky
And they all look just the same.

And the people in the houses
All went to the university,
Where they were put in boxes
And they came out all the same,
And there's doctors and lawyers,
And business executives
And they're all made out of ticky tacky
And they all look just the same.

And they all play on the golf course
And drink their martinis dry,
And they all have pretty children
And the children go to school,
And the children go to summer camp
And then to the university,
Where they are put in boxes
And they come out all the same.

And the boys go into business
And marry and raise a family
In boxes made of ticky tacky
And they all look just the same.
There's a green one and a pink one,
And a blue one and a yellow one,
And they're all made out of ticky tacky
And they all look just the same.

little boxes

1- What are the little boxes on the hillside?

2- How is this poem's message like the one in the "Circle Game?"

3- Does the poet think people's lives fit into patterns? Why?

4- What kinds of boxes are people put into during their lives? List some. (The poem mentions several...)

5- "Ticky tacky" is a nonsense word, it has no real meaning. Why do you think the poet used this word over and over again in the poem?

6- How can the people in the poem be compared to an assembly line in a factory?

7- What do you think is missing from these people's lives, if anything?

8- How important do you think it is to be an individual? Why?

9- Why do you think a lot of people are comfortable or happy with their little boxes?

10- Are there any little boxes in your life? If so, what are they? If not, explain why.

the poet in you ...

You will write five poems (a minimum of <u>ten</u> lines each.) The topics for the poems can be chosen from the following:

1- How you feel about yourself.

2- How you see other people.

3- The part of the city or town you live in that is you.

4- How you fit into your family.

5- How school affects you.

6- The patterns in your life.

7- The patterns of your life in <u>ten</u> years. (Think of how old you will be and what you are likely to be doing.)

The poems do not have to rhyme. It is more important that they be thought out and express your feelings.

follow your star:

Where Do I Go ?
If I Had Wings
Spelling Assignment
Mirror Writing
For Two Cents
Insight

where do i go?

from the musical _Hair_

"Where do I go? Follow the River. Where do I go?
Follow the Gull. Where is the something? Where is the someone? That tells
me why I live and die.
Where do I go? Follow the children. Where do I go?
Follow their smiles. Is there an answer in their sweet faces
That tells me why I live and die?
Follow the wind. Follow the thunder
Follow the neon in young lover's eyes
Down to the gutter, up to the glitter
Into the city where the truth lies
Where do I go? Follow my heartbeat. Where do I go? Follow my hand.
Where will they lead me and will I ever discover why I live and die?
Why do I live? Why do I die? Tell me where do I go
Tell me why
Tell me where
Tell me why
Tell me where
Tell me why!"

1- Is it important to know where you are going in life? Why or why not?

2- Do you think it's better to automatically get what you want in life _or_ to work for it?

3- Does meeting challenges help or hurt you in life? Why?

4- What kinds of things do _you_ follow in your life? _Why_ do you follow them?

5- Do you let yourself be led or do you lead yourself?

6- Do you think people ever discover why they live and die?

7- Answer these questions as they apply to _you_: Where do I go? Who will lead me? How would life be different without me?

8- This song asks a lot of questions and answers very few. What questions do you ask yourself that are still unanswered? List at least three questions like this. Why do think you still _don't_ have the answers?

182

if i had wings

Peter Yarrow and Susan Yardley

If I had wings no one would ask me should I fly
The birds sing, no one asks why.
I can see in myself wings as I feel them
If you see something else keep your thoughts to yourself
I'll fly free then.

Yesterday's eyes see their colors fading away
They see their sun turning to grey
You can't share in a dream that you don't believe in
If you say that you see and pretend to be me
You won't be then.

How can you ask if I'm happy goin' my way?
You might as well ask a child at play!
There is no need to discuss or understand me
I won't ask of myself to become something else
I'll just be me!

If I had wings no one would ask me should I fly
The birds sing, no one asks why.
I can see in myself wings as I feel them
If you see something else keep your thoughts to yourself
I'll fly free then.

1- Do people's opinions of you hold you back from doing things? Why or why not?

2- Do you have difficulty being different from your friends? Why or why not?

3- Do you think that people who go their own way are happy?

4- Why do you think the person in the song says, "There is no need to discuss or understand me"...do you ever feel that way? Why or why not?

5- Is "I did it my way" always the best thing to do?

6- Summarize this song, explaining what each stanza means to you.

mirror writing... ?

1- "Grown up, and that is a terribly hard thing to do. It is much easier to skip it and go from one childhood to another." – F. SCOTT FITZGERALD

2- "It is unjust to claim the privileges of age, and retain the playthings of childhood." – SAMUEL JOHNSON

3- "To be adult is to be alone." – JEAN ROSTAND

4- "The turning point in the process of growing up is when you discover the core of strength within you that survives all hurt." – MAX LERNER

5- "The strongest principle of growth lies in human choice." – GEORGE ELIOT

6- "He who would learn to fly one day must first learn to stand and walk and run and climb and dance: one cannot fly into flying." – NIETZSCHE

CHOOSE ANY THREE OF THE ABOVE QUOTATIONS:

Paragraph #1... Explain its meaning in detail.

Paragraph #2... How does this quotation apply to you?

Paragraph #3... Explain the quotation in terms of id, ego, and super-ego.

Do each of the above for all 3 quotations you pick. You will have a total of 9 paragraphs.

Teacher: This was done after a discussion of id, ego, and super-ego.

---

spelling...

Find the definition, part of speech, and a synonym for each word. Then, write an EXAMPLE for each word. Have your examples deal with some part of your personality, growing up, or your relationship with other people.

1. stereotype
2. rapport
3. tradition
4. unique
5. expectation
6. peer
7. conformity
8. sacrifice
9. identity
10. disillusion
11. heritage
12. maturity
13. pressure
14. consequence
15. prejudice
16. uncertainty

for 2¢...

The human being is made up of oxygen, nitrogen, phosphorous, hydrogen, carbon, and calcium. There are also 12½ gallons of water, enough iron to make a small nail, about a salt-shaker full of salt, and enough sugar to make one small cube. If one were to put all of this together and try to sell it, the whole thing would be worth about one dollar.

1. What do you think is the point of this statement?

2. In what ways are you worth more than $1.00?

3. What are some ways we measure the worth of human beings?

4. How important is the money value of a thing?

insight ooo Answer these questions:

1· How often do you consider the consequences of what you do <u>before</u> acting?

2· How do you <u>know</u> when something is wrong or right?

3· Why should some people get paid more than others for working - or should they?

4· How come so many people want to "get ahead" and are never satisfied?

5· When, if at all, is it right to tell on someone?

6· When, if at all, is it good to take a dare?

7· How often do you do things of which you are <u>not</u> proud?

8· What is one thing you <u>don't</u> want to be when you get older? Why?

9· How often do you do things just because others expect you to do them that way?

10· How often do you hurt people when you really don't mean to?

Many times people only consider <u>one</u> side of an argument. The next four questions ask you to take an <u>unpopular</u> point of view. You don't have to agree with what you write - sometimes it is good to look at "the other side." You might change your mind or you might convince yourself you were right all along.

In one paragraph (or more) for each of the following, <u>defend</u> the point of view that is being represented.

1· What is good about war? (WAR IS GOOD.)

2· What is good about prejudice? (PREJUDICE IS GOOD.)

3· What is <u>not</u> good about being generous? (BEING GENEROUS IS BAD.)

4· What is <u>not</u> good about being smart? (BEING SMART IS BAD.)

IV. tools of the trade...

HOW TO...

WRITE-ON

ooo Okay, you can write (you learned how to do that back in the first grade!) but one of the things that we're after this year is to make your writing interesting to read...

— SOME THINGS TO KEEP IN MIND WHEN YOU WRITE —

1) One of the best ways to improve the quality of your writing is to start thinking about the <u>type</u> of words you choose...some words suggest special <u>moods</u>. Usually, these kinds of words are adjectives. <u>Think</u> before you use a word in a story. Compare these → "The wind blew...", "The wind rattled the empty trees...", "The sun was very hot..." "The blazing sun scorched the earth..." Ask yourself, "Is there a more descriptive way to say it?" Find these words in a thesaurus.

2) Pay attention to <u>details</u>, they can make things come alive.

3) Use <u>specific</u> <u>examples</u>, especially when you are trying to prove a point.

4) Try to answer these questions whenever possible: <u>WHO</u>, <u>WHAT</u>, <u>WHY</u>, <u>WHERE</u>, <u>WHEN</u>, <u>HOW</u>.

5) <u>Describe</u> as much as you can, <u>in</u> <u>detail</u>.

6) If possible, <u>look</u> at things <u>before</u> you write about them...you'll be surprised at how much you can forget - even with familiar things!

7) <u>Feelings</u> make your writing more personal.

8) <u>Always</u> <u>proofread</u> your paper! Whenever you write something, read it over at least <u>one</u> time to be sure it sounds all right and that it makes sense. Then look for spelling and grammatical errors.

perfect paragraphing...

Paragraphs are used in all kinds of writing. A paragraph is a group of sentences (usually 6-8) that talks about and develops <u>one</u> topic.

- The <u>first</u> sentence of a paragraph is called the <u>Topic Sentence</u>. The Topic Sentence tells <u>what</u> the paragraph is going to be about.

- The next few sentences develop (talk about) your topic. The sentences can be many different kinds. They can include facts or specific examples, descriptions, opinions, explanations, or incidents.

- The <u>last</u> sentence of a paragraph is called the <u>Concluding Sentence</u>. This sentence summarizes your paragraph. You can do this by using <u>different</u> words to re-state your Topic Sentence.

-A <u>Sample Paragraph</u> -

Indent ᐧᐧᐧᐧᐧ→ Fort River is an elementary school in Amherst, Massachusetts. ←ᐧᐧ *TOPIC Sentence* The school is a one floor building with classrooms that are called "quads." Each quad has three home corners. Fort River also has a library called the Media Materials Center. The school has two cafeterias and a large gymnasium. The school was built in 1973. Fort River is one of five elementary schools in this town. ←ᐧᐧ *CONCLUDING SENTENCE*

the other word

o oo the quality of your writing depends on the <u>words</u> you choose to use. Instead of always using words like "big," "small," "good," "pretty," etc. develop a vocabulary of more interesting adjectives. For the words below, find words that mean the same thing or nearly the same thing, by looking in a dictionary or thesaurus, or thinking of more interesting words yourself! Use this paper when you write.

BIG
1. gigantic
2. _____
3. _____
4. _____

SMALL
1. _____
2. _____
3. _____
4. _____

OLD
1. _____
2. _____
3. _____
4. _____

YOUNG
1. _____
2. _____
3. _____
4. _____

HAPPY
1. _____
2. _____
3. _____
4. _____

SAD
1. _____
2. _____
3. _____
4. _____

BEAUTIFUL
1. _____
2. _____
3. _____
4. _____

SOUR
1. _____
2. _____
3. _____
4. _____

COLD
1. _____
2. _____
3. _____
4. _____

RED
1. _____
2. _____
3. _____
4. _____

GREEN
1. _____
2. _____
3. _____
4. _____

BLUE
1. _____
2. _____
3. _____
4. _____

HOT
1. _____
2. _____
3. _____
4. _____

RICH
1. _____
2. _____
3. _____
4. _____

FAT
1. _____
2. _____
3. _____
4. _____

THIN
1. _____
2. _____
3. _____
4. _____

<u>Teacher</u>: This assignment can be repeated often. By using different words you help your students expand their vocabulary.

First Lines

ooo What can you tell about these stories from their first lines?

"It was a bright cold day in April, and the clocks were striking thirteen."

1984

"Crossing the lawn that morning, Douglas Spaulding broke a spider web with his face. A single invisible line on the air touched his brow and snapped without a sound."

Dandelion Wine

"A screaming comes across the sky. It has happened before, but there is nothing to compare it to now."

Gravity's Rainbow

"It was a pleasure to burn. It was special pleasure to see things eaten, to see things blackened and changed."

Fahrenheit 451

"I read about it in the paper, in the subway, on my way to work, I read it and I couldn't believe it, and I read it again."

"Sonny's Blues"

"Alan Austen, as nervous as a kitten, went up certain dark and creaky stairs in the neighborhood of Pell Street and peered about for a long time on the dim landing before he found the name he wanted written obscurely on one of the doors."

"The Chaser"

"During the whole of a dull, dark, and soundless day in the autumn of the year, when the clouds hung oppressively low in the heavens, I had been passing alone, on horseback, through a singularly dreary tract of country, and at length found myself, as the shades of the evening drew on, within view of the melancholy House of Usher."

"The Fall of the House of Usher"

"It was late and everyone had left the cafe except an old man who sat in the shadow the leaves of the tree made against the electric light."

"A Clean, Well-Lighted Place"

R. J. Bauman, who for fourteen years had travelled for a shoe company through Mississippi, drove his Ford along a rutted dirt path."

"Death of a Travelling Salesman"

"It was quite a summer. It was hot: the sun, even when it had just come up, was yellow hot and small as a quarter. There hadn't been any rain in nearly two months, and outside of town only the early cotton had come up; and the corn had rust."

"The Bright Day"

Write an <u>opening line</u> for a story about:

1. a circus coming to town.   2. a murder mystery.   3. the first winter snowstorm.

4. an incredibly hot day.   5. a football game.   6. a spaceship landing on the moon.

7. someone who is about to take a test he or she hasn't studied for.

8. someone who is expecting a bike for Christmas and only sees small boxes under the tree.

9. a person who has to get his or her tooth pulled by a dentist.

10. a child running away from home.

the essay

ooo the purpose of an essay is to make clear to the reader the idea which the author has chosen as his or her subject, as well as to make the author's attitude about the subject, clear. The author may, at times, try to challenge the reader to examine his or her own opinion of the subject, and perhaps change that opinion. Since most people like to make up their own minds, a person who writes an essay needs to be as convincing as possible. Essays can be written in many different ways. They can be done in the form of a story that has a definite point of view. (This is not as easy as it sounds.) Or, they can be done as a straight forward argument that fully discusses a subject. The more facts and specific examples in your essay, the more convincing your essay will be.

Choose _two_ topics from the list below and write an essay on _each_ one:

Comic Books are Worthless   The Possibility of Atomic War
The Freedoms We _Don't_ Have   Should Commercials be Allowed on TV?
Computers are Smarter than People   Television This Year

Medical Care in this Country Should be Free
The Importance of the Equal Rights Amendment
Should Chemical Preservatives be Allowed in Food?
The Appeal of the Fast-Food Restaurants
Time – Our Most Important Possession
Advantages or Disadvantages of Growing Up in a City

I THINK...

No matter what topic you choose, first form a definite opinion, then RESEARCH your topic to get facts to support your argument. Next, decide what FORM your essay will take so you will be able to get your point across and convince your reader in the best possible way. Each essay should be about five paragraphs long.

description checklist ☑

*Use this list when you write...

character: ☑

height
weight
hair color
hair texture
hair style
eye color
shape of eyes
shape of nose
shape of mouth
shape of ears
teeth (crooked, braces, etc.)
complexion (color, pimples, etc.)
shape of face
distinguishing features
glasses (shape and color)
birthmarks / freckles
fingernails (long, polished, etc.)

hand size
foot size
cleanliness
jewelry
clothing worn
style
color
fit (baggy, tight, etc.)
amount
habits
type of walk
voice (loud, soft, etc.)
general appearance
personality (shy, friendly, etc.)
intelligence
age
speech patterns (stutter, accent, etc.)

 ☑

description checklist ☑

place: ☑

general shape
height
width
outside appearance
colors
function (job) of the place
things in the place
climate
sounds in the place
smells in the place

temperature
material used (wood, brick, etc.)
arrangement of things
where the place is
what it is near
what it is next to
what it is across from
scenery surrounding it
mood of the place
people in the place (number)

object: ☑

color
shape
size
function
weight
texture
cost

temperature
smell
taste
sound it makes
state of motion
how it works
how many parts it has (list)

description checklist ☑

event: ☑

what action took place
how long did it take
where did it happen
when did it happen
who was there
how did each person participate
under what conditions did it happen
why did it happen
how did it happen
mood of the event (panic, happiness, etc.)
result of the event
what happened before the event
what happened after the event

Feeling Checklist ☑
love, affection, concern:

admired	adorable	affection	agreeable
altruistic	amiable	benevolent	caring
charitable	comforting	congenial	conscientious
considerate	cooperative	cordial	courteous
dedicated	easy-going	empathetic	fair
faithful	forgiving	friendly	generous
genuine	good-humored	helpful	honest
honorable	humane	interested	just
kind	lenient	loving	mellow
moral	neighborly	obliging	open
optimistic	patient	peaceful	polite
reasonable	receptive	reliable	respectful
responsible	sensitive	sympathetic	tender
thoughtful	tolerant	truthful	trustworthy
understanding	unselfish	warm-hearted	well-meaning

feeling checklist ☑

elation, joy:

amused	at ease	blissful	calm
cheerful	comical	contented	ecstatic
enchanted	enthusiastic	excellent	fantastic
glorious	grand	happy	inspired
jovial	jubilant	magnificent	marvelous
overjoyed	pleasant	proud	serene
splendid	superb	thrilled	tremendous
triumphant	turned on	vivacious	witty

potency:

able	assured	authoritative	bold
brave	capable	confident	courageous
daring	determined	durable	dynamic
effective	energetic	forceful	gallant
hardy	healthy	influential	intense
mighty	powerful	secure	self-confident
self-reliant	skillful	strong	tough

feeling checklist ☑
depression:

abandoned	alienated	alone	awful
battered	blue	burned	crushed
defeated	dejected	desolate	despair
despised	despondent	destroyed	discarded
discouraged	dismal	done for	downcast
downtrodden	dreadful	estranged	excluded
forlorn	forsaken	gloomy	grim
hated	hopeless	horrible	humiliated
hurt	in the dumps	left out	loathed
lonesome	low	miserable	mistreated
moody	obsolete	ostracized	out of sorts
overlooked	pathetic	pitiful	regretful
rejected	reprimanded	rotten	ruined
run down	sad	stranded	unhappy
unloved	washed up	whipped	worthless

feeling checklist ☑

distress:

afflicted	anguished	at the mercy of	awkward
baffled	bewildered	confused	disgusted
displeased	dissatisfied	disturbed	doubtful
futile	grief	helpless	hindered
impatient	imprisoned	lost	offended
pained	perplexed	sickened	skeptical
strained	swamped	tormented	touchy
ungainly	unlucky	unpopular	unsure

fear, anxiety:

afraid	agitated	alarmed	apprehensive
desperate	dread	fidgety	frightened
hesitant	horrified	insecure	intimidated
jealous	jittery	nervous	on edge
overwhelmed	panicky	restless	shaky
tense	terrified	uncomfortable	uneasy

feeling checklist ☑

belittling, criticism, scorn:

abused	branded	censured	deflated
diminished	discredited	disgraced	humiliated
jeered	lampooned	laughed at	libeled
maligned	minimized	mocked	neglected
overlooked	put down	ridiculed	roasted
scorned	slandered	slighted	underestimated

impotency, inadequacy:

anemic	broken	cowardly	crippled
debilitated	defective	deficient	demoralized
disabled	exhausted	feeble	fragile
harmless	helpless	incapable	incompetent
ineffective	inept	inferior	insufficient
meek	paralyzed	powerless	shaken
small	trivial	unable	uncertain
unfit	useless	vulnerable	weak

feeling checklist ☑
anger, hostility, cruelty:

agitated	aggravated	aggressive	annoyed
antagonistic	arrogant	belligerent	bigoted
biting	bloodthirsty	blunt	callous
cold-blooded	combative	cantankerous	contrary
cranky	cross	deadly	discontented
dogmatic	enraged	fierce	furious
gruesome	hard	harsh	hateful
heartless	hideous	hostile	inconsiderate
inhuman	insensitive	intolerable	irritated
malicious	mean	murderous	nasty
obstinate	oppressive	poisonous	prejudiced
reckless	resentful	rude	ruthless
sadistic	savage	severe	spiteful
stern	unfeeling	unmerciful	unruly
vicious	vindictive	violent	wrathful

Nathan Levy   Author/Speaker

Applying his experience from over thirty years as a teacher, principal, author, and educational consultant, Nathan Levy has traveled extensively across the United States, as well as South America, Europe, and Asia to bring his message related to thinking and creativity. His workshops cover many topics for a wide array of participants. He offers ideas on how to bring creativity and spontaneity to adults and children while stimulating integrated thinking. Nathan Levy's many publications assist people in their quest for new and creative ways to develop critical thinking skills. Nathan is the author of the famous book series *Stories With Holes,* and *Whose Clues?* as well as several other books. STORIES WITH HOLES is an excellent teaching tool designed to promote *higher order thinking* in the classroom. For more information about workshops and presentations call (732) 605-1643.

Dynamic Workshops

The various topics for the workshops which Nathan Levy presents are of great benefit to educators as well as parents. Nathan allows the attendants to participate in the workshops to give them the skills they need to bring the information with them to their schools and homes. Topics include:

PRACTICAL ACTIVITIES AND STRATEGIES FOR IMPROVING READING, WRITING, AND THINKING IN THE CLASSROOM

USING "STORIES WITH HOLES" AND OTHER THINKING SKILLS

DIFFERENTIATING IN THE REGULAR CLASSROOM

TEACHING GIFTED CHILDREN (in and out of the regular classroom)

And Many More...

N.L. Associates, Inc. | **P.O. Box 1199** | **Hightstown, NJ 08520**
(732) 605-1643
www.storieswithholes.com

Beaded

Treasures

Beaded
Treasures

Dorothy Wood

David and Charles

www.rucraft.co.uk

A DAVID & CHARLES BOOK
Copyright © David & Charles Limited 2010

David & Charles is an F+W Media, Inc. Company,
4700 East Galbraith Road, Cincinnati, OH 45236

First published in the UK and US in 2010
Text and project designs copyright © Dorothy Wood 2010

A catalogue record for this book is available from the
British Library.

ISBN-13: 978-0-7153-3668-7 paperback
ISBN-10: 0-7153-3668-1 paperback

Printed in China by RR Donnelley
for David & Charles
Brunel House, Newton Abbot, Devon

Acquisitions Editors Jane Trollope and Cheryl Brown
Assistant Editor Juliet Lines
Project Editor Ame Verso
Designer Victoria Marks
Photographers Karl Adamson, Ginette Chapman, Kim Sayer,
Ally Stewart, Simon Whitmore, Lorna Yabsley
Production Controller Kelly Smith
Pre Press Jodie Culpin

David & Charles publish high-quality books on a wide range
of subjects. For more great book ideas visit:

www.rucraft.co.uk

Contents

Introduction

Beaded Treasures brings together a diverse collection of attractive and easy-to-make small-scale projects that incorporate beads in a variety of exciting ways. Here you will learn techniques for making beautiful jewellery and embroidering with beads, as well as mastering bead loom weaving, bead knitting and making beaded ropes and cords. The clear project instructions are easy to follow whether you are a novice or an experienced crafter and any templates or charts you need are given on pages 122–3.

The projects are grouped together in five sumptuous chapters according to the type of items created: Bracelets & Bangles, Necklaces & Scarves, Rings & Earrings, Bags & Boxes and Beaded Accessories. The first project in each chapter is illustrated with step-by-step photographs, and the numerous ideas that follow it have clear stepped instructions. Most of the techniques you will need are quick and simple and are described within the projects. Where additional advice is needed you will find it in the Techniques section (pages 90–121), which gives you a thorough grounding in eight different beading techniques.

Beading is often thought of as an enjoyable but time-consuming craft, however, this book focuses on petite projects that use the fabulous decorative qualities of beads and that should be fairly straightforward to make. The projects are many and varied: there are over 50 different projects to choose from – a cornucopia of delights for the bead enthusiast and keen crafter alike – to give everyone the opportunity to widen their horizons and to find new, fun and rewarding ways to work with beads.

Beads

Walk into any bead shop and you will find a wonderful array of beads in all shapes, sizes and colours. It is worth having a good look around first to see what is available, as many shops specialize in particular types of beading; if jewellery is the main focus, the shop will stock mainly large decorative beads, whereas another shop may have a wide range of smaller beads such as seed beads and bugles for loom work and needle weaving. Beads are also available by mail order catalogue and online shopping, and although this can be more economical, nothing beats the experience of walking into an 'Aladdin's Cave' of a really good bead shop and handpicking your beads.

Choosing beads

With such a variety of beads it can be overwhelming deciding what to buy but it is easy to narrow down your choice to make the task less daunting. As different beading techniques often use specific types of beads, once you decide what you are going to bead then the task becomes much easier. Seed beads are ideal for techniques such as bead loom weaving, needle weaving or ropes and cords, whereas larger beads are more suitable for threading and stringing, and wirework. Learning a little about the different types of beads, how they are measured and different finishes will help you make an informed choice next time you visit the bead shop.

Large beads

Glass

Glass is the most versatile of all the materials from which beads are made. It can be made into a wide range of sizes and shapes and the variety of finishes, described on page 11, make for endless possibilities. Pressed glass beads are made in moulds to create lots of different shapes. Powder glass beads are made from recycled glass, which is ground and then fused in moulds to create beads with striped layers. Millefiori beads are made from canes of glass that is then cut into slices to reveal the decorative cross section. Metallic-lined beads are transparent beads with the holes lined in a metallic colour to create a sparkly effect that shines through the surround.

Crystals

The term 'crystal' describes a faceted bead ranging from the finest quality cut glass, such as Swarovski crystals, to inexpensive faceted glass or even moulded plastic beads. There is a huge difference in price but the more expensive crystals have a far superior shine and sparkle. Crystals are available in a wide range of colours and shapes.

Lampwork

These exquisite glass beads are handmade on a workbench using a blowtorch with rods or canes of plain or patterned glass. The beads are formed around a mandrel, a revolving metal rod that determines the size of the hole. The winding process creates distinctive lines of glass wound around the outside. The still soft glass can be pressed with a ribbed tool or crumbs of glass can be sprinkled on the surface to create texture.

Pearls

The lustre on pearls makes them look luxurious even if the beads themselves can be inexpensive. It is easy to distinguish between real and fake pearls because if you rub a real pearl gently against your tooth it produces a grating sensation whereas the surface of imitation pearls is completely smooth. Real pearls, which fall into the organic group, see page 9, can either be cultured (from a pearl farm) or from the wild. Like every other type of bead the price varies with quality. The most valuable pearls have an iridescent lustre and are not too wrinkled. Pearls can be dyed almost any colour but are most often white, cream or pastel shades.

Metal

Metal beads are available in a wide range of materials such as brass, copper, aluminium and different alloys. Some silver and gold beads are plated over a base metal but you can buy precious metal beads in sterling silver. As gold is so expensive, beads are generally a cheaper substitute known as rolled or gold-filled. Metal beads can be moulded, modelled or shaped from sheet metal and often have a distinctive textured surface.

Modelled

Modelling materials for beads include resin, gesso, lacquer, pâpier maché, ceramic, polymer clay and cinnabar. Although many are mass-produced these beads are still in the main handmade and have a quaintness and individuality that is lost with manufactured beads.

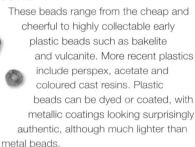

Plastic

These beads range from the cheap and cheerful to highly collectable early plastic beads such as bakelite and vulcanite. More recent plastics include perspex, acetate and coloured cast resins. Plastic beads can be dyed or coated, with metallic coatings looking surprisingly authentic, although much lighter than metal beads.

Gemstones

Gemstones or semi-precious beads are pieces of mineral, which have been cut and polished to make attractive and valuable beads. Often sold in strings, the price varies considerably depending on the aesthetic value and rarity of the mineral. Transparent gemstones are sometimes faceted to add sparkle and opaque gemstones, like opal, are often made into cabochons. Inexpensive chips are small rough pieces of mineral, ideal for jewellery making and bead knitting.

Organic

Organic beads, made from a huge variety of natural materials, were the first beads made by our ancestors for artistic ornamentation. Seeds, nuts, shells, bones and horn were all fashioned into beads then and are still popular now. Some organic materials like ivory, amber, tortoiseshell and jet are now rare but can be found in antique jewellery. Painted wood beads are colourful and cheap but there are also lots of really attractive beads made from unusual woods from around the world.

Small beads

Seed beads

These are round doughnut-shaped beads ranging from size 3 to 15. Larger seed beads are known as pebble or pony beads and the smaller ones as petites. The most common size of seed bead is size 11 (see page 10).

Cylinder beads

Cylinder beads, also known by their trade names delicas, antiques or magnificas, are precision-milled tubular beads. They are ideal for needle weaving and bead loom weaving as the beads sit neatly side by side to make an even bead fabric. Cylinder beads have a large hole, enabling you to pass the thread through each bead several times.

Hex beads

These are cylindrical beads made from a six-sided glass cane. They are like a squat bugle bead (see below) and are useful for creating texture. Twisted hex beads are also called two-cuts.

Drop beads

Drop beads, such as Magatamas, are beads with an off-centre hole that adds interest and texture to many bead projects. They are available in the same colours and finishes as ordinary seed beads.

Triangle beads

These beads have three sides and add an interesting texture to bead fabric, especially herringbone stitch (see page 115). There are two main styles, both from Japan; the geometric sharp-sided Toho triangle and the more rounded Miyuki triangle.

Bugle beads

Bugle beads are glass canes cut to a variety of lengths. The most common sizes are 3–4mm, 6–7mm, 9mm and 15mm. Twisted bugles are five- or six-sided tubes that have been twisted while the glass is still hot.

Bead sizes

When you handpick beads it isn't so essential to know the exact size as you can mix and match on the spot. However, if you are buying online or from a catalogue the beads may not be shown actual size and it is useful to know how different beads are measured. Beads are generally measured in millimetres (mm) but some, especially seed beads and bugles, can also have bead sizes. Beads are measured across the widest point. So if the bead is round it is the diameter, on a square bead it is the width and if oval, cylindrical or rectangular, the beads are measured by length and width.

Seed beads

Many beading techniques use small beads known collectively as seed beads which range in size from the tiny size 15, known as petite beads, to large size 3 pebble beads. Seed bead sizes relate to the number of beads that fit into 2.5cm (1in) when laid out like rows of doughnuts. It is not always accurate but, as shown below, there is an obvious scale of sizes.

Size 15 = 1.3mm
Size 11 = 1.8mm
Size 10 = 2.0mm
Size 9 = 2.2mm
Size 8 = 2.5mm
Size 6 = 3.3mm

Bugle beads

These tubes of glass are measured in millimetres (mm) or by size, depending on where you buy them. To make matters more confusing, Czech and Japanese bugles are measured differently so check before you buy. If you want to match bugles with seed beads, a size 1 bugle is about the same diameter as a size 12 seed bead; other bugles are about the same diameter as a size 11 seed bead.

Czech

Size 1 = 2mm
Size 2 = 4mm
Size 3 = 7mm
Size 4 = 9mm
Size 5 = 11mm

Japanese

Size 1 = 3mm
Size 2 = 6mm
Size 3 = 9mm

Bead quantities

Beads are either sold individually, in a packet of some sort or on a string. Larger beads are more often sold individually although bead strings have become quite popular, especially for semi-precious beads. These strings are generally a standard 40cm (16in) long and so the number of beads varies depending on the size of the individual beads. The table below gives you an idea of the quantities for one string.

Bead quantity for one string

Size	No. of beads	Size	No. of beads
2mm	200	8mm	50
3mm	133	9mm	44
4mm	100	10mm	40
5mm	80	12mm	33
6mm	67	15mm	27
7mm	57	20mm	20

With seed beads the strings are 51cm (20in) long and generally sold as hanks of 12 strings. The quantity varies depending on the size of the beads. Use the table below as a guide.

Seed bead quantity for one string

Size	Beads per 2.5cm (1in)	No. of beads
15	24	480
11	17	340
10	16	320
9	15	300
8	13	260
6	10	200

Seed beads, cylinder beads and bugles are sold in a variety of packets, bags and tubes with no standard bead packet sizes. Packets or containers usually have the weight marked, making it easier to determine how many you require. Some beads are sold in round weights such as 5g or 100g; others are sold with a particular number of beads so have an odd weight like 4.54g. Do check the weight of each different bead – some companies keep the bead quantity the same in each packet and vary the price whereas others keep the price the same and alter the quantity. Many small beads are sold in standard tubes and sold by length of tube usually either 3in (8cm) or 6in (16cm). To give you a rough idea of quantity and weight, the table, right, shows a few examples, but bear in mind that different manufacturers' beads vary.

Bead packet quantity guide

Bead type	Size	Tube size	No. of beads	Weight
Seed beads	15	8cm (3in)	3800	13g
	11	8cm (3in)	1650	15g
	8	8cm (3in)	600	15g
	6	8cm (3in)	150	13g
Cylinder beads	11	2.5cm (1in)	1000	5g
	8	2.5cm (1in)	150	5g
Toho triangles	11	8cm (3in)	1020	12g
Magatamas	4 x 6mm	8cm (3in)	150	14g
Cube beads	3mm	8cm (3in)	240	12g
	4mm	8cm (3in)	140	12g

Bead finishes

Beads, especially small beads like seed beads and bugles, have several descriptive words that explain exactly what the bead looks like. For example, 'SL purple AB' is a silver-lined purple bead with an iridescent, rainbow effect on the surface (AB meaning Aurora Borealis). This information can be extremely useful when you are ordering from a catalogue or on the Internet where you can see lots of different purple beads that all look fairly similar.

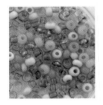

Transparent beads made from clear or coloured glass are see-through and allow light to pass through. **Opaque** beads are a solid colour and don't allow any light to pass through. **Translucent** beads are between transparent and opaque and sometimes referred to as **greasy**, **opal** or **satin** beads.

Gloss beads are very shiny like glass. **Matt** beads are opaque beads that have been tumbled or dipped in acid to give them a dull, flat surface. **Frosted** beads are transparent or translucent beads, which have been treated in a similar way to matt beads.

Lustre beads are opaque beads with a coating that gives the bead a pearl finish. **Ceylon** beads are transparent beads with a milky lustre. **Gold** or **silver lustre** beads have been treated with a gold or silver pearl finish.

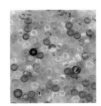

Colour-lined or **inside colour** beads are transparent beads with the hole lined in another opaque colour. **Silver-lined** (rocailles) beads have the hole lined with silver. They are also available with a matt finish that has a frosted appearance.

Iris, **iridescent**, **rainbow** or **AB** beads have been treated with metal salts while the glass is hot to create a coating that resembles an oil slick. Matt beads have an appearance like raku, or pottery-fired clay.

Dyed beads have been painted with a dye or paint on the surface. They often have bright or unusual colours but the dye or paint can wear off in use.

Metallic beads have been heated and sprayed with oxidized tin. **Higher metallic** beads are surface coated with gold and then sprayed with oxidized titanium. The gold gives a brighter finish. **Galvanized** beads are electroplated with zinc for a durable finish.

Materials

All the materials used in the book are readily available from craft or jewellery suppliers. If you don't have a local shop, check the suppliers list on pages 126–7 to find companies who operate a mail-order system or have websites.

Fabrics

Beads can be used to embellish all sorts of fabrics, including **silk**, **felt**, **velvet**, **cotton**, **netting**, **organza** and **prints**. Choose a weight of fabric to suit the project, using the 'you will need' list in each project as a guide for what to buy. If the fabric you want to use is too lightweight, sew or iron interfacing on the reverse side to add body before sewing on the beads.

Threads

Polyester sewing thread is ideal for couching or embroidery techniques (see pages 119–21) but a specialist beading thread is more suitable for all other beading techniques. **Nymo and S-lon threads** are strong, flat, nylon threads available in a range of sizes, or use a round braided thread like **Fireline**. The standard size for seed beads is D and the finer size B is ideal when passing the thread through a bead several times. Both thicknesses are available in a range of colours that can be matched to your beads. **Cord threads** are more suitable for making fringes and tassels (see pages 100–102) as they allow the beads to swing attractively. Refer to the 'you will need' list in each project for the specific thread used.

Ribbons

Ribbons are one of the easiest trimmings to buy, as they are available in such a wide variety of shops. The range of colours and textures is huge – from the sheerest **organza** to heavyweight **twills** and **velvets** – and all are suitable for embellishing. Use a pattern or picot edging to dictate where to place the beads or work freely on a plain ribbon. Try using wide ribbons instead of fabric for making small accessories (see Ribbon Gift Bags, page 74).

Beaded trims

Beads and sequins are not only sold loose but are available ready-made into **trimmings**, **fringing**, **braids** and **motifs**. It is a more expensive way to buy the beads but the effect is instant and you only buy exactly what you need. The clever use of bead products can be quite effective and with careful design the trimming should become an integral part of the completed project (see Sheer 'n' Swinging Scarf, page 42).

Glues

White PVA glue is a good basic craft glue. For fine, detailed work decant some glue into a small plastic bottle with a nozzle and attach a metal gutta nib as illustrated. **Clear superglue** is ideal for securing single beads or ball ends on to hard surfaces such as wire. The gel version is easier to control: apply a tiny drop to the wire then slide the bead over the glue and leave for a few seconds to dry. If you need a strong glue for larger beads use an **epoxy resin**, which has two components that are mixed together to activate the adhesive. **Craft glue dots** are ideal for sticking small bead motifs to a smooth surface. They are available in a range of sizes and different types, such as pop-up glue dots, which raise the motif off the background to give a three-dimensional effect. Mini glue dots are perfect for sticking ribbon. **Jewellery glue** is a clear-drying glue that doesn't harden completely and so maintains the flexibility of the stringing material while holding the bead or knot secure. Refer to the 'you will need' lists in the projects to tell you which products you will require for each item.

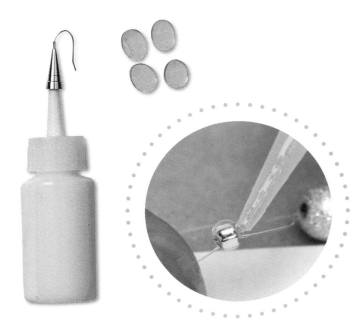

Wire

I have used various types of wire in this book because this material works so well with beads. Wire is measured either in millimetres (mm) or by standard wire gauge (swg) and both measurements are given in the project 'you will need' lists. Wire used for jewellery making ranges from **base metal brass** or **copper** to **sterling silver**. The most popular wires are **silver-** or **gold-plated**, but **coloured enamelled** wires give a coordinated look to a jewellery design. A good standard size that holds its shape in a bead link is 0.6mm (24swg). The higher the swg, the thinner the wire, so 36swg is a very fine 0.2mm, and 18swg is a chunky 1.2mm.

Craft wire

The most popular craft wires range from 1mm (19swg) down to 0.375mm (28swg) and the thinner wires have a larger gauge number. For beading, a good all-round wire to start with is 0.6mm (24swg). Choose from enamelled wire, which has a copper base and is available in a wide range of colours, or silver- and gold-plated wire for a classic finish. Wire cutters are needed for cutting wires (see page 16).

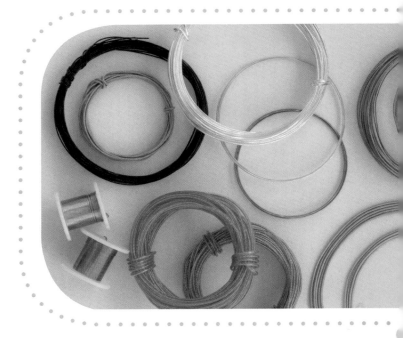

Memory wire

This is a jewellery wire sold in circles of various diameters for necklaces and bracelets and is called memory wire because it retains its shape. You will need to use special memory wire cutters, or failing that a heavyweight wire cutter to cut these hard wires.

Bead stringing wire

This is a tough nylon-covered jewellery wire that is perfect for basic bead stringing and is available in 7, 19 or 49 strands. Wires with more strands are of better quality. The overall thickness of wire in each type ranges from 0.25–0.66mm (0.010–0.026in).

Jewellery findings

Findings are the hooks, fastenings and pins that transform beads into jewellery. There are all sorts of styles, from traditional to contemporary, and it is worth searching for unusual fastenings and clasps to match the particular design. Basic findings are silver- or gold-plated but for a special project ask in your local bead shop for sterling silver or even real gold fitments. Look for clasps and fastenings in an appropriate size and shape to make your jewellery look really stunning.

Head pins

These resemble a large dressmaker's pin and are used to make bead dangles or charms (see page 105). Basic head pins have a flat, plain end, but look out for head pins with decorative ends, which are especially attractive for making earrings (see Ready-to-Wear Earrings, page 60).

Eye pins

These have a round loop at one end and are generally used to make bead links (see page 104). Longer eye pins can be coiled to make decorative ends for earrings or pendants.

Thong ends

Secure to the ends of leather thong or cord using flat-nosed pliers so that a fastening can be attached (see page 113).

Spring ends

Thread ribbons and cords into the springs, then squeeze the end spring only to secure and attach a fastening (see page 113).

Crimp ends

These findings are specially designed for finishing bead stringing wire neatly, but can also be used for fine thong and other threads. Simply insert the wire and squeeze the crimp end with crimping pliers.

Knot covers

Also known as calottes (with a side hole) or clamshell calottes (with a hole in the hinge), these findings hide the knot or crimp at the end of the necklace or bracelet and make it easy to attach a fastening (see page 113–14).

End cones

These are knot covers, usually cone- or tulip-shaped, for thicker threads, ribbons or multiple strands. Choose a size that fits snugly around the beads. See page 114 for how to secure the threads and attach fastenings.

End bars

Use end bars with rings for attaching multiple strands of beads on necklaces and bracelets. Solid crimp bars have tiny teeth for gripping and can be secured to ribbon, yarn or beadwork with flat-nosed pliers.

Spacer bars

These hold strings of beads at an equal distance apart. Use end bars with the same number of rings or holes to finish the item then attach the fastening (see page 113).

Crimps

Round and tubular crimps are generally used on thread that can't be knotted, such as bead stringing wire. They are available in a range of sizes – generally use a larger size of tube than the round style. To attach fastenings and space beads along the wire, see pages 107–108.

Jump rings

These round or oval rings, which have a slit for opening and closing, are generally used to link components and attach fastenings (see page 106). They can also be used for chain maille where rings are linked together in a decorative pattern (see page 109).

Filigree caps

These give a slightly antique appearance to beads. There are lots of different styles and sizes to suit a range of beads (see Pearl Cluster Earrings, page 59). Turn to page 106 for how to fit them.

Split rings

These are formed from a coil of wire. The fastening has to be slotted between the coils and pushed round to secure over both wires. Use split-ring pliers (see page 17) to attach fastenings to prevent breaking your fingernails.

Earring wires

These come in a variety of styles suitable for pierced ears, or you can buy screw or clip fitments. See page 106 for how to attach them.

Solid rings

Available in a diverse range of sizes and shapes, solid rings are used generally as a design element in jewellery pieces, either individually or joined together with jump rings to make a chain.

 Tip Jewellery findings come in a range of metal finishes but use solid silver if you are allergic to nickel or other metal finishes.

Fastenings

These range from the basic lobster claw to ornate toggle and clasp items. Choose one to suit the style or material used to make the item, making sure that it is strong enough for the weight of the beads. Fastenings can have a single hole or multiple holes to accommodate one or more strands. Crimp fastenings are ideal for bead stringing wire or fine thong, as you can slot the threading material straight into the fastening and secure with crimping pliers (see page 17).

Trigger clasp   **Screw fastenings**   **Lobster claw**   **Ornate hook**   **Magnetic fastening**

Toggle fastening   **Multi-strand fastenings**   **Crimp fastening**

Tools and Equipment

As with any craft, if you are new to beading, you will need to assemble a small range of basic tools. As you progress, you can invest in one or two of the more specialist tools and other equipment as required. Beadwork tools and equipment are readily available from craft and bead shops or from one of the many online suppliers, some of which are listed on pages 126–7.

Basic tool kit

Choose a relatively fine set of these tools, as you will usually be working on a small scale. Mini tools are ideal if you have small hands or do not intend to use the tools very frequently.

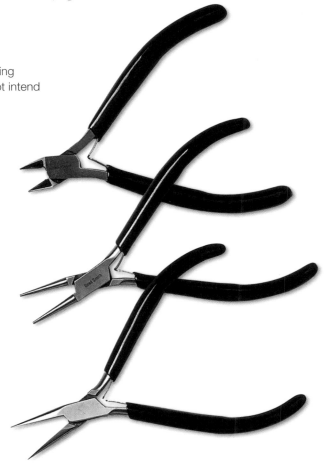

Wire cutters

Many fine wires can be cut to length quite easily with a pair of craft scissors. However, if you are making jewellery or trying to cut wire ends close to a project you will get better results with a pair of wire cutters. Hold the flat edge of the cutters away from the 'tail' of the wire for best results.

Round-nosed pliers

The tapered jaws of these pliers are used to make rings of wire. Hold the wire near the top of the jaws to make a small ring and near the base to make a larger ring.

Flat-nosed pliers

These are ideal for holding small beads and manipulating wire. Look out for those with a fairly smooth surface on the gripping part of the jaws. If they are too serrated the teeth will damage the wire. Some flat-nosed pliers have a snipe nose for fine work.

Beading mat

Textured mats are inexpensive and indispensable for all beading work. The fine pile stops the beads rolling about and lets you pick up directly on to the needle. Once you have finished, it is easy to fold the mat and tip any beads left back into their container.

Embroidery scissors

These small scissors with fine, sharp points are ideal for trimming the ends of threads closely, especially in the case of small-scale work.

Thread conditioner

These are often used to prepare thread for bead stitching or stringing. They reduce the amount of friction as the thread is pulled through beads and makes it less prone to tangling, which in turn helps to prolong the life of beading. Run your thread through the conditioner, avoiding the needle area, and then pull the thread back through between your finger and thumb to remove any excess conditioner and smooth the thread.

Bead reamer

Most bead reamer tools have several different heads encrusted with fine diamond powder so that you can open out bead holes. This tool is ideal for enlarging the occasionally encountered undersized hole in strings of pearls or other semi-precious stones.

Crimping pliers

If you plan to use crimps regularly, crimping pliers will produce a more professional finish than flat-nosed pliers. The latter simply flatten the crimp, while crimping pliers put a dent in one side of the crimp and then you use the pliers to squeeze the bent crimp to make a neat, rounded tube shape (see page 107). The pliers come in three sizes to suit different sizes of crimp.

Split-ring pliers

Split rings are notoriously difficult to open, so if you use them regularly, consider buying these pliers, which have a special tip to open the ring so that you can attach a finding.

Tweezers

Fine-pointed tweezers are useful if you need to untie knots and also for picking up individual small beads from a beading mat or a dish of beads.

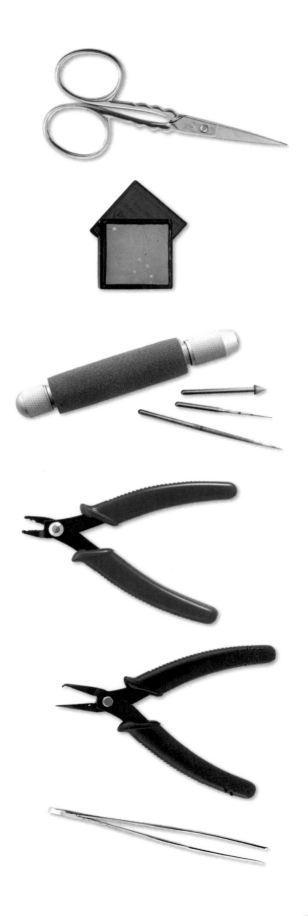

Bead spinner

If you are making a multi-strand necklace or bracelet, this tool will speed up the process considerably. It also makes it easy to mix beads to create a random effect. Larger models are easier to use and will work with fairly small quantities of beads. See page 111 for how to use it.

Bead board

Not essential, but a useful piece of equipment for making necklaces or bracelets. The grooves hold the beads in position so that you can arrange and rearrange them easily, and the curved shape gives a good impression of the finished result. The board is also marked with measurements to make it easy to plan designs and make them the right length.

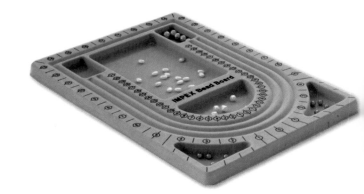

Embroidery hoop

An embroidery hoop or frame keeps the fabric taut while you embroider with beads and prevents puckering. Wrapping the inner hoop with narrow fabric tape keeps the fabric in the hoop tensioned.

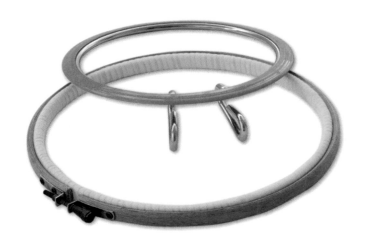

Bead looms

There are several different bead looms available, some are wooden and others have a stiff wire frame. Basic looms are suitable for making bead bands up to 6cm (2½in) wide, although the wire spring restricts the number of warp threads that can be strung on the loom. For weaving bands of beads wider than 30–35 beads, you will need to buy or make a wider loom with a longer spring or coil.

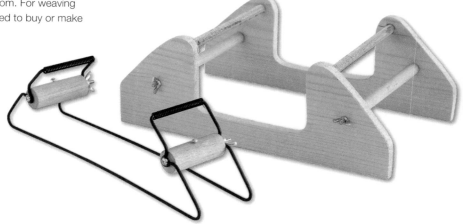

Needles

A variety of different needles are needed, depending on the technique and type of beads used.

1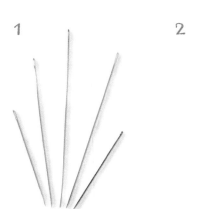

2

3

4

5

1 Beading needles

You can buy bead embroidery needles in short or long lengths. Size 10 or 12 are fine enough for most seed beads, but if you are using petite or size 15 beads (15/0 or 1.3mm) or need to go through seed beads several times, use size 13 or 15. Remember that the finer needles have much smaller holes and you may need to choose a finer thread. Regular quilting needles or sharps are also suitable, which have small, round eyes that are relatively easy to thread. These needles are ideal for embroidery and bead stitches.

2 Bead loom needles

These fine, extra-long needles are designed to go through the small holes in seed beads when working on a loom. The length of the needle enables you to go through all the beads at once, but it does make the needle fragile, so keep a stock in case of breakages.

3 Big-eye needles

Two very fine needles are soldered together at each end to make a needle with a long eye. These needles are ideal for threading thicker yarns and are available in several sizes.

4 Curved big-eye needles

These specialist needles are ideal for threading beads using a bead spinner (see opposite). The curved shape follows the flow of the beads so that they thread on to the needle quickly (see page 111).

5 Tapestry needles

These large-eye needles, which have a blunt tip, are useful for stringing large beads or when working with yarn or wire. They can also be used to guide knots into place (see page 112).

Bead storage tips

It is important to store beads carefully so that they are easy to access, don't spill out and can be returned to the container quickly once the work is done. Follow these practical tips to ensure effective storage.

- Once opened, transfer beads from their original packaging, such as plastic bags, bubble packs and boxes, to stronger containers.
- Tubes are generally adequate for storage as long as the lid is a good fit, but containers with secure screw tops are more suitable for seed beads and other small beads.
- Label boxes of beads carefully with size, colour and finish, as well as where you bought them in case you run out before finishing an item and need to restock.
- Store larger beads in small translucent or clear boxes so that you can see the colours inside, especially useful if you want to mix and match.
- Boxes with a lid and base the same size and shape are particularly useful, as you can tip half the beads into the lid to make it easier to handpick a few.
- Look for inexpensive polythene boxes sold at bead and craft fairs.

The Projects

Necklaces & Scarves
pages 36—49

Bracelets & Bangles
pages 22—35

Bracelets & Bangles

Making beautiful bracelets has never been easier so there is no longer an excuse for not having the perfect beaded bangle to wear with a special outfit – just make one! The projects in this chapter range from simple wire projects that can be completed in a matter of minutes to slightly more intricate woven designs. Using the techniques you will learn along the way, you will be able to adapt the designs in terms of beads and colours to create your own unique pieces too.

Charm Bracelet

Once you realize how easy it is to make a beaded charm bracelet using head pins you will never be out of jewellery to match an outfit for any occasion. A head pin is rather like a very large dressmaker's pin. They can be of varying lengths but remember that it is always easier to bend a long pin rather than a short one. To make this attractive charm bracelet you can add beads to a ready-made bracelet or add bracelet fastenings to a length of silver- or gold-plated chain using jump rings (see page 106). When making a charm bracelet choose a variety of beads in a range of sizes and shapes and attach the beads so that they all hang from the same side of the chain.

Charm Bracelet

You will need...

- Selection of pink, white and turquoise beads
- Crystal bugles, 30mm
- Silver-plated chunky chain bracelet
- Silver-plated wire, 0.6mm (24swg)
- Silver-plated jump rings
- Silver-plated head pins
- Basic tool kit (see pages 16–19)

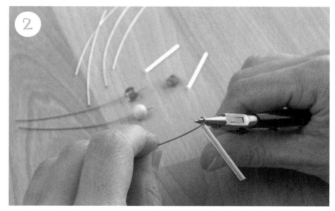

1 Open out the chain bracelet and lay out the beads along the length to achieve an attractive balance of shapes, colours and sizes. Use long beads such as bugles to create depth or position several beads on top of one another.

Tip If you don't have a plain chain bracelet simply buy a length of chain from the bead shop and attach bracelet fastenings at each end using jump rings (see page 106).

2 Make the beads into charms using head pins or wire. If the bead has a small enough hole, simply thread it on to a head pin. Using round-nosed pliers, hold the head pin close to the bead and wind the wire around once or twice. Trim the wire end close to the loop and then hold the loop in the round-nosed pliers and bend back slightly to straighten (see also page 105).

3 If you like, you can pick up several beads on the head pin to make a longer charm. If the bead hole is slightly larger than the head pin, pick up a seed bead before the larger bead so that it doesn't come off the end. Make a ring at the top as described in step 2.

4 Beads with larger holes can be attached using silver-plated wire. Cut a short length of wire and place the bead in the middle. Fold the wire in half and twist the two ends together for 5–7mm (¼–⅜ in) (see also page 104).

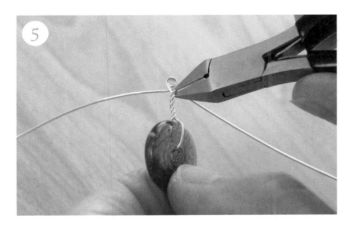

5 Wind one end of the wire around the round-nosed pliers twice to form a loop. Carefully cut off the ends of the wire close to the ring.

6 Lay the bracelet out so the chain is not twisted. Lay out the beads along the length. Open the jump rings one at a time and attach the charms (see tip below). The beads should be attached on the same side of the chain so that they hang in the right way.

tip To open a jump ring, hold it on either side of the join with two pairs of pliers. Push the ends away from one another to open them. Once the charm is attached reverse the process to close the jump ring.

Ribbon Chain Bracelet

This unusual bracelet is made by weaving lengths of sheer ribbon through chunky chain to create an interesting effect. These are then paired with lengths of chain punctuated with bead links to make a fun and festive design.

You will need . . .

- 3 pebble beads, 15mm
- 10–12 medium-sized mixed beads
- 7 gold washer-style beads
- 2 gold tube beads
- Gold-plated chain with 5mm links, 1.25m (1¼yd)
- Sheer burgundy ribbon, 1m (40in) of 6mm
- Gold-plated wire 0.6mm (24swg)
- 10 gold tube crimps, 3mm
- 16 gold-plated jump rings
- 2 toggle fastening rings, 7mm
- Toggle fastening, 12mm
- Basic tool kit (see pages 16–19)

1 Cut five 15cm (6in) lengths of chain. Bend a 10cm (4in) piece of scrap wire in half and twist one end tightly to make a 'needle'. Thread a 25cm (10in) length of ribbon on to the needle and weave it through the chain links on one length. Repeat on all the lengths.

2 Thread the ribbon through a large tube crimp and then a jump ring and back through the crimp. Thread it through the last link in the chain and back through the crimp. Pull the ribbon with both ends to manoeuvre the chain, crimp and jump rings close together. Trim the ribbon tail and then squeeze the crimp to flatten and secure the ribbon. Repeat at both ends of all the chains.

3 Make three bead links by picking up two small beads on gold-plated wire then add a pebble bead and two more small beads. Use round-nosed pliers to make an eye pin loop at each end of the wire (see page 104).

4 Cut three pieces of chain 13cm (5in) long. Cut one in half and cut the other two 4cm (1½in) from one end. Attach a bead link between the cut pieces of chain. Arrange the bead lengths between the ribbon chains so that the beads step down the bracelet.

5 Attach the chains to the small toggle ring with jump rings. Repeat at the other end. Attach a bracelet toggle fastening to each of the small toggle rings. Make four bead charms and attach to the end of a five-link chain. To finish, attach the chain to the jump ring at the large round toggle fastening.

Hundreds and Thousands Bracelet

Inexpensive silver-lined seed beads are mixed with focal beads of cracked horn, ceramic and silver in a restricted colour palette to make this bold contemporary bracelet. The large beads are strung on elastic cord adjoining the strands.

You will need . . .

- 5g silver-lined transparent grey seed beads, size 9
- 5g mixed matt greys and clear off-white lined cylinder beads, size 11
- 5g matt grey Toho triangle beads, size 11
- Antique silver round bead, 18mm
- 2 cracked horn round beads, 15 x 12mm
- Ceramic round bead in brown, 20mm
- Bead thread in smoke, size D
- Elastic cord in black, 25cm (10in) of 1mm
- Organza ribbon in cream, 30cm (12in) each of 6mm and 9mm
- Bead spinner
- Curved big-eye needle
- Jewellery glue
- Basic tool kit (see pages 16–19)

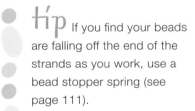 **Tip** If you find your beads are falling off the end of the strands as you work, use a bead stopper spring (see page 111).

1 Mix the small beads in the bead spinner and string fifteen 15cm (6in) lengths of beads on the bead thread (see page 111), leaving an 8cm (3in) tail at each end.

2 Lay the strands in a bundle and tie each end in an overhand knot (see page 99) about 6mm (¼in) from the beads. Trim the tails and put a drop of jewellery glue on the knots to secure.

3 Loop the elastic cord through the middle of the bead strands at one end, then feed both ends through the antique silver bead and tug to pull the knot inside the bead.

4 Take both ends through a cracked horn bead then take a single tail through the brown bead and other cracked horn bead.

5 Loop the elastic through the other end of the beaded strands and back through the last two beads. Pull tight, then tie the cord with a reef (square) knot (see page 99) and trim the ends.

6 Cut the ribbons into three and tie in pairs between the beads.

Friendship Bracelet

This simple bracelet is made using tiny cylinder beads, which are very even and when woven lock together tightly to make a smooth bead fabric. The fastenings are made entirely of beads so no clasps or hooks are required. The picot edging down either side of the bracelet is optional.

You will need . . .

- 2g white cylinder beads, size 11
- 1g lime cylinder beads, size 11
- 1g aqua cylinder beads, size 11
- 1g bright blue cylinder beads, size 11
- Bead loom
- Beading needle
- Nymo thread in white
- Basic tool kit (see pages 16–19)

1 Set up the bead loom with six 76cm (30in) long white Nymo threads (see page 91). To calculate the length of the bracelet, measure the circumference of your wrist and take off 1cm (½in) for the fastening. Following the beadwork chart on page 122, work the bead design to this length ending with two white rows. Put the needle back through the second last row of beads.

2 Bring the needle out between the first two beads on the last row. Pick up three aqua cylinder beads and fit under the centre four threads. Take the needle back through the beads. Work another two rows avoiding the outside threads.

3 Wind the loom back to the other end of the bracelet and add a block of nine aqua cylinder beads to that end as well. Take the beadwork off the loom. Sew the thread ends back into the bracelet leaving one thread next to the centre aqua bead at each end.

4 To make a toggle, pick up five lime beads and put the needle back through the last three to make a circle. Pick up a bead and put the needle through the centre of the circle. Keep adding beads, putting the needle through the cluster until you make a 6mm (¼in) toggle.

5 At the other end of the bracelet pick up enough lime cylinder beads to make a loop that will pass over the toggle snugly. Put the needle back through the other side of the centre aqua bead and then back through the loop before securing the end in the bracelet.

6 To add a picot edge, attach a thread at one end and bring it out at the edge of the bracelet opposite the centre lime cylinder bead. Pick up three lime cylinder beads and put the needle back through the same bead, bringing it out on the other side of the bracelet.

7 Pick up another three beads and put the needle back through the first two in the bracelet. Feed the needle down to the next coloured centre bead and then out to the edge. Make a picot on either side and continue down the bracelet adding matching picots either side. Secure the end of the thread in the bracelet to finish.

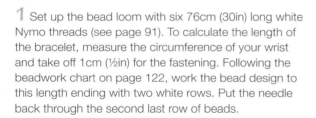

Chain Maille Bracelet

These exquisite beads have a crushed ice finish with a pretty silvery effect that makes the beads and chain maille really come together. The chain maille flowers are shown on page 109 and the bead links technique is shown on page 104. Use a plain silver toggle fastening made from a similar thickness of wire as that used for the chain maille so that it blends in to the design.

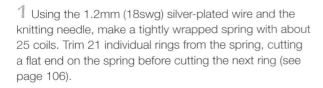

You will need...

- 4 crushed ice wine cube beads, 8mm
- 4 crushed ice wine round beads, 10mm
- Silver-plated wire, 1.2mm (18swg)
- Silver-plated wire, 0.6mm (24swg)
- Silver-plated toggle clasp
- Knitting needle or rod, 7mm (⅜in) diameter
- Basic tool kit (see pages 16–19)

1 Using the 1.2mm (18swg) silver-plated wire and the knitting needle, make a tightly wrapped spring with about 25 coils. Trim 21 individual rings from the spring, cutting a flat end on the spring before cutting the next ring (see page 106).

2 Tension all the rings to make closed jump rings and then open two out of every three. Make seven flower shapes using the flower chain technique on page 109 and arrange on the work surface.

3 Using round-nosed pliers, make a large eye pin loop with 0.6mm (24swg) silver-plated wire. Pick up a cube bead. Make a loop at the other end and trim the end (see page 105). Make four cube bead links and four round bead links in total.

4 Open one loop of a bead link and pick up a flower shape, then close the loop. Attach a different bead link to the other side. Continue joining flower shapes and bead links until the chain is complete. If the chain is too short for your wrist make another flower shape and bead link. Attach a toggle fastening to the end bead link loops to finish the bracelet.

Tip When making the jump rings, cut the end of the spring with the flat side of the wire cutters so that the ends butt together neatly.

Spiral Bracelets

Although they look very delicate, these spiral bracelets are made with a strong beading stitch that is unlikely to break. You can use any beads you like to make the bracelets but it is better to choose contrasting colours or textures for the inside and outside beads so that the spiral design is obvious.

You will need...

- 2g grass green seed beads, size 11
- 3g mint green seed beads, size 11
- 3g aqua seed beads, size 8
- Toggle fastening
- Nymo thread in white
- Beading needle
- Basic tool kit (see pages 16–19)

1 Thread the beading needle with a 2m (2yd) length of white Nymo thread. Pick up four grass green beads, then one mint green bead, one aqua bead and another mint green bead. Tie the beads into a circle, leaving a 15cm (6in) tail.

2 Pass the needle through the four grass green beads. Pick up one grass green bead, one mint green, one aqua and another mint green. Let the beads drop down to the work.

3 Pass the needle back through the last three grass green beads and the one just added. Pull the thread tight and position the beads next to the previous group of mint green/aqua beads.

4 Pick up one grass green bead, one mint green, one aqua and one mint green. Let the beads drop down to the work. Repeat steps 3 and 4. The spiral will only become obvious when you have made about eight repetitions.

5 Continue adding beads until the spiral is the length required, approximately 17cm (6¾in). Oversew the two halves of the toggle fastening to the ends of the bracelet. Feed the needle back down through three or four beads, tie a double half-hitch knot (see page 99) and feed the needle through another three or four beads. Trim the thread close to the beads.

Tip Create a different effect using hex beads to make a helter-skelter pattern, placing dark beads on the outside and pale beads on the inside.

Waxed Cotton Bracelet

Waxed cotton is a fabulous material for stringing beads. It is available in a wide range of colours that you can co-ordinate with beads to make really stylish pieces. The beads in this bracelet are spaced using overhand knots (see page 99) and clever sliding knots (see page 112) so that you can adjust the diameter to take it on and off.

You will need...

- Five decorative beads – a single large bead and two pairs of beads
- Four small ring beads
- Waxed cotton in two toning colours, 76cm (30in) of 1mm
- Basic tool kit (see pages 16–19)

1 Thread the largest bead on to one strand of waxed cotton. Hold the second strand over the top of the bead and tie an overhand knot (see page 99), using both strands at each end close to the bead.

2 Thread the first pair of beads on to the other strand of waxed cotton, one on each side, and then tie the strands together again. Thread on the second pair of beads on the first strand and tie the threads together.

3 Overlap the two sets of cords so that the beads and cord form a bracelet-sized oval. Tie one end with an overhand knot over the cords and then repeat with the other end in the opposite direction to make a sliding knot fastening (see page 112).

4 Adjust the position of the knots so that the bracelet can go over your hand. Thread a small ring bead on the end of each cord, tie an overhand knot and trim neatly.

Tip Check that the bead holes are big enough to thread the waxed cotton through. If the bead holes are slightly too small use a bead reamer to enlarge them (see page 17).

Bugle Bracelet

This simple bead loom bracelet is made from bugles and hex beads that fit together beautifully in adjacent rows because they are both the same width. It is a great project to experiment with the loom weaving technique because there is no chart to follow. Use several shades of bugle beads to create the mottled appearance.

You will need . . .

- 5g each of purple iris matt, lilac satin and white satin bugles, 3mm
- 5g silver-lined clear hex beads, 3mm
- Nymo or S-lon thread in white
- Beading needle, size 10
- 24mm bar crimp ends and fastening
- Bead loom
- Glue
- Basic tool kit (see pages 16–19)

1 Set up the bead loom with eight 45cm (18in) individual warp threads so that the threads are about 3mm (⅛in) apart. Tie the weft thread to a side thread about 15cm (6in) from one end (see page 91).

2 Mix the different short bugles on a beading mat (see page 16) and pick up seven in a random order. Position the bugles under the warp threads and take the needle back through the beads so that it passes over the warp threads.

3 Weave six rows of bugle beads and then pick up seven hex beads and weave as before. Continue adding rows of bugle beads and hex beads to create a random pattern. Work the bead band about 15cm (6in) long or to suit your wrist measurement.

4 Weave thread across both ends of the bracelet (see page 92) and then take off the loom. Tie the thread ends together in pairs and trim.

5 Open a bar crimp end and apply a little glue inside. Position the end row of beads inside the teeth and tuck in any stray threads. Apply a little more glue and then carefully close the bar crimp end with flat-nosed pliers. Repeat at the other end.

Tip Depending on which beads you choose you can use this technique to create a whole selection of bracelets that all look totally different.

Square Stitch Bracelet

Although these top-quality seed beads have quite large holes it is essential to use a fine beading needle (size 13) as thread passes through each bead several times. If you are choosing your own beads, make sure two seed beads side by side are the same width as the cube beads, as sizes vary between manufacturers.

You will need...

- 28 steel gold iris cube beads, 3mm
- 2g gold lustre green tea Toho seed beads, size 11
- 5g rainbow metal matt Toho seed beads, size 11
- 3 pale creamy yellow round glass beads, 12mm
- 5-hole gold-plated multi-strand bar clasp
- S-lon beading thread in dark gold
- Bead stop spring
- Beading needle, size 13
- Basic tool kit (see pages 16–19)

1 Pick up seven steel gold iris cube beads on a 3m (3yd) length of beading thread and drop down to the middle. Secure the beads one side with a bead stop spring (see page 111). Thread a long fine beading needle on the other end.

2 Pick up two gold lustre seed beads and pass the needle through the first cube bead again, then through the seed beads again. Continue working square stitch (see pages 94–5) with these beads to the end of the row. Pass the needle back through the cube beads and the row just worked.

3 Change to the matt rainbow beads and work four rows of square stitch. On the next three rows decrease by two beads at each end to leave two beads (see page 95). Bring the thread out between the two beads. Remove the stop spring from the other end and thread with a needle. Work the other side to match.

4 Make a second panel exactly the same then work two panels with only one pointed side. Join the two large panels together by picking up a gold lustre seed bead, a large round bead and another seed bead. Take the thread through the two seed beads at the top of the second panels and then weave through the bead fabric and secure with one or two half-hitches (see page 99).

5 Take the thread from the other side and pass through the beads just added and secure in the bead fabric. Join an end panel to each side in the same way. Check the size of the bracelet and add extra rows at each end if required before sewing to the rings of the multi-strand bar clasp.

Chain Maille Watch

A standard watch face can be transformed using this simple chain maille technique, which involves linking large solid rings with jump rings. A selection of beads is then attached, with the colours carefully mixed, together with some organza ribbon, to create a flamboyant design.

You will need...

- Watch face in a gold finish with end link holes
- Selection of large and small beads in bright blue, purple, purple/black and golden yellow
- 16 gold solid rings, 15mm
- Organza ribbon in blue, purple and yellow, 10cm (4in) of 15mm each
- 25 gold-plated jump rings, 5mm
- 30 gold-plated head pins
- Gold-plated toggle clasp
- Basic tool kit (see pages 16–19)

1 Cut through two solid rings using wire cutters and open like a jump ring (see page 106). Slot these rings into each hole at either end of the watch face.

2 Lay the watch flat and arrange six solid rings in pairs out from each single solid ring. Link each pair with a jump ring and then join the pairs together using single jump rings.

3 Attach a single solid ring at each end with jump rings to make the strap. Tie a piece of ribbon through the first and last pairs of solid rings and trim.

4 Make about 30 head pin or drop bead dangles, using a mixture of the different-coloured beads, about five or six in each colour. Thread the beads on to head pins, trim to 7mm (⅜in) and make a plain loop in the top (see page 105).

5 To attach drop beads to the chain maille, pick a drop bead up on a length of the gold-plated wire and fold the tail back on itself. Make a wrapped loop by winding the tail around the main wire two or three times and trimming the end (see page 105). Trim the wire to 7mm (⅜in) and make a loop with round-nosed pliers (see page 24).

6 Start attaching drop beads around the chain, with the head pin dangles attached to each solid ring and each jump ring. Join the round end of the toggle clasp to the top end with a single jump ring. Link two jump rings together and use to attach the end bar at the bottom of the strap.

Quick Ideas

Sparkly stripes

Mixing larger beads and smaller beads in a bead loom weaving project appears to be impossible but you simply choose small beads that fit in twos or threes across the width of the larger bead. In this design two small beads are woven between each warp thread. Create an interesting texture with matt cube beads and colour-lined triangle beads, then finish the bracelet with a toggle and loop fastening (as described for the Friendship Bracelet, page 28).

Memory bangle

To make this simple bracelet, coil a length of memory wire (see page 13) around your wrist to get the right size and mark. Using memory wire cutters, or heavyweight wire cutters, cut the wire at the mark. Stick a memory wire ball end on one end of the bracelet using superglue or other strong glue. Pick up a selection of beads in toning colours and in a variety of shapes and sizes, leaving enough room to fit the second ball end. Trim the wire if necessary and then glue a second ball end in place to finish.

Chunky charm

Picot edging (as described for the Friendship Bracelet, page 28) adds an elegant touch to a simple bead loom woven bracelet made with triangle beads. These beads have a crinkly texture that contrasts with the metal beads, which are added after the bracelet has been woven. As the metal beads are heavy, make sure you sew them securely using two strands of thread. Finish the bracelet with a woven thread panel at each end (see page 92) and attach bar crimp ends, an extension chain and a clasp.

Necklaces & Scarves

Wearing a beaded necklace or scarf can make the ultimate fashion statement. An exquisite necklace can make an otherwise ordinary outfit something out of this world, while a beautiful beaded scarf will not only keep the chill off your shoulders, but will also add glamour and movement to your silhouette. The projects in this chapter encompass a diverse range of easy-to-master techniques and, as always, you can make your own bead and colour choices to personalize the designs.

Jadeite Pendant

We think of a pendant as a type of necklace, but this old French word actually refers to the ornament that hangs from it. The necklace style goes back to ancient times when it was a symbol of wealth or represented the religious beliefs or tribal status of the wearer. A pendant can be simply strung on a plain thong or cord, or attached to a necklace. Pendants usually have a hole at the top, but you can explore other innovative approaches like using a large ring to suspend a collection of smaller beads and charms, as in this design in which a jadeite bangle makes an unusual centrepiece. Pick up the dark veining in one of the bead colours and then add complementary coloured beads to create a stunning design. Antique silver charms add the finishing touch.

Jadeíte Pendant

You will need . . .

- Jadeite bangle, 50mm
- 2 antique silver washer-style spacers, 6mm
- Selection of beads in pink/wine, 6–12mm
- Selection of beads in blue/green, 3–12mm
- 4 antique silver tube beads, 3 x 8mm
- Antique silver butterfly and dragonfly charms
- Resin leaf in burgundy, 12 x 15mm
- 6 silver-plated small round beads
- Waxed cord, 1m (39in) of 2mm
- 5 silver-plated head pins, 7cm (2¾in)
- Silver-plated wire, 0.6mm (24swg)
- 2 silver-plated jump rings
- Basic tool kit (see pages 16–19)

Tip Make the wrapped loops around the jadeite bangle tight to space the bead dangles. Alternatively, keep the loops loose so that they bunch together.

1 To make a wrapped-loop bead dangle, pick up a few beads on a head pin. Hold the head pin near the tip of a pair of flat-nosed pliers and bend the wire over at right angles about 3mm (⅛in) above the top bead.

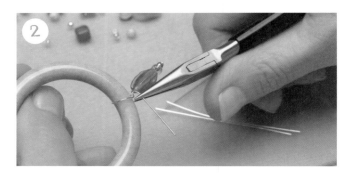

2 Curl the rest of the head pin around the jadeite bangle to form a loop. Using flat-nosed pliers, wind the wire around the stem of the head pin about three times (see page 105). Trim the end of the tail close to the coil.

3 To make a bead dangle with wrapped loops at both ends, pick up a washer-style spacer or a leaf bead on the end of a length of the wire, bend the wire back on itself about 2.5cm (1in) from the end and wrap the short tail around the main wire two or three times. Trim the tail close to the coil.

4 Pick up a selection of beads on the wire, then bend the wire at right angles 3mm (⅛in) above the last bead. Wrap the wire around the jadeite bangle and then wrap the tail two or three times around the straight section. Trim the tail close to the coil. Make about seven different wrapped-loop bead dangles in total.

5 To make a charm dangle, make a loop on the end of a length of wire (see page 104). Pick up a selection of beads and then follow step 4 to attach it to the bangle. Open the loop, then attach the butterfly charm and close the loop again. Make a second charm dangle and attach the dragonfly to the loop. Repeat with the resin leaf.

6 To hang the pendant, make a wrapped loop at the end of a length of wire (see page 105). Bend the wire over 3mm (⅛in) below the coil and wrap the long tail around the jadeite bangle. Wrap the wire tail around two or three times under the previous coil to secure the wire, then trim the end.

7 Tie the waxed cord through the wrapped pendant loop. Make two bead dangles using head pins, picking up a small silver-plated bead and then either a small pink or a small green bead and finishing with a loop. Attach these to the cord knot with jump rings (see page 106).

Tip For a more decorative fastening, add a bead to each cord tail, tie an overhand knot after the beads and trim the tail.

8 To fasten the necklace so that it can be adjusted, overlap the ends by 15cm (6in). Tie each end over the other cord using an overhand knot (see page 99). Pull the knots away from each other to shorten the length (see also page 112).

Luscious Links

The wire technique used to make this pretty necklace is so versatile that once you know how to make the simple link you will easily be able to make matching bracelets and earrings too.

You will need . . .

- Selection of mixed pink beads
- Selection of mixed pink seed beads
- Silver-plated wire, 0.6mm (24swg)
- 7 silver-plated head pins
- 7 silver-plated jump rings
- Silver-plated necklace fastening
- Basic tool kit (see pages 16–19)

1 Cut 15cm (6in) of the silver-plated wire. Hold the wire in your round-nosed pliers so it is about 6mm (¼in) down from the tips of the pliers and you can just feel the end of the wire jutting out between the blades. Bend the wire around the blades using your thumb until it is flat on the other side. Take the wire off the pliers and bend the tail back to straighten.

2 Pick up beads to make the link, for example: two seed beads, a larger bead and another two seed beads. To make the loop at the other end of the bead link, trim the wire to 7mm (⅜in) and bend over at an angle after the last bead.

3 Hold the short tail in round-nosed pliers as before and bend around until it touches the main wire again to make a loop. Hold both rings between finger and thumb, and twist until the rings are level. This is the basic bead link – now simply make enough links to go around your neck and join them all together.

4 To open the links, hold the ring at one end in flat-nosed pliers and bend up slightly to open. Join a second link on and then bend the ring down again to close. Attach a necklace fastening to each end (see page 113).

5 To make the drop attachment at the bottom of the necklace open the jump rings then join them all together in a chain (see page 107). Attach the end one to the centre link of the necklace. Make seven bead charms using the head pins (see Charm Bracelet pages 24–5) and attach one to each ring.

Tip Look out for tubes of mixed beads in toning colours – this saves agonizing over which individual beads to buy.

Love Heart

This choker-length bib necklace is made with coin beads and shimmer beads with a stunning silver heart charm as the focal point. It is made with simple bead links and head pin dangles.

You will need . . .

- 7 opaque ivory with silver coin beads, 15mm
- 36 silver-plated irregular spacer beads, 6mm
- 3 transparent gold shimmer oval beads, 30 x 15mm
- 2 transparent gold shimmer round beads, 18mm
- 7 ball beads in a silver finish, 3mm
- 6 opaque ivory with silver round beads, 12mm
- Heart charm in a silver finish, 3cm
- Silver-plated wire, 2m (2yd) of 0.6mm (24swg)
- Silver-plated chain, 38cm (15in) of 3mm links
- 7 silver-plated head pins
- Silver-plated hook fastening
- Basic tool kit (see pages 16–19)

1 Make bead links (see page 104) with the coin beads on the wire, adding a spacer bead on either side. Make a similar bead link with each of the transparent shimmer beads.

2 For the head pin dangles, pick up a small silver ball, a spacer bead, an opaque ivory round bead and a spacer bead. Bend the tail over and trim the head pin to 7mm (⅜in), then make a loop on the end with round-nosed pliers (see page 104).

3 To make the heart dangle, pick up the heart bead with a silver ball on both sides on a head pin and make a loop as before. Join the bead links and dangles as shown (see page 104).

4 Attach the bead strand with the heart link in the centre of the chain and the others spaced about 2cm (¾in) apart. Attach a hook fastening to the ends of the chain to finish.

Hip For extra security you can make the bead links and head pin dangles with wrapped loops instead.

Sheer 'n' Swinging Scarf

Make a gorgeous scarf in sheer silk organza to match your favourite evening outfit and add a touch of luxury with some subtly shaded bead fringing – a quick fix for instant glamour!

You will need . . .

- Cream organza, 46 x 112cm (18 x 44in)
- Metallic cream organza, 46 x 30cm (18 x 12in)
- Ready-made bead fringing, 46cm (18in)
- Sewing machine with zipper foot
- Sewing machine thread in cream
- Dressmaker's pins
- Basic tool kit (see pages 16–19)

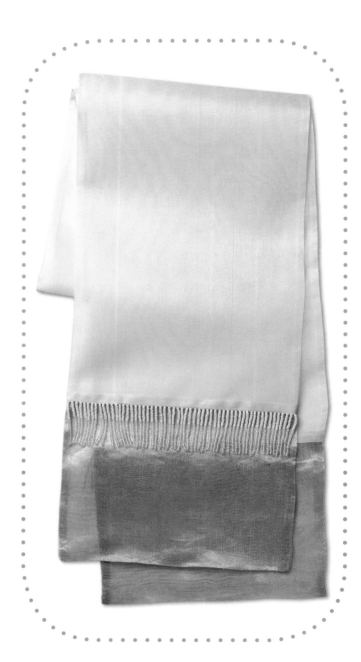

1 Cut two pieces of cream organza 23 x 112cm (9 x 44in) and two pieces of metallic organza 23 x 30cm (9 x 12in). Cut two 23cm (9in) lengths of bead fringing. Carefully remove two or three strands from each end to leave 20cm (8in) of fringing in the middle. Make sure the remaining fringing is quite secure.

2 Pin a length of bead fringing along both short ends of one piece of cream organza so that the tape is near the raw edge. Using a zipper foot on your sewing machine and cream sewing thread, stitch as close as possible to the beads. Pin a piece of metallic organza over the bead fringe and machine stitch the seam again.

3 Pin the second piece of cream organza to the free end of the two pieces of metallic organza (so it makes a tube), making sure all seams are on the outside, and machine stitch. Trim all seams to 6mm (¼in) and press towards the metallic organza.

4 With right sides facing, fold the scarf so that the seams match and pin the side seams. Machine stitch the side seams leaving a gap on one side for turning through. Trim the seams to 6mm (¼in) and turn through. Ease out the corners, press the edges and slipstitch the gap.

Wood Works

Giant wood beads would have been rather dark and dull on their own in a necklace, but teamed with paler wood beads with a pretty painted design changes the look completely. The blue and brown colour scheme is echoed in the knotted waxed cord to add to the overall effect.

You will need . . .

- 5 dark wood oval beads, approx. 50 x 32mm
- 4 dark wood round ribbed beads, 24mm
- 8 pale blue beads, 20mm
- 5 dark blue beads, 20mm
- 4 dark blue beads, 10mm
- 8 painted wood beads, 30 x 15mm
- Waxed cotton cord in pale blue and brown, 2m (2yd) of 1mm each
- Tapestry needle
- Jewellery glue
- Basic tool kit (see pages 16–19)

1 Arrange the beads on a beading mat (see page 16) so that you have a dark wood bead with two or three coloured or painted wood beads in between.

2 Holding both cords together, tie an overhand knot about 15cm (6in) from one end (see page 99). Thread a large dark wood bead on the long ends and drop it down to the knot.

3 Tie a second overhand knot on the other side of the bead, using a tapestry needle to guide the knot to the right position (see page 112). Continue picking up beads in the order you have chosen, tying a knot after each one, until the necklace is about 90cm (35in) long.

4 Untie the knot after the first large bead and take it off again. Thread just the brown cord through. Thread the other end of the brown cord through in the opposite direction. Tie an overhand knot both sides of the large bead, keeping the cord taut. Use jewellery glue to secure the knot and then trim the ends.

Tip If you prefer you can make a shorter necklace, leaving tails at each end, then attach a fastening (see page 113).

Delightful Discs

These donut beads are generally used individually as pendants, but as they are not expensive, five or seven donuts look absolutely stunning strung together with several strands of toning seed beads. You can make the multi-strands longer or shorter to vary the design.

You will need . . .

- 40g teal metal iris seed beads, size 11
- 7 light jade donut pendants, 40mm
- Multifilament or braided thread in green, size B
- Craft wire, 0.6mm (24swg)
- 2 bell end cones
- Hook fastening
- Bead spinner
- Curved big-eye needle
- Jewellery glue
- Basic tool kit (see pages 16–19)

1 Pick up the seed beads on to the reel of thread using a bead spinner and a curved big-eye needle (see page 111).

2 To link the donut beads together, cut off three groups of 45 seed beads, leaving 5cm (2in) of thread at each end. Tie the strands of beads around two donuts using a reef (square) knot (see page 99) then pass the thread ends through a few beads and secure with a half-hitch knot (see page 99) and a drop of jewellery glue.

3 Tie loops of 22 seed beads between the donuts, securing the threads as before. Join all seven donuts in the same way. Separate six 36cm (14in) strands of seed beads. Loop three through each end donut and tie the ends together.

4 Add a 22-seed bead loop around each bundle and drop down to the end donuts. Secure the threads with wire and attach a bell end cone (see page 114), making a plain or wrapped loop to attach a hook fastening.

Tip To save time stringing beads yourself buy beads on hanks and transfer them onto the reel of thread.

Devoré Scarf

A net fringe adds colour and sparkle to a plain scarf. Devoré velvet is made from silk georgette with a viscose pile. The pattern is created by removing the viscose pile with etching fluid, leaving the plain silk georgette in some areas.

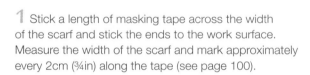

You will need . . .

- Silk/viscose scarf
- 20g gold pearls, 4mm
- 28g dark brown pearls, 4mm
- 28g burnt orange seed beads, size 9
- 28g orange seed beads, size 9
- 28g apricot seed beads, size 9
- Masking tape
- Pencil and ruler
- Cord thread
- Beading needle
- Basic tool kit (see pages 16–19)

1 Stick a length of masking tape across the width of the scarf and stick the ends to the work surface. Measure the width of the scarf and mark approximately every 2cm (¾in) along the tape (see page 100).

2 Beginning at one corner, attach a length of cord thread and pick up one dark brown pearl, six seed beads (one burnt orange, one orange, two apricot, one orange and one burnt orange), one gold pearl, six seed beads (as before) and one dark brown pearl. Take a tiny stitch into the scarf below the second mark then put the needle back through the dark brown pearl. Work across the scarf adding the same loop of beads between the marks. Sew in the end.

3 Secure a second thread with a couple of tiny stitches on the reverse side and bring it out through the first dark brown pearl. Pick up eight seed beads (one burnt orange, two orange, two apricot, two orange and one burnt orange), then one brown pearl. Repeat three times. Add another string of beads down the other side.

4 Take a new length of thread up through the second dark brown bead at one side. Pick up six seed beads (order as in step 2) and take the needle through the gold pearl. Pick up another six seed beads (as before) and one dark brown pearl. Continue across the width.

5 At the other end, take the needle down through the dark brown pearl at the end. Work back across, feeding the needle through the dark brown beads. Continue adding rows of bead netting until you reach the last dark brown bead at each side.

6 Pick up 21 seed beads (order as in step 3 until there are 21 beads), one dark brown pearl and one burnt orange seed bead. Take the needle back through the dark brown pearl, the seed beads and the next dark brown pearl. Pick up six seed beads (as in step 2), feed the needle through the gold pearl at the bottom of the netting and pick up another six seed beads (as before) and one brown pearl. Repeat until the fringe and last row of netting is complete. Sew in thread ends securely.

Rock 'n' Roll

In this 'Y'-shaped necklace, the translucent rocks and wheel-shaped ceramic beads perfectly complement each other, and when linked with copper wire and beads, the design really comes together. Use copper eye pins to make the links rather than copper wire, as the eye pins have an antique finish.

You will need...

- 6 pink ice rock beads, 20mm
- 7 pink glaze ceramic beads, 23 x 7mm
- 32 copper beads, 6mm
- Copper head pin
- 28 copper eye pins, 4.5cm (1¾in)
- Copper toggle fastening
- Basic tool kit (see pages 16–19)

1 Feed the head pin through the largest rock bead, trim the end to 7mm (⅜in) and use round-nosed pliers to make a loop (see page 24).

2 Use the eye pins to make the bead links with the remaining large beads (see page 104). Use eye pins to make links with the small copper beads – you should be able to use the cut-off section to make bead links for half the beads.

3 Join the head pin rock to a copper bead link (see page 105), then add a ceramic bead link, a copper bead link and a rock bead link to make the tail of the 'Y' shape.

4 Attach two copper bead links to the rock bead loop, then add alternate ceramic and rock bead links with copper bead links in between. After the last large beads, join the remaining copper bead links together. Finish the necklace with a toggle fastening.

Tip To give this design a completely different look, use antique silver eye pins and beads with cooler tones such as blue and green.

Beaded Scarf

This gorgeous knitted scarf uses a fine yarn to add beads into the knitting. The beads are strung on to fine cotton perlé in a similar shade to the main yarn so that it is almost invisible when knitted. You can simply add beads to the border at each end but knitting in size 8 seed beads on the main body of the scarf adds extra texture and sparkle. The finished scarf is (90cm) 36in long.

You will need . . .

- No.12 cotton perlé colour 524, two balls
- RYC natural silk aran colour 464, three balls
- Knitting needles, size 7
- Light seafoam AB seed beads, size 8 (15cm / 6in tube)
- 50 smoke grey faceted beads, 4mm
- 15 each of smoke grey, transparent and matt turquoise AB faceted beads, 6mm
- Basic tool kit (pages 16–19)

1 Using the no.12 cotton perlé straight off the ball, pick up a seed bead, a 4mm smoke grey bead, a seed bead, a 6mm turquoise bead, a seed bead, a 6mm smoke grey bead and a seed bead. Repeat, alternating between transparent and matt turquoise beads until you have added about twenty 6mm beads in total.

2 Hold the cotton perlé with the silk aran yarn together and cast on 40 stitches (see page 116). Knit two rows (see page 116). On the next row knit one stitch then add a bead every two stitches using bead knitting (see pages 117–18). Knit the next row with both yarns but without adding beads.

3 On the next row knit two stitches and then add a bead. Work along the row adding a bead every two stitches. Knit a row without beads again. Repeat these four rows three times.

4 Break the perlé thread and pick up size 8 seed beads on the thread straight off the ball. Change to knit one, purl one for every row to work the main part of the scarf. Work one row knit one, purl one.

5 On the next row knit four stitches before beginning to add the beads. Add the beads on every second knit stitch. Alternate between the two bead rows so that the beads are on the same side as the bead border and are spaced attractively.

6 Once the scarf is the length required break the cotton perlé and add the same beads for the border as before. Knit the border to match the other end and cast off (see page 118).

Netted Scarf

One of the easiest ways to embellish a simple scarf is to add a netting fringe. The bead netting adds weight and gives a sheer scarf body. Add interest by threading alternate colours of seed beads and varying the size. Use beads in a contrasting colour to the scarf for impact, or use toning colours for a subtler effect.

You will need . . .

- Scarf, 25cm (10in) wide
- 5g hematite cube beads, 4mm
- 15g pewter seed bead mix, size 15–6
- Strong fine beading thread
- Beading needle
- Dressmaker's pins
- Stop bead
- Basic tool kit (pages 16–19)

1 Measure across the bottom of the scarf approximately every 3.25cm (1¼in) to divide it into eight equal sections and mark with pins (see page 100).

2 Secure two threads on one corner of the scarf, then pick up a cube bead and a large seed on both threads. Remove one thread from the needle. On this thread pick up 15 seeds, a large seed, 15 seeds and a large seed then add a stop bead to secure temporarily (see page 111). Add a single thread on the other corner and add the same beads with a stop bead at the end. These two strands of beads are for the straight edges at each end of the netting.

3 On the other thread at the first corner, * pick up five small seeds, a large seed, five small seeds, a large seed and a cube bead. Pick up another large seed then repeat from * to complete the other side of the loop.

4 Take a small stitch through the fabric at the first pin. Take the needle back through the cube and large seed bead. Repeat from * to make loops all the way across the scarf.

5 Take the needle back through the large cube and then through the last beads added, to come out of the large seed bead on the other side of the cube bead in the middle of the last loop. Pick up the seed bead sequence to make the next loop missing out the large seed and cube at the end.

Tip Twisted beading threads with a round cross-section have a better drape than flat or braided threads.

6 Feed the needle through the three beads in the middle of the next loop. Continue to the last loop. Pick up five seeds, a large seed and five seeds and then take the needle through the next large seed on the end string of beads. Work loops across the scarf again, going through the first large seed bead on the end string from bottom to top. Pick up the five seeds, a large seed and five small seeds and take the needle through the middle three beads on the last loop of the first row. Leave this thread to tie in later.

7 Join a new thread on the right-hand side below the second large seed. Bring the thread out above the large seed and work another row of netting all the way across. When you come out of the last large seed on the left hand-side strand, work another row of netting.

8 For the final row of netting, work a half-hitch (see page 99) above the last large seed bead on the right-hand side and take the thread back through the last loop to the other side of the middle three beads. Work the last row of netting. Secure the thread end with several half-hitches.

Tip Remember to match the size of the beads used in the netting to the weight of the scarf so that it isn't too heavy.

Rings & Earrings

When it comes to accessorizing, rings and earrings are a simple but dramatic way to enhance the look of any outfit. If, like I did, you doubt whether a ring made from beads can ever be comfortable to wear, have a go at making any of the four rings in this chapter and you will be pleasantly surprised! The earring designs range from classic pearl drop earrings to wear with a string of pearls, to sparkling stardust earrings, which appear to float on illusion cord. There are designs for every occasion and plenty of ideas for you to develop and adapt.

Peyote Stitch Rings

These pretty rings are quick to make and, as you finish the band before joining it into a ring shape, it is easy to get it just the right size. Use small seed beads or bugles for the band so that it is not too bulky and sits comfortably between your fingers and then go to town embellishing the band to create a unique ring. Add semi-precious stones, Swarovski crystals or pearls for a luxury look or have fun using seed beads and various bead techniques to make these funky designs. These rings are made with peyote stitch, worked back and forwards across the width making it easy to adjust the size of the ring. The ring can be embellished as you work or once the band is completed.

Peyote Stitch Rings

You will need . . .

- Nymo thread
- Beading needle
- Basic tool kit (see pages 16–19)

Frilly Ring

- 5g rainbow metal matt seed beads, size 11
- 2g silver-lined rose seed beads, size 9

Pink Ring

- 5g pale pink and dark pink short bugles, 2mm
- 12 multi iris drop beads, 3 x 4mm

Spiky Ring

- 5g emerald raspberry gold lustre seed beads, size 11
- 2g dark pink short bugles, 2mm

Frilly ring

1 Pick up six matt rainbow seed beads for the first two rows. To begin the third row, pick up another seed bead and take the needle through the second bead from the end.

2 Continue adding beads to work an even-count peyote stitch band (see page 97) long enough for a ring. This will be about 6cm (2⅜in) depending on the size of your finger. Bring the ends together – the beads should lock together neatly although it may be necessary to add or take away a row to get the right bead sequence. Take the thread back and forwards across the gap to 'zip' the beads together then sew in the ends securely.

3 To make the frilly circular peyote stitch, pick up three silver-lined beads and take the needle back through the beads to make a circle. Pick up a silver-lined bead between each of these three beads. Continue working rounds (see page 97), to make a circle about 15mm (⅝in) in diameter. To create a slightly frilly circle squeeze in beads as you near the finished size. Pick up a matt rainbow bead between each bead in the final round and sew in the ends.

4 Bring a thread out in the middle of the frilly circle at the end of one of the three centre beads. Pick up ten matt rainbow beads and take the needle back through the centre bead from the other end. Add a loop of beads over each centre bead. Add two more loops in the very centre. Sew the embellishment to the ring band and sew in the thread ends securely.

Tip The rings are worked in peyote stitch, but could also be worked in brick stitch (see page 96). In brick stitch you would need to work the band lengthways instead of back and forwards.

Pink ring

1 Begin with four dark pink beads and then work the next two rows in pale pink. Work alternate rows in dark and pale pink to make the even-count peyote stitch ring band (see page 97). Join the ends but don't sew in the tail.

2 Take the tail thread through the adjacent bugle on the edge. Pick up a drop bead on the tail thread and take a backstitch through the bugle and then take the needle through a bugle in the next row in from the edge, which is slightly offset. Pick up a second drop bead and work a backstitch through that bugle. Add two more drop beads in the same way.

3 Continue working back and forwards across the ring band to add three more rows of drop beads. Sew in the ends to finish.

Spiky ring

1 Pick up eight lustre seed beads and work an even-count peyote stitch band (see page 97) long enough for a ring and join the ends together as above.

2 Take the thread through the beads to come out in the middle of the band. Pick up three short bugles and a rainbow seed. Take the needle back through the bugles only then bring it out one bead across. Add another two fringe strands with three bugles along the centre of the ring band.

3 Work your way around the three long strands creating strands with only two short bugles and a seed bead. Finally add single bugle bead strands on the outside. Sew in the thread ends.

Tip The ring will be much stronger if you keep the join in the peyote stitch beaded band at the top of the ring, under the embellishment.

Pearl Drop Earrings

These graduated earrings are easy to make and are a great way to use up any leftover beads and pearls. The beads are simply slotted on to a silver-plated head pin and a loop is made at the end to attach the earring wire.

You will need . . .

- Pearls in white: two 10mm, two 8mm, two 6mm and four 3mm
- 2 flat, round white turquoise beads, 20mm
- 2 silver-plated head pins, 7cm (2¾in)
- 2 silver-plated earring wires
- Basic tool kit (see pages 16–19)

1 On a head pin, begin by picking up a 3mm pearl, and then add a white turquoise bead.

2 Continue adding the other pearls one at a time, from the largest to the smallest.

3 Trim the end of the head pin to 7mm (⅜in), bend it over using flat-nosed pliers and then use round-nosed pliers to rotate the end around to form a loop (see page 104).

4 Open the loop of an earring wire with flat-nosed pliers (see page 106), attach the earring and close the loop. Make two.

Tip To make these earrings extra special, look out for fancy head pins with a ball or a decorative end. If you can't find decorative head pins long enough, make a bead dangle with the large bead and a bead link with the pearls and join the two together.

Aztec Fringe Earrings

These bold diamond-shaped earrings are worked in square stitch with added fringes, which can be altered in length as desired. Because they are such a simple design you can easily change the colour of the beads to suit the colour of your outfit – this red-and-gold design has a real Aztec feel.

You will need . . .

- 6g matt red seed beads, size 10
- 3g matt gold seed beads, size 8
- 2 gold-plated earring wires
- Nymo thread in red
- Beading needle
- Basic tool kit (see pages 16–19)

1 Thread your needle with a length of red Nymo thread. To make the block of 56 beads in square stitch (see pages 94–5), string on eight red seed beads. Take the needle back through the eighth bead and pull the thread tight so that the ninth bead is suspended below the eighth bead.

2 Put the needle back through the ninth bead and pick up another bead, the tenth. Put the needle back through the sixth bead and through the tenth bead again so that it is also suspended below the first row. Add the eleventh and twelfth beads in the same way.

3 Take the needle back through the first eight beads and down the second row to stabilize the block. Add another row of eight beads and stabilize again. Continue in this way until you have seven rows of eight beads, stabilized after every row has been added.

4 To add the fringe, thread the needle with another long length of Nymo thread. Take the needle through the first block of beads and out at the first corner of the block.

5 Pick up alternate red and gold beads to add a fringe strand of nine red and eight gold beads in total. Add a further four fringe strands at the centre points and corners of the block.

6 Finish by stitching an earring wire to the top corner of the block. Make a second earring in the same way to match.

Clustered Berries Ring

Cluster rings may look complicated, but are quite easy to make, as they are simply lots of head pin dangles attached to a ready-made looped ring base. Add two or three dangles to each loop of the ring for a chunky effect.

You will need . . .

- 30 silver-plated round beads, 3mm
- 18 metal-lined beads in pink, 6mm
- 3 flower drops in pink, 12mm
- 4 antique silver tube beads, 3 x 8mm
- 4 antique silver washer-style spacers, 6mm
- Silver-plated ring with 10 wire loops
- 30 silver-plated head pins
- Basic tool kit (see pages 16–19)

1 Make bead dangles using the head pins, picking up a small silver bead and then a pink or antique silver bead and finishing with a loop (see page 105).

2 Open the loop with flat-nosed pliers, attach it to one of the ring loops and close the loop again.

3 Make a few dangles using the washer-style spacers with a wrapped loop at one end and a plain loop for attaching to the ring loops (see page 105).

4 Add the large flower beads towards the middle of the ring base and mix the antique silver beads in with the pink metal-lined beads.

Tip When you put the ring on your finger, the bead dangles will all push together to make a solid cluster. If the cluster ring seems too loose and floppy, add a few more bead dangles.

Herringbone Earrings

Work tubular herringbone stitch (see page 115) with a variety of beads such as cylinders, twisted bugles and short bugles beads in the same colourway to create a pair of unusual loop earrings. The earring wires attach through a bead, which is more secure than simply sewing over the wire loop.

You will need . . .

- 2g silver cylinder beads, size 11
- 2g nickel matt short bugles, 3mm
- 48 gun metal twisted bugles, 7mm
- 2 nickel matt beads, size 6
- 2 sterling silver earring wires
- Nymo or S-lon thread in black
- Beading needle
- Basic tool kit (see pages 16–19)

1 Work the base band of ladder stitch (see page 94) as follows: pick up four cylinder beads and go back through all four, leaving a long tail. * Pick up two more cylinder beads and go back through the previous two and the two just added. Repeat from * until there are eight pairs of cylinder beads in a row. Join the ends together in a circle by going back through the first two beads and the pair just added.

2 To begin the herringbone stitch, pick up two twisted bugles and go down through the next cylinder bead and back up through the next cylinder bead along. Add pairs of twisted bugles all the way round. Step up at the end of the round through the next cylinder bead and the bugle stacked on top.

3 Continue working herringbone stitch in rounds, stepping up each time. Work two rounds of cylinder beads, two with 3mm bugles, two with cylinder beads, two with 3mm bugles and two with cylinder beads. Add a round of twisted bugles and then complete the second side in reverse order up to the twisted bugles.

4 On the next round add cylinder beads to create a two-drop ladder stitch border. Pick up four cylinder beads and pass the needle through the next twisted bugle and back up through the previous twisted bugle and the first two cylinder beads again. Pass the needle back down through the other two cylinder beads and twisted bugle again. Come up through the next bugle along and pick up two cylinder beads. Continue going through the previous stack and the one just added to the end.

5 To finish the ends, pick up one cylinder bead and go down through the next one. Come up through the next and add one until there are four cylinder beads. Flatten the tube and take the needle through all four cylinder beads. Using the long tail, repeat at the other end to add a row of four cylinder beads.

6 Join the two pairs left on either side together by looping the thread through the opposite rows and bring the thread out in the middle of each row. Pick up two 3mm bugles and a size 6 seed bead. Pick up a third 3mm bugle and take the needle back through the other two bugles (these are essentially inside the size 6 seed bead). Attach an earring wire through the top bugle and then sew in the thread ends. Make a second earring to match.

Stardust Sparkle Earrings

The glittering beads in these glamorous earrings are hollow and extremely light so can be strung on very fine illusion cord, appearing to float in mid-air. Tiny silver-lined seed beads and twisted hex beads give extra sparkle.

You will need . . .

- 16 clear silver-lined seed beads, size 6
- Silver-plated stardust round beads, four 8mm, ten 6mm and nine 4mm
- 50 silver-lined twisted hex beads, size 8
- Illusion cord, 0.3mm
- 2 silver-plated earring findings
- Cyanoacrylate instant glue
- Tapestry needle
- Basic tool kit (see pages 16–19)

1 To make one earring, cut five 35cm (13¾in) lengths of illusion cord and insert into the loop of the earring finding.

2 Fold the cords in half, thread on a seed bead and apply a drop of instant glue. Add an 8mm stardust bead then loop the illusion cord back through the bead. For extra security take the tail back through the loop on the side of the bead and through the loop just formed to make a half-hitch knot (see page 99). Pull taut, add a drop of glue and tug to hide the knot inside the bead.

3 Add beads to each strand. To secure the size 8 hex beads or smaller, simply secure with a drop of instant glue. Pick up a hex bead on one strand, add a drop of instant glue where you want the bead to lie and then use a tapestry needle to slide the bead over the drop of glue. Leave for a few moments until the glue sets.

4 To secure the size 6 beads or small round stardust beads, loop the illusion cord back through the bead as described in step 2.

5 Continue adding beads on all strands, alternating between small and larger beads. Vary the lengths of the strands, with the longest about 10cm (4in). To finish, add a hex or one of the other small beads to each strand and secure with a drop of instant glue. Trim the tails close to the beads once the glue has dried. Make a second earring to match by copying each strand in turn from the first earring.

Pearl Cluster Earrings

Beautiful pearl earrings fit for a queen! Filigree caps (see pages 15 and 106) look absolutely stunning against the subtle pastel shades of the pearl beads. Look for antique silver leaf charms to add a finishing touch to the fabulous focal pearl cluster.

You will need . . .

- Approx. 16 pearls in white, cream, blue and coffee, 6mm
- 2 pearls in blue, 15mm
- Approx. 16 silver-plated filigree caps, 6mm
- 2 silver-plated filigree caps, 15mm
- Silver-plated leaf beads, six 10 x 6mm and four 12 x 8mm
- 28 silver-plated jump rings, 5mm
- 18 silver-plated head pins
- 2 silver-plated earring wires
- Basic tool kit (see pages 16–19)

1 Make each of the pearls into a head pin dangle, as follows. Pick up a pearl and then a filigree cap (use the large filigree caps for the large blue pearls) and insert a head pin from the pearl side. Bend the head pin at an angle and trim to 7mm (⅜in). Use round-nosed pliers to make a loop (see page 104).

2 Make two lengths of chain using nine jump rings in each (see page 107). Attach an earring wire to the top of each jump-ring chain (see page 106) and attach a large blue pearl to the bottom of each chain.

3 Beginning at the top ring, attach a pearl charm and a small leaf using another jump ring. Continue down the chain, adding pearl charms to every jump ring, alternating sides.

4 Attach the remaining leaf charms using jump rings so that they are evenly spaced down the chain. Make a second earring to match the first.

Tip You can change the earring wires to screw or clip fittings to adapt these earrings for wearers without pierced ears.

Ready-to-Wear Earrings

It can be frustrating looking for the ideal earrings to go with a special outfit but it is much easier to buy just the right beads and make your own. These earrings are made using the bead link technique on page 104 and finished with a head pin bead dangle with a plain loop. The head pins have a decorative end, which inspired the choice of cylinder beads, but the earrings can be made with any similar size and shape of beads.

You will need . . .

- Glass multicolour beads, two 12mm and two 15mm
- 4 gold metal-effect cylinder beads, 3 x 7mm
- 2 gold-plated head pins with decorative end
- Gold-plated wire, 0.5mm (25swg)
- 2 gold-plated earring wires
- Basic tool kit (see pages 16–19)

1 Pick up a large multicolour bead on the head pin and then a gold metal-effect cylinder bead. Bend the end of the wire over at about 90 degrees close to the top of the cylinder bead. Trim the end to 7mm (⅜in). Use round-nosed pliers to bend the wire around to make a loop on the end of the head pin (see page 104).

2 Make an eye pin loop on the end of the gold-plated wire. Pick up small multicolour bead and then a gold metal-effect cylinder bead. Make a loop at the other end of the link and trim the wire (see page 105).

3 Open the loop below the small multicolour bead and attach the head pin dangle made earlier. Attach an earring wire to the top end of the bead link. Make a second earring to match.

Tip If you can't find head pins like these, add two tiny metal donut-shaped beads to a plain gold-plated head pin before you add the large bead.

Quick Ideas

Turquoise and lime

To make these simple earrings, cut two 15cm (6in) lengths of seven-strand bead stringing wire (see page 13) and loop each through a sterling silver earring wire. Feed on a size 2 silver-plated crimp and squeeze flat where the wires cross, close to the earring loop. Add a tubular crimp, seed bead, large bead, seed bead and crimp to each end and squeeze the crimps so that the beads lie about 3cm (1¼in) from the earring wire (see page 107). Trim the ends.

Funky spirals

To make these quick and clever designs, simply bend 0.7mm (22swg) enamelled copper wire in green and blue into interesting shapes with round-nosed pliers (see page 108). Bend the tails at 45 degrees and apply a dot of glue just above the bends. Add the beads, make a loop at the end of the wire and attach earring wires to finish (see page 106).

Beaded bows

Make this pair of fetching earrings using two pebble beads, four smaller beads, two five-link lengths of gold-plated chain, earring wires and some narrow sheer ribbon. Make a large charm with the pebble bead at the bottom and one or two small beads on top. Attach the charm to a five-link length of gold-plated chain and attach an earring wire to the top (see page 106). Tie a length of sheer ribbon through the bottom link of the chain and trim diagonally.

Bags & Boxes

When it comes to beaded treasures nothing is more prized than a beautiful trinket box or a stunning beaded bag, whether to present a gift in, to keep your valuables in or to wear with pride. The projects in this chapter use bead techniques including needle weaving, bead embroidery and bead loom weaving, together with wonderful materials such as silk, organza, ribbons, sequins and tassels to create some truly exquisite bags and boxes – your only dilemma will be which one to make first!

Amulet Purse

An amulet is a charm, something worn as protection from misfortune or evil spirits. Traditionally, these delightful purses were hung around the neck with the charm tucked safely inside. Nowadays an amulet purse has a more decorative purpose and is worn as a rather unusual necklace. It is worked in brick stitch from a chart, with the design repeated twice so that the back and front are identical. The purse is rather tiny and doesn't hold very much, but it could still protect you from misfortune: keep a little money folded up inside and you should get home safely!

Amulet Purse

You will need...

- 4g silver-lined clear crystal bugle beads, 3mm
- 2g white cylinder beads, size 11
- 10g light pink cylinder beads, size 11
- 8g pink cylinder beads, size 11
- Nymo thread in white
- Cord thread
- Two beading needles
- Basic tool kit (see pages 16–19)

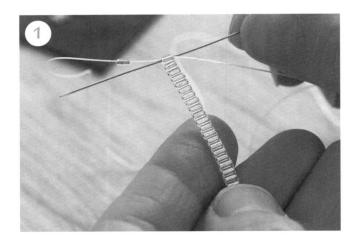

1 Thread a long length of white Nymo thread with a beading needle at each end. Work ladder stitch (see page 94) using the bugle beads until there are 50 beads and then join the strip into a circle.

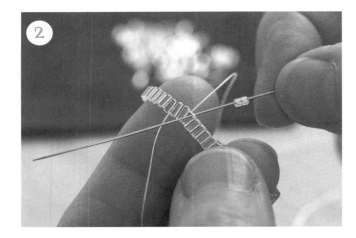

2 Working in brick stitch (see page 96) follow the chart on page 123, starting on Row 1. Pick up two light pink cylinder beads and put the needle through the first loop and back through the second bead. Continue working brick stitch, repeating the chart twice until you reach the first bead again.

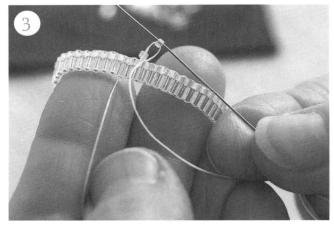

3 Stitch these two beads together and then begin the next row as in step 2. Keep following the chart, working tubular brick stitch until you complete Row 30. Now fold the purse in half so that the hearts are in the centre.

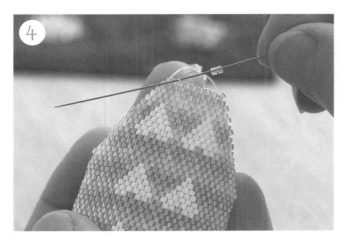

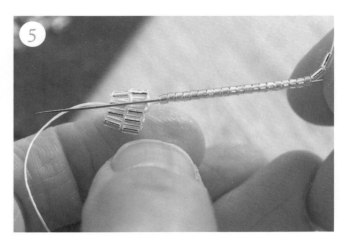

4 From now on you will not be stitching a tube but should continue working brick stitch one side at a time, decreasing the beads at each edge, as shown on the chart. To decrease, pick up two beads as usual but put the needle through the second loop from the edge and work across the row as normal. Now join on a thread on the other side of the purse and complete the back in the same way. Once both sides are complete, stitch the seams together invisibly (see page 98).

5 For the tassel, make an eight-bugle strip in ladder stitch and join into a tube. Add a second row using brick stitch. To make a tassel strand, cut a 2m (2yd) length of cord thread and pick up 20 light pink cylinder beads and two bugles. Take the needle back through the cylinder beads and through next loop below the bugle tube.

6 Continue adding tassel strands around the bugle tube, alternating between dark and light beads and making the strands different lengths until there are 16 strands in total. Sew the tassel to the bottom of the amulet purse.

Tip Use cord thread for the tassel fringe so that it drapes nicely. Nymo thread is ideal for the brick stitch but will give a much stiffer effect if used for the tassel.

7 The strap is made using chain stitch (see page 98). Start by picking up eight cylinder beads (alternate colours in pairs) and tie the beads into a circle. On the next and subsequent chains, pick six cylinder beads. Put the needle through the two pink beads at the top of the previous link and through the first two light pink and pink beads just added. Work chain stitch until the strap is 60cm (23½in) long. Attach the strap securely on either side of the amulet purse.

Starry Nights Jewellery Pouches

Turn plain little gift bags into something really special with a few well-placed sequins. Sequins are ideal for gift bags as they are flat, come in all sorts of shapes and sizes and in a wide range of lovely colours.

You will need . . .

- Organza fabric, 14 x 46cm (5½ x 18in)
- Fine cord, 75cm (30in)
- 13 silver star sequins, 1.5mm
- 12 silver round sequins, 6mm
- Fine embroidery thread in silver
- Dry adhesive tape or fabric glue
- Sewing machine
- Needle and bodkin
- Basic tool kit (see pages 16–19)

 **Tip** If you are short of time, look out for ready-made organza bags in your local gift shop. They are sold in a variety of colours and sizes.

1 To make the bag, fold the organza in half widthways and machine stitch the side seams. Trim the seams to 6mm (¼in) and turn through. Fold down the top edge by 6cm (2⅜in) and machine stitch a 1.25cm (½in) casing 4cm (1½in) down from the top edge.

2 Snip into the side seams between the casing lines. Cut the cord in half and, using a bodkin, thread one piece through from one side and back out the same gap. Thread the other end through from the other side. Knot the ends together.

3 Stick the sequins in rows across the organza bag as shown. Use a tiny dot of fabric glue (not near the hole in the sequin) or use a dry adhesive tape. If you use wet glue to stick the sequins, tuck baking parchment inside the bag to prevent the fabric layers sticking together.

4 Sew running stitch along in rows, backstitching through the holes of the sequins to secure. Sew in the ends on the reverse side to finish.

Flower Cluster Box

Plain card gift boxes can be transformed into exquisite beaded jewellery boxes. You can buy a satin-covered box with a padded lid insert that can be covered with beaded fabric or make your own.

You will need . . .

- Floral print fabric, 25cm (10in) square
- Lightweight iron-on interfacing, 25cm (10in) sq.
- Assortment of beads including seed beads, bugles and larger beads
- Gift box, 11.5cm (4½in) diameter
- Thin wadding (batting), 12 x 36cm (4¾ x 14in)
- Double-sided tape, 1.25cm (½in) wide
- Thin card
- Tapestry needle and toning sewing thread
- Grosgrain ribbon to tone with fabric, 40cm (16in)
- Basic tool kit (see pages 16–19)

1 Choose an area of fabric with an attractive pattern. Cut it out at least 5cm (2in) larger all round and iron interfacing on the reverse. Lay the fabric on a soft surface and press the box lid into the fabric to make an indented mark. Tack (baste) around the marked line.

2 Thread a tapestry needle with a double length of toning thread and secure on the reverse of the fabric with a couple of backstitches. Bring the needle to the right side, pick up a bugle, lay it flat and take the needle back through at the end of the bead. Stitch further beads around the petals in an irregular way (see page 119).

3 At the flower centres, bring the needle up and pick up a large round bead and then a seed bead. Take the needle back through the large bead and fabric. Add several more large beads and then fill in with smaller beads.

4 For the fronds, bring the needle out between two petals and pick up three to five seed beads. Put the needle back in the fabric at the end of the beads and backstitch along the line, back two or three beads. Pull the thread through and feed the needle back through the beads again.

5 To add three or four spikes to each flower centre, bring the needle out between larger beads. Pick up five seed beads, a large round bead and another seed bead. Miss the seed bead just added and take the needle back through the other beads and fabric.

6 Stick double-sided tape around the rim of the lid. Cut three pieces of thin wadding (batting) the same size as the lid. Use double-sided tape to stick the bottom piece on to the lid. Position the beaded fabric over the wadding (batting) and stretch down on to the rim of the lid. Use the tacked (basted) line as a guide for how far to stretch. Trim the fabric neatly just above the bottom edge of the lid. Remove the tacking (basting). Cut a strip of thin card to fit around the rim and tape in place.

7 To finish, tape the grosgrain ribbon over the card around the rim; trim neatly where the ribbon overlaps and stick down.

Trinket Box

Three different bead techniques are combined to make this beautiful trinket box. The rim is covered with a stunning piece of bead loom weaving, the padded lid is decorated with hand-embroidered beads and the box is finished off with an exquisite, three-dimensional beaded blackberry.

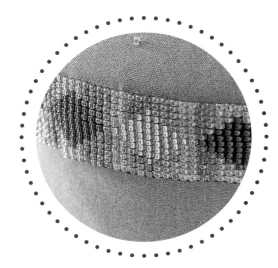

You will need...

- 6g each of iridescent pale aqua and green/blue iris seed beads, size 11
- 5g iridescent blue rainbow seed beads, size 11
- 3g each of deep blue, blue/green, dark olive green and pink seed beads, size 11
- Circular papier mâché box, 12cm (4¾in) diameter
- Double-sided tape, 1.25cm (½in) wide
- Lilac georgette, 30cm (12in)
- 50g (2oz) wadding (batting)
- Organdie, 15cm (6in) diameter circle
- Wooden bead, 7mm
- Bead loom
- Nymo thread in petrol blue
- Beading needle
- Dressmaker's pin
- Spray adhesive
- Thin card
- Co-ordinating ribbon, 15mm (⅜in) wide
- Basic tool kit (see pages 16–19)

1 Fit fourteen 1m (39in) lengths of petrol blue Nymo thread into the bead loom (see page 91) and work the design following the chart on page 122. You will need four repeats plus one extra diamond for this box. Take the beading off the loom and check the length against the box rim. Allow 6mm (¼in) for the fabric covering. Put the beadwork back on the loom and weave the fabric ends (see page 92).

2 Stick double-sided tape around the inside and the outside of the lid rim. Cut a 5 x 40cm (2 x 15¾in) strip of georgette and stick it halfway down the rim on the outside. Fold over the raw edge of the overlap and use double-sided tape to secure. Smooth the strip of fabric over to the inside of the lid.

3 Cut six circles of wadding (batting) the same size as the lid. Cut another slightly larger and two smaller circles. Stick another piece of double-sided tape around the rim of the lid. Pile the wadding (batting) on top of the lid beginning with the smallest circle and finishing with the largest one.

4 Position the organdie over the wadding (batting) and stretch it gently on to the double-sided tape. Adjust until the top is a smooth dome and trim any excess fabric. Stick more double-sided tape around the rim of the lid. Stretch a 15cm (6in) diameter circle of georgette on to the double-sided tape and trim off the excess fabric. Tie off the threads on the bead strip and fold the woven fabric under. Stick the bead strip around the rim, butting the ends together.

5 Using the point of a pair of embroidery scissors, make a hole in the centre of the lid from the inside. Tie a knot in the end of a length of Nymo thread and feed it through the hole. Leaving a 1cm (½in) circle in the centre clear of beads, begin to stitch green/blue iris beads in the middle of the lid. Work out from the centre, spacing the beads out further and using progressively lighter iridescent beads.

6 To make the blackberry, thread the beading needle and pick up the wooden bead, tying the thread to it, leaving a 10cm (4in) tail. Cover the bead with rows of eight dark olive green seed beads. Begin to fill the gaps with some of the other colour beads, threading the needle under the dark olive green rows. Keep adding beads until the wooden bead resembles a blackberry. Feed the thread ends through the centre of the lid and out of the hole on the reverse side.

7 From inside, lay a dressmaker's pin across the hole. Push down on the blackberry to sink it into the wadding (batting) and tie the threads across the pin using a surgeon's knot (see page 99).

8 Cut a strip of georgette fabric 3cm (1¼in) deeper than the box base and long enough to wrap around it. Stick double-sided tape on the inside of the rim and around the base. Stick the fabric around the box and then tuck the excess inside. Stretch the fabric gently on to the base of the box.

9 Cut two circles of thin card the same size as the base of the box and trim one slightly smaller. Spray adhesive on one side of each circle and stick to a piece of georgette. Trim the fabric to 1cm (½in) and snip into the card all round. Spray with adhesive and stretch the fabric on to the reverse side.

10 Stick the larger covered circle inside the lid and the smaller circle on to the base of the box. To finish the inside of the box simply cover the raw fabric edge with a piece of co-ordinating ribbon.

 Tip Use double-sided tape or spray adhesive to secure the ribbon inside the box.

Spiral Bag

A spiral rope makes a lovely handle for a little evening bag. Spiral twist (see page 115) is one of the strongest rope techniques making it ideal for a bag handle. Choose beads that match one of the colours in the bag fabric so that the elements of the design work together.

You will need...

- Small ready-made clutch bag
- 5g teal matt turquoise seed beads, size 6
- 5g blue-lined triangles, size 11
- 2g dark brown seed beads, size 11
- 6 turquoise washer beads
- 3 brown flat oval beads, 8 x 6mm
- Nymo thread in turquoise
- Beading needle
- Basic tool kit (see pages 16–19)

1 Pick up four dark brown seed beads and this three-bead sequence; a triangle, a size 6 seed bead and a triangle on to Nymo thread. Tie in a circle, leaving a long tail, and take the needle back through the four dark brown seed beads again.

2 Pick up one dark brown seed bead and the same three-bead sequence as in step 1. Take the needle through the last three dark brown seed beads on the spiral. Pull the thread up and then take the needle through the last dark brown seed bead.

3 Repeat step 2 to add a second loop of beads. Continue repeating step 2, making sure that the loops lie right next to each other. After four or five repeats the spiral effect will be quite obvious. Continue until the rope is about 20cm (8in) long and leave a tail at both ends.

4 Pick up two dark brown seed beads, a washer bead, a large brown bead, a washer bead and a flat oval on one tail of the rope. Sew the thread through at the top of the side seam of the bag and then back through the beads just added. Secure the thread in the spiral rope. Repeat to attach the handle to the other side of the bag.

5 To make a co-ordinating fastening on the bag flap, attach a thread to the centre of the flap. Pick up a washer bead, a large brown bead, a washer bead, a flat oval and a dark brown seed bead. Miss the seed bead and take the thread back up through the other beads. Secure the thread end in the fabric.

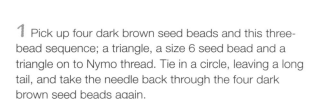

Beaded Tweed Bag

Tweed fabric makes a pretty background for this gorgeous selection of glass beads, which almost seem to merge into the fabric. Stitch the beads on to the fabric individually, before the bag is made up.

You will need...

- Pink tweed fabric, 20 x 36cm (8 x 14in)
- Seed bead mix, size 12–6 (size 6 plum, size 9 pink and white, size 11 red, metallic rainbow, pink and white, size 12 pinky-red)
- 10g pale pink round crystals, 6mm
- Beading needle, size 10
- Ribbon, 30cm (12in) of 15mm
- Perlé cotton thread, no.5 in deep fuchsia
- Sewing machine with zipper foot
- Cord maker (or pencil)
- Basic tool kit (see pages 16–19)

1 Fold the fabric in half crossways and press to mark the centre line. Using single stitch (see page 119), sew beads densely for the first 2cm (¾in) above the crease line, making the bead panel 15cm (6in) wide. Sew the crystal beads first spacing them out every 1cm (½in) and then add the size 6 plum beads. Sew pink and white size 9 seeds between the larger beads and then fill any gaps with smaller white and pink beads, adding some deep red and brighter pinky-red beads to liven the mix.

2 For the next 2cm (¾in) add the same number of crystal and size 6 plum seed beads adding fewer smaller beads in between. Over the next 6cm (2½in) space the beads out further.

3 Fold the fabric with beads inside in half and sew the side seams by hand or zigzag with a zipper foot on a sewing machine. Turn inside out. Trim around the top edge, following the weave, to 16cm (6½in) deep. Fray the last 1cm (½in) on the front and back. Sew a mix of beads along the frayed edge every 6mm (¼in).

4 Cut the ribbon in half and pin on the inside 4cm (1½in) from the top edge. Sew along both edges with matching sewing thread. Fold the perlé cotton in three and tie a knot in each end. Secure one end to a door handle and then twist tightly using a cord maker or pencil. Fold the tightly twisted thread in half, hold the knots and allow the cord to twist from the other end. Tie the ends together.

5 Smooth out the twists, tape the centre point and cut in half. Thread one length through the tweed at the side seam and then along the ribbon to the other side. Go back along the ribbon channel on the reverse side. Repeat on the opposite side.

6 Tie the cord ends together and unravel the thread ends. Sew single beads all over the knots to make beaded tassels. Trim the ends neatly.

Dolly Bag

The dolly or Dorothy bag is a classic shape that can be brought bang up to date by making it in a rich coloured silk, embellished with a funky sequin trim. The sequins make more impact as a wider band created from three rows of sequin trim linked together with a luxury sheer ribbon in a toning colour.

You will need . . .

- Turquoise silk dupion, 32 x 36cm (12½ x 14½in)
- Medium weight iron-on interfacing, 32 x 36cm (12½ x 14½in)
- Lining fabric, 32 x 29cm (12½ x 11½in)
- Decorative sequin trim, 64cm (25in)
- Plain sequin trim, 32cm (12½in)
- Sheer ribbon, 64cm (25in) of 15mm
- Turquoise satin ribbon, 112cm (44in) of 7mm
- Sewing machine with buttonhole setting
- Dressmaker's pins
- Needle and tacking (basting) thread
- Basic tool kit (see pages 16–19)

Tip To reduce bulk on the back seam of the bag, cut away the sequins from the trim inside the seam allowance.

1 Cut a piece of silk dupion 25 x 32cm (10 x 12½in). Cut one piece of interfacing 15 x 32cm (6 x 12½in) and another 9 x 32cm (3½ x 12½in). Iron the two pieces of interfacing, one on top of the other, along the longest edge of the silk dupion.

2 Cut the sheer ribbon in half and pin one piece 5cm (2in) from the bottom edge of the bag panel. Leave a 1.25cm (½in) gap and pin the second piece in place. Catch down the ribbon with tiny stitches along both edges.

3 Lay the plain sequin trim between the ribbons and attach it by sewing invisibly through the sequins (see page 121). Cut the decorative sequin trim in half and sew one piece to each outside edge of the ribbons.

4 Measure 9.5cm (3¾in) from the top edge in the centre of the bag panel and mark the position with a pin. Iron a 5cm (2in) square of interfacing on the reverse side with the pin mark in the centre. Tack (baste) the position of two horizontal 1.25cm (½in) buttonholes on the right side either side of the pin. Set the machine to the buttonhole setting and make two buttonholes. Snip along the slit to open the buttonholes.

Tip If your sewing machine doesn't make buttonholes, just feed the ribbon tie through the fabric between the casing lines using a large needle.

5 Fold the bag panel with right sides together and stitch the back seam to create a tube. Cut an 11cm (4¼in) circle from silk dupion and two circles the same size from interfacing. Iron the interfacing to the reverse side of the silk. Mark the bottom of the bag tube and the circle in quarters with notches. Pin the circle into the bottom of the bag, matching the notches. Tack (baste) and then machine stitch together.

6 Turn down the top edge of the bag by 5cm (2in) and press. Machine stitch a 1cm (⅜in) casing 3cm (1¼in) from the top edge. Make a lining in the same way as the bag, from an 18 x 32cm (7 x 12½in) piece of lining and 11cm (4⁵⁄₁₆in) circle. Turn down the top edge and press.

7 For the bag handle, cut a 35cm (14in) length of satin ribbon and sew the ends securely on the inside of the bag, level with the lower casing line. Turn the bag outside in and pull on the lining. Pin along the lower edge of the casing and slipstitch in place. Thread a 76cm (30in) length of satin ribbon through one buttonhole on the casing line and back out the other. Trim the ribbon ends at an angle, then pull up and tie in a bow.

Quick Ideas

Sumptuous sachets

These bags are so gorgeous they are almost a gift in themselves! Make a simple bag from lightweight crushed polyester fabric with a strip of organza ribbon across the bottom edge on the front then use stranded embroidery cotton (floss) the same shade as the bag to make the cord and tassel (see page 102). The cord is drawn through an organza ribbon casing sewn inside the bag. Sew seed beads, bugles and square beads along the bottom of the bags in a funky diamond design, and add a few extra beads to the tassel to finish.

Romantic pouch

To make this ring purse or scented sachet cut a heart-shaped piece of silk large enough to fit in an embroidery hoop, mark the design in the centre and iron interfacing on the back. Work the beading by couching (see page 121) strings of pearls in heart shapes and filling the centre using single stitch (see page 119). Cut a second piece of silk and with right sides together, stitch the shaped side seams. Trim seams and turn through. Fold the top edge inside, stitch a casing and thread organza ribbon through.

Ribbon gift bags

To make these festive gift bags take some wide wire-edged organza ribbon, fold in half and stitch the side seams together. Add bead fringing or bead netting to the bottom edges (see pages 100–101) in contrasting colours to the ribbon bags. Fill the bags with your presents, attach a few bead strands to a short length of craft wire and secure around the neck of the bag before tying a ribbon bow to match the bead colours.

Padded box

Make a pretty beaded box using a ready-made box with a lid insert or make a padded box like the one shown here. Cut a piece of silk at least 5cm (2in) larger than the lid, mark any design you like with a vanishing marker and embroider as desired (see pages 119–21). Once the beading is complete, trim the fabric to 2.5cm (1in) from the beading and stretch over the lid insert, lacing the edges together in both directions. Finish with a pretty coordinating tassel (see page 102).

Wedding bag

This glamorous handbag would be ideal for a bride or bridesmaid. Run up a simple bag on the sewing machine then add a row of fringing across the front using seed beads to coordinate with the fabric (see page 101). Make a handle from a length of bead stringing wire (see page 13), feeding sufficient seed beads on to the wire to cover it. Attach the ends of the wire securely to the front of the bag so they will be hidden under the feather trim. Make a handle for the back in the same way and then oversew marabou feather trim all around the top edge.

Beaded Accessories

From twinkling tiaras to sparkling shoes, this chapter shows you how to create an array of beautiful beaded accessories to make sure you get noticed wherever you go. Simple wirework techniques can create stunning headgear, while shoes can be enlivened with two different beaded motifs worked in brick stitch. For a break from the norm, why not try weaving your own beaded belt? A duo of key rings completes the beaded look, ranging from simple bead-embroidered shapes to statement tassels.

Wild Berry Tiara

Tiaras have become quite fashionable in recent years and although usually worn by brides or bridesmaids, they can be quite fun to wear at elegant parties. This tiara has an unusual autumnal look with its beautiful beaded berries and bugle leaves and was inspired by the way brambles twist and tangle in the hedgerows. It would be ideal for a winter party or an autumn wedding but would look just as stunning made in more traditional colours of white and cream.

Wild Berry Tiara

You will need . . .

- Purple enamelled wire, 1m (1yd) of 0.9mm (20swg) and 2m (2yd) of 0.2mm (36swg)
- Green enamelled wire, 3m (3yd) of 0.7mm (22swg) and 3m (3yd) of 0.315mm (30swg)
- 5g each wild blueberry, heather mauve and matt lilac seed beads, size 11
- 5g each brilliant shamrock, citron and autumn green seed beads, size 11
- 3g each willow bugle beads, 6mm and 9mm
- 3g each rainbow bugle beads, 9mm and 14mm
- 4 purple beads for berry centres, 12mm
- Needle
- Basic tool kit (see pages 16–19)

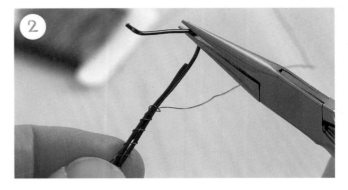

1 Cut two 40cm (16in) lengths of 0.9mm (20swg) purple wire. Bend 1cm (½in) over at one end and lay the second length just into the loop. Wrap 0.2mm (36swg) purple wire tightly around to cover the cut ends, leaving a loop for hairpins. Wrap the fine wire in a more open manner to hold the two thicker wires together.

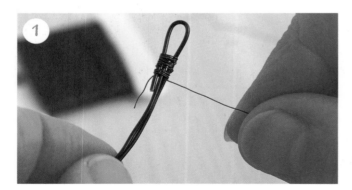

2 At the other end, bend one wire over again and trim the second length if required. Wrap the cut ends tightly and then tie off the fine wire and trim neatly. Bend the wire into a hairband shape to create the tiara base.

3 To make a leaf, cut a 25cm (10in) length of 0.7mm (22swg) green wire. Using flat-nosed pliers, bend the wire into a spiky leaf shape and wrap the ends together leaving a long stem.

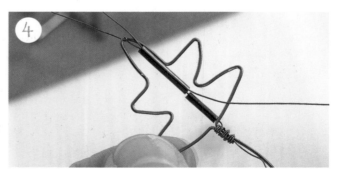

4 Trim the short end of the leaf to 6mm (¼in). Wrap the 0.315mm (30swg) green wire around the base to secure. Pick up a 9mm willow bugle and a 14mm rainbow bugle on the long end of the fine wire. Wrap the wire around the top of the leaf twice and feed it back through the longer bugle. Pick up a 9mm willow bugle and wrap the wire around the middle point of the leaf. Feed the wire back down the bugle. Continue adding bugles to create the leaf veins and snip off any excess wire.

5 To make a berry, tie the end of a 1m (1yd) length of 0.2mm (36swg) purple wire through the hole of a large purple bead. Pick up eight heather mauve seed beads and feed the wire back through the hole. Add seven more rows of eight beads. add shorter rows of wild blue berry between these rows to cover the bead. Add texture to the berry by adding three beads at time, looping the needle under the previous bead strands. Cover the bottom hole with three beads.

6 Cut a 25cm (10in) length of 0.7mm (22swg) green wire. Bend one end over to make a 6mm (¼in) loop and feed it inside the berry. Wrap the end of the fine wire around the wire stem to secure. Hold the berry stem against the leaf stem and twist the wires together for about 2cm (¾in). Make the long tail into a slightly smaller leaf shape and then use short bugles to make the veins on this leaf, as in step 4. Make two more large berry stems with two leaves each. Make two smaller stems with only one small leaf on each.

7 To make small leaf sprays, cut a length of 0.315mm (30swg) green wire. Pick up eight green seed beads in a random order. Bend the wires over to form a loop of beads and twist the wires together to create the top leaf. Pick up eight more beads to make a second loop and then eight more to make a third loop on the other side. Twist the ends of the wires together. Make the last two leaves with ten seed beads.

Tip When twisting two wires to make a stem, keep the tails at right angles and hold between your finger and thumb to get an even finish.

8 Take one of the larger stems and holding it in the middle of the base, wind the tail around to secure. Secure one of the other large stems on one side. Make some wire tendrils by cutting 15cm (6in) of 0.9mm (20swg) purple wire. Hold each end of the wire with round-nosed pliers and bend around to make a small loop. Wrap the wire around a knitting needle to create a spiral at each end. Make four double tendrils in all. Wind one or two tendrils around between the berry stems and add a small leaf spray in between. Add a large berry spray on the other side and then shape the tiara with two small sprays at the end. Fill in with tendrils and leaf sprays to complete.

Heart's Desire Key Ring

A hook fastening is ideal for making key rings, and because it opens on a spring on one side it can also be attached as an embellishment to a belt, trouser loop or even a bag.

You will need . . .

- Scraps of dark blue velvet, dark blue organza and metallic blue organza
- Rainbow metallic and dark blue machine embroidery threads
- Mixed denim blue beads
- 4 silver-plated head pins, 8cm (3in) long
- Short lengths of silver-plated chain
- Silver-plated wire, 0.6mm (24swg)
- Swivel-hook fastening
- Dressmaker's pins
- Needle and tacking (basting) thread
- Sewing machine with a darning or freestyle embroidery foot
- Basic tool kit (see pages 16–19)

Tip To make large jump rings, bend one of the head pins around a knitting needle or rod to make a tight coil. Use wire cutters to snip on one side of each coil to separate into rings (see page 106).

1 Lay the dark blue organza over a piece of velvet. Cut a 3cm (1¼in) wide strip of metallic organza and pin on top. Trace the heart from page 122 and cut out. Pin the heart on the fabrics and tack (baste) around the edge to hold the layers together and mark the shape.

2 Using rainbow metallic embroidery thread in your sewing machine and a darning or freestyle embroidery foot, sew a swirling pattern inside the heart. Change the thread to dark blue and repeat a similar pattern on top.

Tip You can simply stitch a swirly pattern inside the heart outline using backstitch if you don't want to embroider by machine.

3 Cut two heart shapes smaller than the original template in velvet for padding and lay on the reverse side inside the tacking (basting) lines. Lay a larger heart of velvet on top. Tack (baste) through all layers again. Machine stitch in a narrow satin stitch in dark blue around the tacking (basting) line. Trim the excess fabric and then zigzag again over the previous stitching.

4 Cut a short length of silver-plated chain and sew it to the top of the heart. Now fit a large jump ring (see tip left) to the other end and fit on to the hook fastening.

5 Pick up a few mixed denim beads on a head pin and make a ring at the end with round-nosed pliers (see page 105). Make another with different beads. Pick up about 3cm (1¼in) of beads on two head pins. Make a ring at the end and trim off excess wire. Attach one of the short head pins to a short length of silver-plated wire. Fit all the embellishments to the hook fastening with jump rings.

Beaded Mules

Transform a pair of plain mules with these delightful paisley-pattern motifs. The motifs are worked in brick stitch (see page 96) using petite beads with a pretty picot edging around the outside, which are then stitched or glued on to the front of each shoe.

You will need . . .

- 2g each crystal, green rainbow, dark rainbow, crystal pink and pale mauve petite seed beads
- 4g crystal aqua petite seed beads, size 15
- Silk mules
- Nymo thread in pale pink
- Beading needle, size 13
- Basic tool kit (see pages 16–19)

1 To work the ladder stitch start, thread the needle with a 1m (1yd) length of Nymo thread. Pick up a dark rainbow bead and put the needle back through the bead again. Pick up a second dark rainbow bead and put the needle back through the previous bead and then back through the one just added.

2 Add a further four dark rainbow beads and three aqua crystal beads. Take the needle through the last crystal bead again and then begin brick stitch (see page 96) by picking up two aqua crystal beads. Put the needle through the first loop and back through the second bead. Work brick stitch down the first side. Work three aqua crystal beads in the loop on the first rainbow bead and then work back up the second side in brick stitch.

3 Bring the needle out at the top crystal bead and pick up two green rainbow beads. Work one row of brick stitch. To keep the motif flat, increase the number of beads around the bottom curve by working a second bead into a loop twice.

4 Work a second row of brick stitch. At the point end pick up a green rainbow bead and take the needle back through the bead on the opposite side to make a point. Add a row of dark rainbow beads.

5 Beginning at the top bead on the motif work three rows of crystal aqua beads, tapering the beads to shape the motif. Add six crystal aqua beads to the point in the same method as step 1. Work a row of brick stitch back down to the motif and then feed the needle back through the beads to add a row of five more beads at the top then another row of three.

6 To make the picot edging, pick up five pale mauve beads. Miss a bead on the motif and take the needle down through the next. Bring it out at the next bead and pick up five crystal pink beads. Work round the motif alternating the colours. Make three motifs for each shoe.

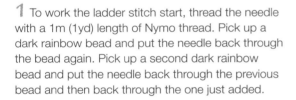 Tip Make a matching brooch by stitching a beaded paisley motif and sticking it to fabric-covered card. Attach a brooch fastening to the back.

Tasselled Key Rings

It will be difficult to misplace your keys when they are attached to wonderful tasselled key rings that are not only practical but decorative too. The tassels can be made in a single colour to match your décor or in a combination of mixed colours for a different effect. Attach a beaded tassel to your key with some beautiful sheer ribbon for an elegant, artistic touch.

You will need...

- Wooden bead, 22mm
- 10g lime or fuchsia seed beads, size 11
- 12g lime or fuchsia bugles, 6mm
- Quilting thread to match beads
- Beading needle
- Basic tool kit (see pages 16–19)

1 Thread a length of quilting thread on to the beading needle and feed it through the centre of the wooden bead and tie with a surgeon's knot (see page 99). Pick up approximately 17 seed beads and put the needle back through the centre of the wooden bead. Hold your finger and thumb over the holes to stop the beads going in and then pull the thread tight.

2 Continue adding 17 beads at a time until the bead strands touch near the holes with gaps in the middle – about 12 altogether. Now pick up 13 beads each time and fill every second gap around the bead. Fill the remaining gaps with groups of nine beads. Tie the thread ends together with a surgeon's knot and trim the ends.

3 To make the tassel loop, pick up 25 beads on a length of quilting thread. Feed the needle back through the beads to form a circle and then take it back through again for extra strength. Put both ends into the needle and take them through the wooden bead.

4 Thread the needle with a 2m (2yd) length of quilting thread. Pick up two seed beads and a bugle bead. Repeat until there are eight bugle beads on the thread. Pick up another seed bead. Leaving the last seed bead take the needle back through the other beads. Ease the bead string down the thread to leave a 10cm (4in) tail.

5 Keep adding further strands of beads and bugles until there are ten strands altogether. Tie the thread ends together and split the tassel strand bundle in two. Loop the threads sticking out from the bottom of the wooden bead around the tassel strands and tie off using a surgeon's knot (see page 99). Trim the thread ends.

6 Thread another 2m (2yd) length of thread and secure the end to the base of the wooden bead close to the tassel strands. Thread on the seed beads and bugles to make a tassel strand as in steps 4 and 5. To make a fuller tassel, sew in 20 extra strands of beads individually around the bottom of the bead (see also page 102).

Brick Stitch Rosettes

Brick stitch worked in a circular shape makes a super bead medallion that can be worn as a brooch or attached to a bag. High-quality Swarovski crystals elevate this embellishment into the luxury class and will transform a pair of plain pumps into the perfect party shoes.

You will need . . .

- 2 wine round crushed glass beads, 10mm
- 5g raspberry bronze iris seed beads, size 11
- 28 rose Swarovski xilion crystals, 4mm
- 32 rose Swarovski xilion crystals, 6mm
- Nymo thread in wine or black
- Beading needle
- Strong glue
- Basic tool kit (see pages 16–19)

1 Thread the beading needle with a long length of Nymo thread. Take the needle through the hole in the large round bead twice and then tie the tail to the main thread with a reef (square) knot (see page 99) so that the knot ends up next to the hole.

2 Ease the threads round so that there is a thread on opposite sides of the round bead. Work brick stitch along the threads with seed beads (see page 96). Begin by picking up two seed beads and then continue adding one each time. Take the thread through the first and last beads to complete the circle.

3 Add two small crystals to begin the next round of brick stitch, missing some loops so that the crystals are spaced evenly. Add single crystals thereafter and join the last to the first as before.

4 Work another round of brick stitch with the seed beads and then work a round of crystals adding 16 large crystals.

5 To work the picot edge pick up three seed beads and take the needle back through the last seed bead added and pull up to create the picot. Continue in brick stitch alternating between adding one seed bead and then two seed beads, taking the needle through the second seed bead only all the way round. Sew in the thread ends. Make a second rosette in the same way and attach to your shoes using strong glue.

Tip Take care spacing the larger beads so that they have plenty of room otherwise the medallion will buckle rather than lie flat.

Crystal Tiara

Tiaras have always been associated with royalty and wearing one, whether it is for a ball or on your wedding day, will always make you feel like a princess. This tiara is extremely easy to make using the twisting techniques shown on page 104 and simple wire wrapping to attach the Swarovski crystals and imitation pearls. Use a ready-made tiara band or make your own by twisting two lengths of 0.8mm (21swg) wire together.

You will need . . .

- Clear AB Swarovski round crystals, one 10mm, seven 8mm and nine 6mm
- 35 clear AB Swarovski xilion crystals, 4mm
- Ivory round pearls, three 8mm, seven 6mm and forty-five 4mm
- Silver-plated tiara band
- Silver-plated wire, 8m (8yd) of 0.4mm (27swg) and 1m (1yd) of 0.2mm (36swg)
- Basic tool kit (see pages 16–19)

1 Pick up the 10mm crystal on a long length of 0.4mm (27swg) wire and drop down to the middle. Hold the crystal between your finger and thumb and twist the wire to create a 4cm (1⅝in) stem. The amount of twist is crucial to the look (see tip, below).

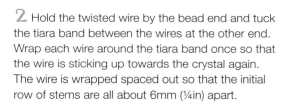

Tip If you want the stems to be straight only twist until the wire is evenly twisted and begins to look like tiny seeds. For slightly crooked stems, as shown in the finished design, twist a few more times and the wire begins to twist in on itself.

2 Hold the twisted wire by the bead end and tuck the tiara band between the wires at the other end. Wrap each wire around the tiara band once so that the wire is sticking up towards the crystal again. The wire is wrapped spaced out so that the initial row of stems are all about 6mm (¼in) apart.

3 Pick up an 8mm pearl on one wire and fold the wire over to the other side of the tiara from where it emerged. Hold the bead just above the pre-twisted stem and twist to create the stem. Repeat with a 6mm pearl on the other side.

4 Continue adding alternate round crystals and the two larger pearls for about 9cm (3½in) on each side to make a total tiara beading length of 18cm (7in). Vary the heights from stem to stem and taper down to the outer edges. When you get to the end of the wire, wrap it once around the tiara band and trim so that the cut end is facing up towards the beads otherwise it will scratch the wearer.

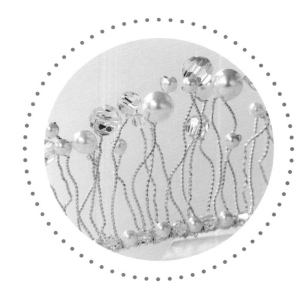

5 Using a 6mm round crystal, twist a long length of wire to make a 3cm (1¼in) stem. Tuck the beaded tiara band between the wires so that the stem is in the middle and wrap to secure as before.

6 Work out from the centre as before, adding 4mm pearls and 4mm xilion crystals alternately, to create shorter stems that sit in front of the main stems. Add the occasional 6mm crystal to add variety as you go.

7 Pick up alternate 4mm pearls and 4mm xilion crystals until there are 21 pearls on a 30cm (12in) length of 0.4mm (27swg) wire. Fold over the ends of the wire to prevent the beads falling off.

8 Hold the wire across the tiara band so that the centre pearl is in the middle. Beginning in the middle of the 0.2mm (36swg) wire, secure the beaded wire to the band, wrapping between the stems and each pearl and crystal in turn. Add or remove a few beads if required till you reach the end of the stems on either side.

9 Wrap the wires neatly a few times at each end to secure, remembering to keep the cut ends facing up towards the beads. Arrange the stems and if necessary, bend each a little more, bringing some slightly to the front to create the effect you desire.

Tip Work a smaller sample and attach to hair combs for the bridesmaids or make a similar tiara in funky colours for a hen night or special birthday.

Summery Sandals

That basic of the summer wardrobe, a pair of flip-flops, can be made into something quite special with the addition of a quick bead embellishment. Choose some pretty, big beads in a matching colour to make a quick star shape.

You will need...

- 24 pony beads, 3mm (⅛in)
- Assortment of big beads in pinks and red
- Pink wire, 0.7mm (22 gauge)
- Pair of sandals or flip-flops
- Epoxy resin glue
- Basic tool kit (see pages 16–19)

1 Cut a length of pink wire and wrap the end around some round-nosed pliers (or a fine knitting needle) to make a short spring (see page 108). Trim off the tail end.

2 Pick up a pony bead and then five or six larger beads in a range of shapes and sizes. Pick up another pony bead and wrap the wire around the pliers again to make a short spring at the other end. Make another two beaded wires in the same way.

3 Lay the beaded wires so they overlap in the middle of the beads. Wrap a second length of wire around where they cross to secure, leaving two long ends. Pick up two or three larger beads on each end and then a pony bead and secure with a spring as before. Trim off the tail of the wire. Wrap another piece of wire around the middle and add fewer beads to create the 'centre' of the star.

4 Make a second bead embellishment for the other sandal. Attach the beads to the strap using a strong adhesive such as epoxy resin.

Tip If you want the bead embellishments to be more temporary, stick them in place with a few large craft glue dots instead (see page 13).

Medallion Belt

This funky hipster belt puts a new spin on bead loom weaving with its long fringing and polka dot medallions, made using decorative beads to create texture. You can simply weave square or rectangular panels across the threads or use increasing and decreasing (see page 93) to create the circular bead motifs.

You will need...

- 5g each of colour-lined lime and chartreuse AB triangle beads, size 10
- 90 cube beads, 4mm
- Space dyed mixed yarns, 2m (2yd) long
- Nymo or S-lon thread in taupe
- Bead loom
- Basic tool kit (see pages 16–19)

Tip If you can't find triangle beads, use seed beads instead, so long as two threaded side by side are the same width as the cube beads.

1 Cut ten 2m (2yd) lengths of mixed yarns. Tie an overhand knot (see page 99) about 15cm (6in) from one end of the yarn and hook over the pin on the bead loom. Wind the dowel ready to begin the first bead panel about 30cm (12in) from the end of the yarn (see page 91).

2 Space the threads every 4mm (scant ¼in) and secure on the other side of the loom. Cut a long length of matching Nymo or S-lon thread and knot to the fourth warp thread in from the edge.

3 To work the first half of the bead motifs, pick up six mixed triangle beads and position under the warp threads so that there are two beads between the four centre threads. Take the needle back through the beads over the warp threads.

4 Increase two beads at each end (see page 93) on the next two rows of triangle beads. Work one row then increase at each end of the next row and work a final row. Add nine cube beads on the next row.

5 For the second side of the circle motif, work two rows of triangle beads, then decrease by two beads at each end of the next row (see page 93) and work two rows. Decrease two beads at each end of the next two rows. Sew in the weft thread ends.

6 Lift the 'belt' off the loom and untie the first knot. Re-tie so that the knot sits about 3cm (1¼in) from the bead motif. Hook this knot over the pin on the loom and set up the loom again. Measure 10cm (4in) from the last bead motif and tie a thread on the fourth warp thread in again. Make a second bead motif.

7 Lift the belt off the loom and tie a knot between the bead motifs. Continue using the new knot to secure the beading. Ten bead motifs will make a 90cm (1yd) length plus loose ends for tying. Tie the threads at each end to match the other knots and trim as required.

Dragonfly Pin

I love watching dragonflies flitting back and forth. These exquisite dragonflies look very realistic although they are made entirely in wire and beads, with their wings formed from a fine metallic mesh ribbon. You can make your dragonflies in realistic colours or make them to match your favourite outfit. Glue a brooch pin to the back so it can be worn as a brooch, or simply push a hatpin through the wires at the back and pin it to a straw hat.

You will need...

- 11 each of antique cranberry, desert peach, cherry sorbet and ice seed beads, size 11
- 16 ice petite seed beads, size 15
- 2 burgundy crystals, 6mm
- Enamelled copper wire in wine, pink and silver, 2m (2yd) each of 0.45mm (26swg)
- Silver-plated wire, 50cm (20in) of 0.8mm (21swg) and 50cm (20in) of 0.2mm (36swg)
- Tubular mesh ribbon, 25cm (10in) of 7mm
- Knitting needle, size 11 (3mm)
- Needle
- Hatpin or brooch fastening
- Micro glue dots
- Epoxy resin glue
- Basic tool kit (see pages 16–19)

Tip Use a narrow tubular mesh ribbon for the wings so that it stretches to fit snugly over the wings.

1 Cut a 50cm (20in) length of 0.8mm (21swg) silver-plated wire. To create the wing shape, hold the wire in the middle and bend it over flat-nosed pliers about 4.5cm (1¾in) from the centre point in each direction. Use the pliers to make a slight bend on the bottom edge near the tip to give the wings an authentic look.

2 Bend the wires up at 90 degrees in the middle and fold over the top of the wings. Bend out again at 90 degrees below the wings ready to make the second set of wings. Shape the lower wings so they are slightly longer and deeper than the top wings. When you bring the wires into the centre again, twist the ends together, bend up and wind one end over the top wings to secure. Snip off any excess wire.

3 Cut four 5–6cm (2–2½in) lengths of tubular mesh ribbon. Unravel one end of each length slightly, thread the tail end into a needle and feed through the loops. Pull up to gather the end and then sew in to secure. Slide the ribbon lengths over the wings so they meet in the middle. Sew together with fine wire.

Tip Use a desk magnifying lamp to see the tiny loops of wire more clearly when you are gathering the tubes of wire mesh.

4 To create the tail, hold all three colours of the 0.45mm (26swg) enamelled wires together and wind around the knitting needle. Begin about 8cm (3in) from the end and keep wrapping right to the end of the point. Snip the wires neatly at both ends.

5 Feed 0.45mm (26swg) pink and silver wires through the two burgundy crystals and pull the wires together so the crystals lie side by side. Wrap the long end of the wires around the tail and then over the top between the beads several times to create the head of the dragonfly. Feed the tail end into the top of the wrapped wire body and wrap the long end around several times to secure. Snip off the ends neatly.

6 On the wine wire, pick up 16 ice petite beads, 11 ice, 11 desert peach, 11 cherry sorbet and 11 antique cranberry seed beads. Beginning with cherry sorbet, repeat the beads in the reverse order. Secure the end of the wire just below the head. Wrap the beaded wire around the body to create the abdomen.

7 Lay the body on the wings and wrap the silver-plated wire around and between the wings to secure to the body. As a finishing touch, apply a tiny amount of glue, such as micro dots, on individual petite beads and stick to the wings. Finally, feed a hatpin through the back of the dragonfly or attach a brooch fastening with epoxy resin glue.

Techniques

If you are new to beadwork it is worth working through this section to learn the skills required for some of the projects. Although most of the projects have full instructions enabling you to work the project from the step-by-step instructions, this section has useful tips and diagrams as well as detailed instructions for the eight key techniques used in the book.

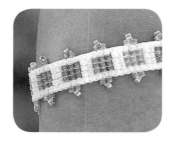

Bead loom weaving

Use this simple technique to weave a flat band of beading, ideal for pretty bracelets, funky belts and embellishments. See pages 91–3.

Needle weaving

Weaving beads together off the loom is known as needle weaving. Some projects require only one stitch while others make use of two or more stitches. See pages 94–9.

Netting, fringing and tassels

Create your own netted or fringed scarves and use tassels to add a touch of class to any project, from bags and boxes to key rings. See pages 100–102.

Wirework

Wirework techniques will need to be mastered for all kinds of jewellery, from simple charm bracelets, necklaces and earrings to more intricate tiaras. See pages 103–109.

Threading and stringing

This is an easy technique for making necklaces and bracelets. You will need to learn to space beads and how to add fastenings. See pages 110–14.

Ropes and cords

This versatile technique is used for bracelets, necklaces and also for earrings and bag handles. Two different stitches are used in this book. See page 115.

Bead knitting

Using beads in knitting can transform a plain scarf or bag into something truly scrumptious. Learn the basic steps of knitting here, plus how to add the beads. See pages 116–18.

Bead embroidery

Embroidering beads turns fabric projects into stunning pieces in an instant. There are several techniques to learn including couching and stacking beads. See pages 119–21.

Bead Loom Weaving

Bead loom weaving is a quick method of producing flat bands of beading. The width of the band is only restricted by the width of the loom. The beads are arranged in straight rows and so the design can be worked out on a square grid in the same way as cross stitch. There are two sets of threads on a bead loom. The warp threads run lengthways through the beadwork and are fitted to the loom. The weft threads are crossways threads, which carry the beads and are woven in with a beading needle.

1 Count the number of beads across the design and add one to find the number of warp threads required. Add 60cm (24in) to the finished length of the project for attaching the threads to the loom and finishing off. Cut the warp threads and tie an overhand knot (see page 99) at one end.

2 Split the bundle in two and loop the knot over the tack on the top roller. Loosen the wing nut and, holding the threads taut, wind the warp threads on to the roller, stopping when there is just enough thread to tie on to the other roller.

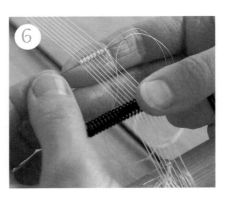

3 Hold the threads firmly and arrange along the top spring. Use a 'T' pin to sort one thread into each coil. Line the threads up across the bottom spring in the same way, so that they run parallel to one another and don't cross at any point.

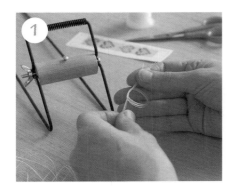

4 Tie an overhand knot and loop the knot over the tack on the bottom roller. Wind the rollers back until there is 30cm (12in) on the bottom roller and tighten the wing nuts.

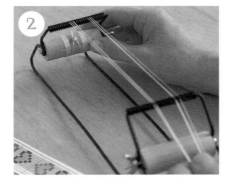

5 Thread a needle with a 2m (2yd) length of thread and tie to the right-hand side warp thread with an overhand knot leaving a 15cm (6in) tail. Beginning at the bottom, read the chart from right to left and pick up the correct number of beads in the right order.

6 Hold the beads under the warp threads and push them up between the warp threads so that there is a thread either side of each bead.

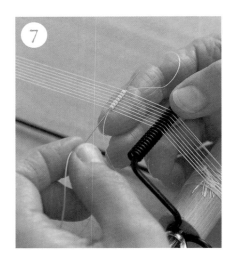

7 Feed the needle back through the beads from left to right, making sure that the needle passes on top of the warp threads. If the needle goes below the warp thread the beads will not be secured.

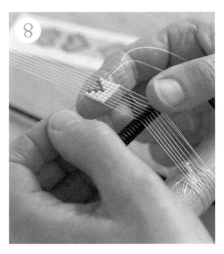

8 Pick up the next row of beads according to the chart and repeat the process, passing the needle back through the beads above the warp threads. After the first few rows it will become much easier to work.

9 When you have about 13cm (5in) of thread left on the weft thread remove the needle and leave the thread hanging. Thread a new length of thread and feed through five or six beads, leaving a 13cm (5in) tail hanging below the beadwork. Both ends can be woven in later.

10 To finish the beadwork, weave the weft thread, without any beads on it, back and forwards across the top of the beads to create a narrow fabric band. Roll the beadwork to the other end. Now attach another length of thread and weave this thread to create a narrow band of fabric at the beginning of the beadwork.

11 Lift the beadwork off the loom. Tie pairs of warp threads together using a surgeon's knot (see page 99). Take the thread ends left over right, twice, and then right over left, twice, and pull tight.

12 Weave the ends of the thread into the beadwork for at least five beads and then double back for at least five beads. Trim the ends close to the beadwork on the reverse side and then trim the warp threads at each end to 6mm (¼in).

Increasing and decreasing

Rather than simply working a straight panel you can change the shape of the loom work by increasing or decreasing the number of beads in each row. You can only increase by the number of warp threads on the loom so this has to be taken into consideration when setting up.

To increase

You can simply pick up one or two extra beads at the end of every row, but to increase at both ends in the same row use the technique below.

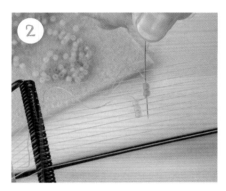

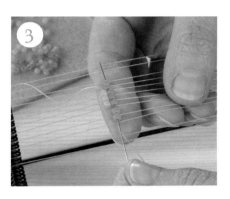

1 At the end of a row pass the weft thread under the warp thread at the end of the bead row and bring it out above the beads. Pick up the number of beads you want to increase by, in this case, two.

2 Lay the beads in position on top of the warp threads. Push the beads down and pass the needle through the beads under the warp threads.

3 Pick up the remaining beads for this row, including the beads you need to increase by at the other side, and slot into position. Take the needle back through all the beads including those added at the other end.

To decrease

To decrease the amount of beads used at both ends in the same row, simply reverse the technique used for increasing beads, so use fewer beads instead of picking up more at each end.

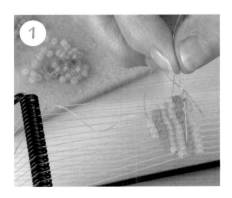

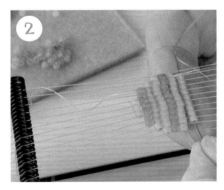

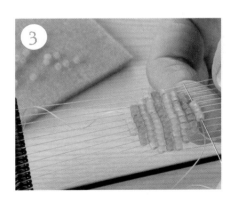

1 At the end of the last full row, take the needle over the outer warp thread and through the number of beads to be decreased. Bring the needle out on the upper side and wrap around the new outer warp to the underside.

2 Pick up the beads for the next shorter row, press up between the warp threads and weave these in place as usual.

3 Continue decreasing beads at each end, to create the shaping.

Needle Weaving

Needle weaving is a way of stitching beads together to create a flat or tubular beaded fabric. There are lots of different stitches that can be used, each with distinct characteristics that determine the finished look and feel of the beadwork. The stitches may appear to be similar in samples but are not readily interchangeable, as their different characteristics become evident in larger pieces. Ladder stitch, square stitch, brick stitch, peyote stitch and chain stitch are described here.

Ladder stitch

This simple stitch is often used to make the base for brick stitch (see page 96). It is usually worked with bugle beads but seed beads can also be used.

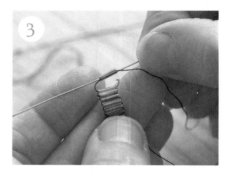

1 Cut a 2m (2yd) length of thread and thread a needle on to each end. Pick up two bugle beads and let them drop down to the middle of the thread. Now put the other needle through the second bead in the opposite direction.

2 Pull the threads tight. Pick up another bead with one needle and put the other needle through the bead in the opposite direction.

3 Continue adding beads in the same way until the band is the length you require. To make the band into a tube, pass each needle through the first bead again and pull tight.

Square stitch

Beads worked in square stitch look similar to beads woven on a loom. The needle passes through each bead several times and so you may need to use a size 13 needle and a fine thread in a toning colour. Square stitch has a wonderful draping quality and is ideal for bracelets.

1 Pick up the required number of beads for the first row. For the second row, pick up a bead and pass the needle back through the last bead on the first row.

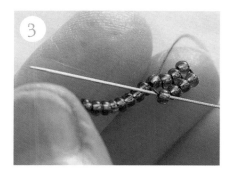

2 Pass the needle through the first bead on the second row again and back through the bead just added. The bead should be suspended below the first row.

3 Pick up a second bead and take the needle back through the second last bead on the previous row. Continue working along the row adding on one bead at a time.

4 To strengthen and stabilize the bead fabric, at the end of the row go back through the previous row and the one just worked, ready to begin the next row.

Increasing

When working in square stitch the beads are usually increased on the edge, but you can pick up an extra bead at any point along the row if it suits the design better.

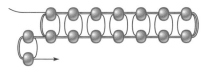

1 Pick up the number of beads you want to increase by, in this diagram, one. Pick up another bead and add it below the last bead as normal. Continue adding beads along the row.

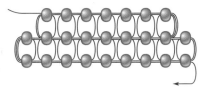

2 At the other end of the row pick up the number of beads you want to increase by at this side. Pick up a bead and work the square stitch on top of the end bead instead of below. Pass the needle through the remaining beads on that row and the one below.

Decreasing

You can reduce the number of beads in a row by stopping short at each end or going from two beads to one at any point along the row.

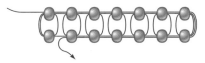

1 Pass the needle through the previous row as usual and then, when passing through the row just added, bring the needle out between two beads where you want the decrease to begin.

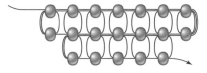

2 Work square stitch along the row as usual, stopping where you want before the end of the row. Take the needle between beads to pass the thread through the previous row and the one just worked.

Brick stitch

Brick stitch is one of the easiest stitches to work and is so called because it looks like a brick wall. The stitch is flexible crossways but rather stiff lengthways and can be worked flat or in a tube. It is used to make the Amulet Purse (see page 62).

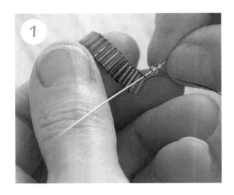

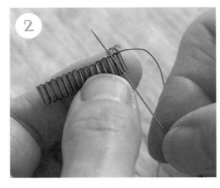

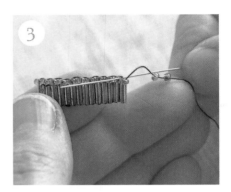

1 Make the foundation row the required length in ladder stitch (see page 94), using either seed beads or bugle beads. For the first row of brick stitch, pick up two beads and pass the needle under the first loop of thread joining the foundation row of beads.

2 Pass the needle back through the second bead you picked up. Pick up another bead. Pass the needle under the next loop and back through the bead again. Continue adding one bead at a time in this way to the end of the row.

3 Turn the beading round and pick up two beads to begin the next row. Repeat steps 2 and 3 until the beadwork is the size that you require.

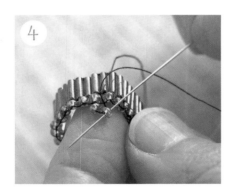

4 To work in a tube, make a foundation tube with the ladder stitch (see page 94). At the beginning of each round pick up two beads, then one at a time thereafter. At the end of the round join the beads together and bring the thread out ready to begin the next round.

Circular brick stitch

A flat brick stitch circle with a small bead in the centre iis the ideal base for a round container or a mat, or you can begin with a larger bead or a row of ladder stitch for different effects. This technique is used for the shoe embellishments on pages 81 and 83.

1 Thread a needle and pick up the centre bead. Drop down to about 15cm (6in) from the tail. Pass the needle back through the bead twice so that there is a thread on both sides. Pick up two beads and pass the needle under the thread loop on one side. Take the needle back through the second bead added, as in regular brick stitch. Continue around the bead, working brick stitch into the loops on both sides.

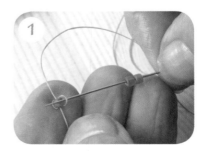

2 Loop the thread through the first and last beads at the end of the round so that the thread finishes on the outside. Begin each new round with the two-bead start. If you are working single bead brick stitch increase by sharing a loop.

Peyote stitch

Peyote stitch is a versatile stitch that can be worked flat or in a tube. It is easiest to work with an even number of beads in each row. Peyote stitch is ideal for bags with a flap, as the fabric is very flexible along its length.

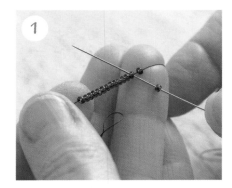

1 Pick up a bead and anchor it by taking the needle back through it again leaving a 15cm (6in) tail. Pick up enough beads to give the required width for the first row, ending up with an even number. Pick up a bead and, missing the last bead on the first row, pass the needle through the next bead.

2 Pick up another bead, miss a bead on the first row and pass the needle through the next bead. Continue to the end of the row missing every second bead.

3 In subsequent rows the beads are in a more obvious zigzag pattern. Work back and forwards in the same way, picking up one bead at a time and passing the needle through the next 'dropped down' bead.

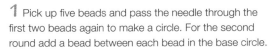

Circular peyote stitch

This technique creates a flat disc that can be used as an embellishment such as in Peyote Stitch Rings (page 50) or could be used to create the base of a vessel or bowl.

1 Pick up five beads and pass the needle through the first two beads again to make a circle. For the second round add a bead between each bead in the base circle.

2 'Step up' by passing the needle through the last bead of the base circle and the first bead added in the second round again.

3 Pick up two beads between each bead added in the last round. 'Step up' by passing the needle through one of the two beads added again ready to begin the next round.

4 Add one bead between each 'up' bead in the next round then two beads between each of these beads in the following round. Step up through the first bead (or pair of beads) added in the previous round ready to start the new round.

Chain stitch

Chain stitch is an ideal stitch for making straps and can be embellished to make more ornate bracelets and necklaces. The number of beads can be varied in each chain to create different effects.

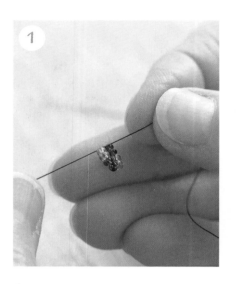

1 Pick up two light beads, two dark beads, two light beads and two dark beads. Tie the beads into a circle using a reef (square) knot (see page 99), leaving a 15cm (6in) tail.

2 Pass the needle back through two dark, two light and two dark beads. Pick up two light, two dark and two light beads and put the needle back through the top two dark beads on the previous chain.

3 Pass the needle through the first two light and two dark beads just added, ready to add the next chain. Continue adding six beads at a time until the chain is the length required.

Joining pieces of beadwork

From time to time it is necessary to make a seam and join two pieces of work. In beadwork it is possible to make an almost invisible join. Most bead stitches have at least one straight side and these can be butted together. Pass the needle through one bead at a time alternating from side to side to join the seam.

Brick stitch and peyote stitch both have two straight edges and two jagged edges where the beads jutt out on alternate rows. When the two opposite edges are brought together, the beads slot in side by side rather like a zip. To sew up the edges, put the needle through the jutting-out bead on one side. Take it through the jutting-out bead on the opposite side and pull tight. Continue working down the seam.

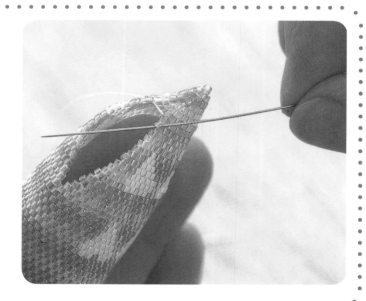

Knots

There are several simple knots used in beading to anchor threads or for tying off ends securely and it is worthwhile learning these knots so that your beadwork remains intact and fastenings firmly attached during use. For extra security, use a cocktail stick to add a drop of jewellery glue on the knots and leave to dry before trimming the tails.

Half-hitch knot

To secure the tail of your thread, work one or two half-hitches over another thread within the beading. To work, take the needle behind a thread in the beadwork and leave a loop. Pass the needle back through the loop and pull up to make the half-hitch. Repeat for extra security or add a drop of jewellery glue over the knot. Feed the tail through several beads before trimming.

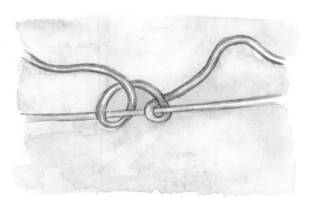

Reef (square) knot

This is the basic knot for tying two threads of equal thickness. It is fairly secure, but can be loosened by tugging on one end. To tie, pass the left thread over the right and tuck under. Then pass the right thread over the left and tuck under the left thread and out through the gap in the middle.

Overhand knot

Use this knot to tie a bundle of threads together or to knot between beads on a string. To tie, simply cross the tail over the main thread to make a small loop, then pass the tail under the thread and back through the loop.

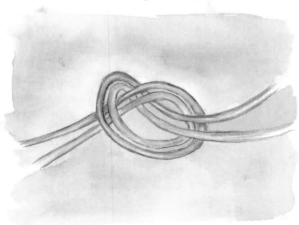

Surgeon's knot

This knot is similar to a reef knot but each thread end is taken over and under twice. The knot is more secure than a reef knot and doesn't loosen while it is being tied.

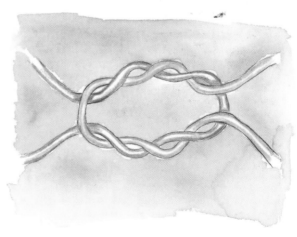

Netting, Fringing and Tassels

Adding fringing, bead netting and tassels to your accessories will transform them into stunningly beautiful beaded pieces. Consider the weight of the bead fringing or netting before beginning and make sure that the colours of the beads tone in with the fabric. Add beads to a ribbon or tape to be incorporated in a design or use a ready-made item such as a scarf or shawl.

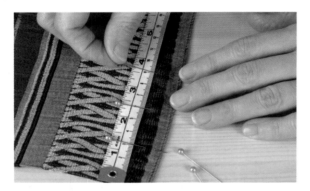

Measuring and marking

Lay the fabric or ribbon flat on the work surface. Measure the width of the item or mark the length of beading required. Work out the spacing remembering that you will get one more strand than the measurement – i.e. on a 10cm (5in) length with 1cm (½in) gaps you will have 11 strands. Insert the first pin the required distance from the side edge. Work along the bottom edge of the fabric, inserting pins as necessary.

Attaching a single thread

On a narrow hem scarf insert the needle about 2.5cm (1in) from the side edge and take a 1cm (½in) stitch through the hem only. Work two tiny backstitches in the hem on the reverse side and then feed the needle through the hem to the side edge ready to begin.

Attaching multiple threads

Cut a double length of thread and thread the cut ends into a needle. Make a small stitch through the hem and pass the needle through the loop on the end of the thread. Pull through to secure. Add a double thread at each mark.

Bead terms for netting

- **Shared beads** are the beads that link the rows of netting and have two threads passing through them.

- **Bridge beads** sit between the shared beads and generally have one thread passing through them.

Horizontal netting

This method of netting is worked from one side to another. When worked flat, this style of netting naturally forms a 'V' shape as each row gets shorter by half a loop at each end. To keep straight sides a new string of beads has to be added at each end; the rows of netting link into the side strands to create a straight-sided piece (see step 4).

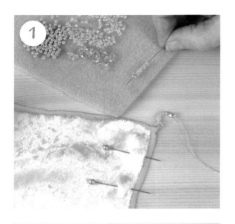

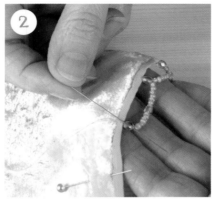

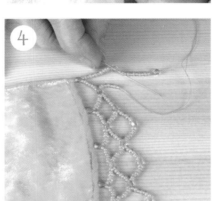

1 Begin with a long thread at the edge of the work. Pick up a shared bead, the required number of bridge beads (in this case seven), a shared bead, seven bridge beads and a shared bead (see box, opposite).

2 Take the needle through the fabric at the next mark and back through the last shared bead. Beginning with the bridge beads, pick up the same sequence of beads to make the next loop and continue to the end of the fabric.

3 To make a shaped net fringe: take the needle back through the beads in the last loop to the other side of the shared bead at the bottom of the loop. Work back across, adding bead loops as before. This time, however, instead of passing through your fabric, you will stitch through the bead at the bottom of each loop.

4 To make netting with straight edges bring a new thread and needle through each end shared bead. Pick up sufficient bridge beads and a shared bead to link into the next row of netting. Add more beads to the end threads as required when you work more rows of netting.

Making a fringe

A fringe is a decorative border of strands that are held closely together at one end and loosely at the other. You can attach a fringe to ribbons, fabric, ready-made items or beaded fabric made using bead stitches or loom work. You can use smaller beads at the top of the fringe and large beads for weight at the bottom.

1 To make the fringe, bring the thread out at the edge of the fabric or beadwork. Pick up the beads for the fringe strand from top to bottom and let them drop down to the fabric or beadwork.

2 Pick up a pivot bead and take the needle back through the other fringe beads on the strand only. Take a short stitch through the edge of the fabric or bead fabric ready to begin the next strand.

Simple tassel

Beaded tassels can be as simple or as ornate as you like. The easiest tassels to make are simply lots of fringe strands tied together with an end cap used to cover the thread ends.

Simple tassel

Beaded bead tassel

1 Pick up the selection of beads for the fringe strand. Pick up a pivot bead and then take the needle back through the other beads. Cut the thread, leaving a long tail.

2 Make sufficient strands to create the size of tassel you require. Feed the threads through an eye pin and tie with an overhand knot (see page 99). Secure the threads with a little clear glue and trim the ends.

3 Feed an end cap on to the eye pin so that the threads are completely covered. Trim the end of the wire to 7mm (⅜in) above the end cap and bend to one side. Make a loop with round-nosed pliers (see page 105).

Beaded bead tassel

Pressed cotton balls are ideal for tassel tops as they are lightweight and can be painted or dyed to match the bead colours. Round wooden beads are a suitable alternative but make sure the hole is large enough to attach the threads from the beaded strands.

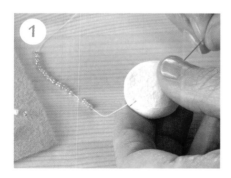

1 Tie a long thread through the hole in the large bead or pressed cotton ball. Pick up sufficient beads to reach round from one hole to the other. Take the needle back through the hole. A good tip is to insert a cocktail stick to stop the beads going down through the hole.

2 Keep adding rows of beads all the way round. Go back, filling in with shorter bead rows, and then tie the thread ends together. Try to keep the shorter bead rows evenly spaced around the ball.

3 Make several bead strands (see above). Tie the threads through an eye pin with an overhand knot and apply glue to secure. Trim the ends. Feed the eye pin up through the hole in the beaded bead, making a wrapped loop at the top. Attach a ribbon loop or cord.

Wirework

Wire-based jewellery or wirework projects are one of the most satisfying crafts to learn as the techniques are easy but produce stunning results in a minimal amount of time. Once you have a basic set of jewellery tools, you can use all the techniques explained here on different thicknesses and colours of wire to make your own unique pieces.

Cutting wire

You can always use strong craft scissors to cut finer wires, but it is better to invest in a pair of good-quality wire cutters, available from most beading shops (see page 16). Wire cutters have a flat side and an angled side.

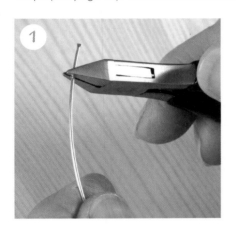

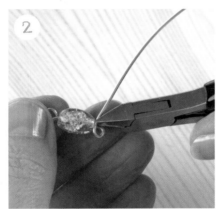

1 Cut with the flat side towards the work to get a straight cut on the end of the wire.

2 When cutting a wire that crosses over another wire, use the very tips of the blades to get as close as possible to the crossover point.

Bending wire

You need to apply firm pressure to get wire to bend where you want it to. Avoid pliers with a serrated surface, which will damage the wire.

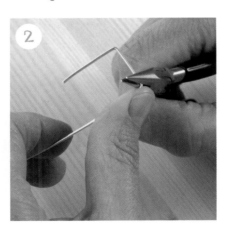

1 Hold the wire firmly with flat-nosed pliers so that the edge of the jaw is exactly where you want the wire to bend. Rotate the pliers to create the desired angle.

2 To create a right angle (90 degrees), hold the tail of the wire and push up against the jaws of the pliers with your thumb.

Twisting wire

You can use this technique to create texture, add body to the wire and make coiling and bending much smoother, as the wire is less likely to kink.

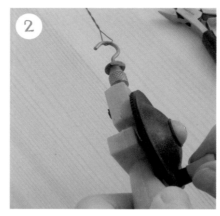

1 Use a bead to give you leverage for twisting the wire. Hold the bead between your finger and thumb and roll it round and round until the wire is evenly twisted along its length.

2 A cord maker or hand drill is ideal for twisting lengths of wire. Loop the wire over the hook, secure the ends in a vice and turn the handle to twist. Take care when releasing the wire, as it can spring up.

Making a bead link

Bead links have a loop at each end of the wire with one or more beads in the middle. This technique is easy to learn and ideal for beginners, but you can also use the head pin plain loop method shown opposite. If you use an eye pin to make the link, begin at step 2 or use the plain loop method opposite.

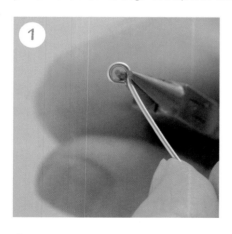

1 To make the first loop, hold the wire about 6mm (¼in) from the end of the round-nosed pliers so that the tip of the wire is level with the jaws. Rotate the pliers to make a loop. Change the position of the pliers and bend the wire back slightly to straighten the loop.

2 Feed the beads you require on to the end of the wire. Hold the wire in the jaws of the round-nosed pliers about 1mm (¹⁄₁₆in) from the beads. Wind the wire around the pliers to make a loop.

3 Cut the wire where it crosses using the very tip of the wire cutters (see page 103). Hold the ring with flat-nosed pliers and bend back to straighten.

Joining a link to a bead dangle

Use flat-nosed pliers to open one of the loops by pushing the cut end back, attach the other section and then close by reversing the action.

Using head pins and eye pins

Resembling large dressmaker's pins, head pins are used to make bead dangles or charms that can be hung from bracelets and necklaces or attached to bead links to make earrings. Eye pins are similar but have a large loop at one end.

Plain loop

This is an easy way to make a loop in head pins and eye pins, as they are made with a harder wire than normal jewellery wire. If the bead slides over the head pin, add a smaller bead such as a seed bead first.

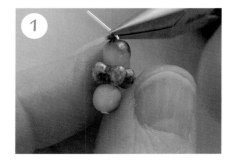

1 Trim the wire to 7mm–1cm (⅜–½in) above the top bead. The distance will depend on the wire thickness and the size of the loop required. Make a right-angled bend close to the bead (see page 103).

2 Hold the tip of the wire with round-nosed pliers and rotate the pliers to bend the wire partway around the tip.

3 Reposition the pliers and continue rotating the pliers until the tip touches the wire and the loop is in the centre.

Wrapped loop

This is stronger than the plain loop and ideal for beads with slightly larger holes.

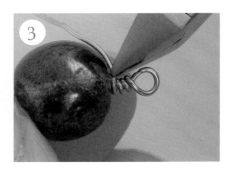

1 You will need at least 3cm (1¼in) of wire above the last bead. Hold the wire 1–2mm (¹⁄₁₆in) above the bead with snipe-nosed pliers and bend the wire at a right angle.

2 Hold the wire close to the bend with round-nosed pliers and wrap the tail all the way around to form a loop.

3 Hold the loop firmly in round- or flat-nosed pliers and wind the wire tail around the stem, covering the gap between the loop and the bead. Trim the tail.

Using filigree caps

These delicate metal caps are available in several sizes to suit different beads and look especially good with pearls. They give a piece of jewellery a more ornate and slightly antique look. Select the correct size to fit the beads you are using. Add the filigree cap at one or both ends of the bead and then continue adding other beads.

Attaching earring wires

Earring wires have a split loop at the bottom that can be opened and closed in a similar way to jump rings (see below). Hold the earring wire in one hand and the loop with flat-nosed pliers. Bring the pliers towards you to open. Attach the earring and reverse the action to close the loop.

Jump rings

One of the most versatile jewellery findings, jump rings are usually round and sometimes oval. They should never be pulled apart to open, as the shape will be distorted.

Opening and closing

Hold the jump ring with two pairs of pliers, ideally both flat-nosed pliers, or use round-nosed with a pair of flat-nosed pliers. To open the ring, bring one pair of pliers towards you. Attach another ring, chain or jewellery finding. Reverse the action to close.

Making jump rings

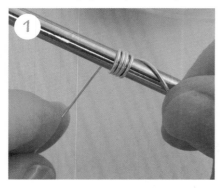

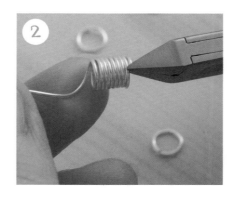

1 Choose a rod of the required diameter – knitting needles are ideal. Hold the end of the wire at one end and wrap tightly around the rod.

2 Slide the closely wound spring off the needle. Use wire cutters to cut each jump ring in turn. Flip the wire cutters over to trim the end each time with the flat edge of the cutters before cutting the next ring.

3 To tension the jump rings so that they stay closed, push the ends slightly so that they overlap on one side and then the other. Pull back and the ends will spring together.

Making chain with jump rings

This is an easy technique, and to speed up the process, you can join rings together in groups of three.

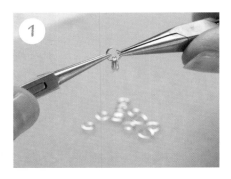

1 Open one jump ring using two pairs of flat- or snipe-nosed pliers, and pick up two more jump rings. Close the jump ring using a reverse action.

2 Make several groups of three rings. Open another jump ring and add two groups of three rings. Close the ring again.

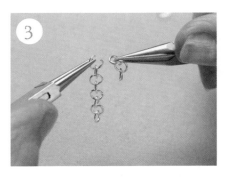

3 Continue adding groups of three with a single jump ring until the chain is as long as you require.

Spacing beads with crimps

Bead stringing wires such as Tigertail, Softflex and other coated wires can't be knotted and so the beads are spaced using crimps, which are available in a range of sizes. You can use flat-nosed pliers to secure the crimps or special crimping pliers for a more professional finish.

Secure a crimp on the wire. * Add a bead and a second crimp. Hold the wire up so that they drop down against the secured crimp. Squeeze the second crimp in position. Pick up another crimp and secure the desired distance from the first bead. Repeat from * until all the beads are added.

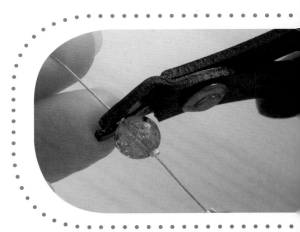

Using flat-nosed pliers

Squeeze the crimp with flat-nosed pliers until it is flat. The edges can be sharp, but as the crimp remains quite wide, this is often the best technique for beads with large holes.

Using crimping pliers

Squeeze the crimp in the oval with the dip to make it curl. Move the crimp to the other oval and compress it into a rounded shape. This is the neatest technique for crimps that are used as a decorative feature in a jewellery design.

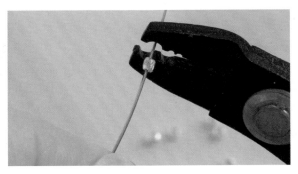

Attaching fastenings with crimps

Use this secure method to create a loop in bead stringing wire or monofilament thread so that you can attach a jump ring or fastening.

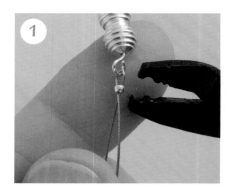

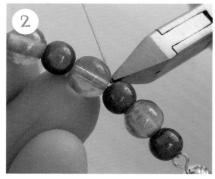

1 Thread the crimp on to the wire, pick up a jump ring or fastening and feed the tail back through the crimp to create a loop. Compress the crimp (see page 107) so that it sits 1–2mm (1/16–1/10in) from the ring or fastening.

2 Continue stringing beads. At the other end, pick up a crimp and the jump ring or fastening. Feed the tail back through the crimp and a few beads. Compress the crimp as before and trim the tail between the beads.

Making a spring

Wrap wire around a knitting needle or similar object to make a tight spring.

1 Hold the tail of the wire in the palm of your hand and carefully wrap the other end around the knitting needle so that the wires fit tightly together.

2 Slide the spring off the needle and trim the ends neatly using the flat side of the wire cutters.

Coiling wire

Coils of wire add a decorative touch to jewellery making. Use round-nosed pliers to begin and flat-nosed pliers with smooth jaws to bend the wire in a loose or tight coil.

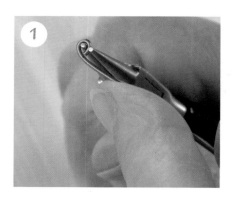

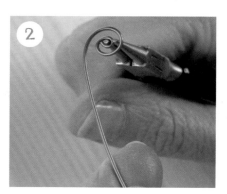

1 To begin use round-nosed pliers to make a small loop at the end of the wire. Hold the wire at the very end of the pliers and bend the wire round until it touches the tail again.

2 To make the coil hold the wire 2.5cm (1in) from the pliers and bend the wire gently round, moving the pliers in the loop until it is the size required.

Chain maille

Linking jump rings together to make chain or jewellery is known as chain maille. This ancient technique is still used to make chain mail garments today. There are simple patterns such as two-in-two chain and flower chain but you can experiment and create some of your own (see Chain Maille Bracelet, page 29).

Two-in-two chain

Jump rings can be linked to make a length of chain. You can simply link single jump rings together or link together in pairs or even threes to make a more ornate chain. Have a supply of open and closed rings ready to make this chain.

1 Open two jump rings and loop one through four jump rings. Close the ring with two pairs of pliers (see page 106). Attach a second ring through the four rings in the same way.

2 Hold so that you have a chain of pairs of jump rings (three to start). Pick up two closed rings on an open ring and loop through the top pair on the chain. Close the ring just added and add another through the same four rings. Repeat until the chain is the required length.

Flower chain

Interlink three jump rings together to make little 'flower' shapes and then join all the flowers together to make a pretty chain with jump rings.

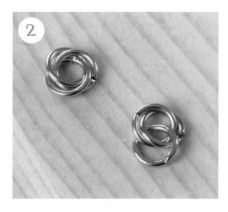

1 Join two rings together. Open a third ring and loop it through where the first two overlap. Close the ring.

2 Group the rings into a flower shape. If the flower shape isn't compact, like the sample on the right of this image, you need to flip the loose ring so that they all nestle close together, like the sample on the left.

3 Make several flowers. Loop an open jump ring through two flower shapes and close. Pick up further flowers one at time with a jump ring, loop through the end flower in the chain and close.

Threading and Stringing

There are many ways to string beads and lots of different materials, so how do you choose what to use? The first consideration is the style you are looking for – perhaps a fun piece, or a more substantial design in an ethnic, classic or contemporary style. This can give an indication of the stringing material such as elastic for a fun bracelet, waxed cotton for an ethnic style, silk thread for a classic design or organza ribbon and bead stringing wire for a contemporary look. Take into account the beads you have chosen too; their weight and the size of the holes determines the strength and thickness of the threading material as you don't want the jewellery to stretch, break or fray.

Making a continuous loop

Necklaces over 61cm (24in) don't need a fastening, so select from the following methods to join the ends according to whichever type of stringing material you are using.

Elastic thread

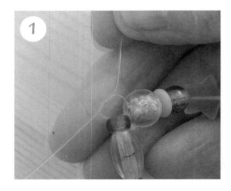

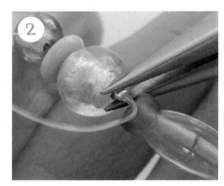

1 Tie the ends of the thread together, working two reef (square) knots (see page 99) one after the other, and hide the knot inside one of the beads with a large hole.

2 Alternatively, feed the opposite ends through a crimp and squeeze to secure (see page 107). Two crimps spaced a few beads apart is even more secure.

Bead thread or cord

Tie the ends with a reef (square) knot (see page 99) and hide the knot in a bead with a larger hole, or use the following more secure technique.

1 Before you begin, make sure you can pass a double length of thread through the bead holes. String the beads, leaving 10cm (4in) at each end. Pass one end of the thread through five or six beads.

2 Using the tail thread, work a half-hitch knot (see page 99) over the main thread. Pass the end through another two beads and knot again. Secure each knot with a drop of jewellery glue. Repeat with the other tail, working in the opposite direction. Pass the ends through a few more beads and trim the ends neatly.

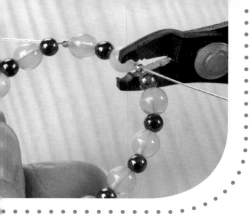

Bead stringing wire

As this stringing material can't be knotted, thread a crimp between two beads and add another crimp a few beads along. Thread the wire from the other end through both crimps. Pull the wire taut and secure the crimps with flat-nosed or crimping pliers (see page 107).

Bead stoppers

When working some bead designs, it is essential to stop the beads falling off the end of the thread or bead stringing wire. Bead stopper springs are a great little tool for this purpose, or use a stop bead instead.

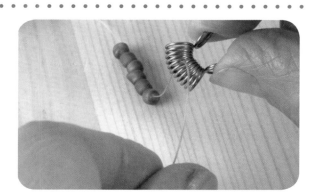

Using a bead stopper spring

Squeeze the levers on the bread spring and slot the thread or wire between the coils. You can move the spring up and down the thread as required.

Using a stop bead

Pick up a bead on the thread or wire and hold the bead about 10cm (4in) from the end. Take the needle back through the bead two or three times to secure.

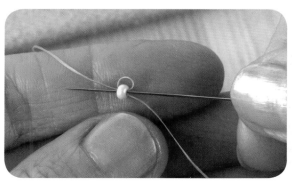

Using a bead spinner

It takes a little practice to become proficient, but this tool, used in conjunction with a curved big-eye needle (see page 19), will enable you to string beads surprisingly quickly. Thread the needle. Pour beads into the spinner. Turn the handle slowly to get the beads spinning (they do not need to be moving quickly). Lower the threaded needle into the beads so that it is fairly horizontal and the beads should whiz up the needle.

Spacing beads with knots

Bead strings are usually knotted to prevent the beads from rubbing together and also to stop the beads falling off if the thread breaks. There are two methods – overhand or reef (square) knots. Whichever method you use, allow an additional 3mm (⅛in) for each knot on finer threads and more for thicker threads.

Using overhand knots

This method is often used for stringing pearls. Add fastenings using a calotte/knot cover (see opposite).

1 Tie an overhand knot after the calotte or clamshell calotte by looping the tail over and under the main thread (see page 99). Pick up the first bead and then tie another loose overhand knot.

2 Slip a tapestry needle into the loop, then manoeuvre the knot along the cord until it is sitting next to the bead. Remove the needle as the knot tightens. Continue adding beads, tying a new knot after each bead.

Using reef (square) knots

This is an easier technique to work, but the knots aren't quite as neat. It is ideal for necklaces and bracelets with chunky beads.

1 Attach a fastening so that there is a double thread and tie a reef (square) knot (see page 99). Use a big-eye needle (see page 19) to take both threads through the first bead.

2 Tie a reef (square) knot on the other side of the bead. Pick up another bead using the big-eye needle and tie another reef (square) knot. Repeat as required.

Sliding knot fastening

With thicker cords and thongs you can make simple slide fastenings to allow you to take the jewellery on and off. Cut the cord long enough to go over your head or hand and allow about 20cm (8in) extra for the knots and slide fastening. Thread beads on to the length of cord and position them in the middle.

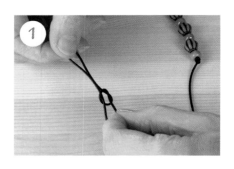

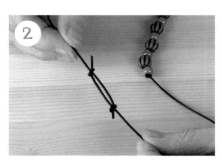

1 Arrange the cords so that they are parallel and the ends are at opposite sides. Pass the left end under the other cord and then work an overhand knot (see page 99).

2 Repeat with the right-hand end, tying the knot so that the end is facing in the opposite direction to the first knot. Pull the knots apart to shorten the necklace and away from each other to lengthen. Adjust the knots along the length until you get a good fit.

Adding fastenings

Depending on the stringing material you are using, choose one of these techniques to attach the fastening.

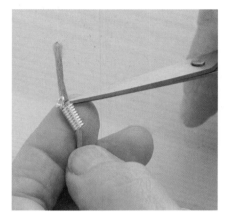

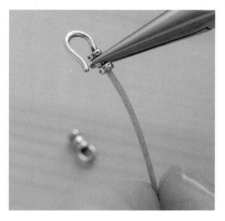

Spring ends

Feed the end of the cord right through the spiral crimp and trim the end. Move the spiral crimp slightly to hide the raw edges and squeeze only the bottom end ring to secure.

Thong ends

Slot the leather thong between the lugs on the fastening and squeeze one side down and then the other with flat-nosed pliers to secure.

Decorative crimp fastenings

These have a crimp incorporated into the design, and are ideal for finishing bead stringing wire or fine waxed cord. Insert the end of the wire into the fastening and squeeze the crimp ring with flat-nosed or crimping pliers to secure (see page 107).

Adding a knot cover

Calottes or clamshell calottes are used to cover the raw ends of thread, wire, cord or fine ribbon when stringing beads. Calottes have a hole in the side and clamshell calottes have a hole in the hinge.

Using a knot

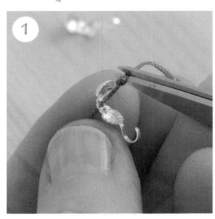

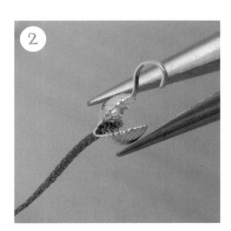

1 Feed the open calotte on to the thread or cord and tie a figure-of-eight or overhand knot (see page 99). Trim the end close to the knot.

2 Bring the calotte down so that it covers the knot. Close the calotte with flat-nosed pliers.

Using a crimp or a seed bead

Bead stringing wires or other coated wires that cannot be knotted easily can be secured inside the calotte with a crimp or a seed bead.

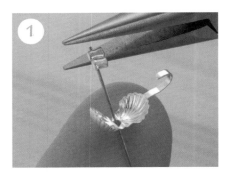

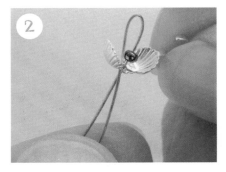

1 Thread the wire through the clamshell calotte, pick up a crimp and squeeze to flatten it. Close the clamshell with flat-nosed pliers. Then pick up the beads and repeat at the other end.

2 Alternatively for heavy beads, pick up a clamshell calotte and a seed bead. Feed the end back through the clamshell. Close the clamshell with flat-nosed pliers.

3 String a few beads over both the wire and tail and add a crimp. Squeeze the crimp, add a few more beads then trim the tail.

Using end cones

These decorative findings are used to cover large knots at the end of necklaces or bracelets. They are particularly useful for multi-strand necklaces or for thick yarn or ribbon. Pick a style and size of end cone that will completely hide any knots or raw ends but fit snugly around the beads.

Bead stringing wire

1 Finish multi-strand necklaces by making a loop on the end of each strand with a crimp. Attach the loops to an eye pin and feed the end through the end cone.

2 If you are planning to go from a multi-strand to a single-strand, make a crimp loop on a length of bead stringing wire and thread through the multi-strands.

Cord or ribbon

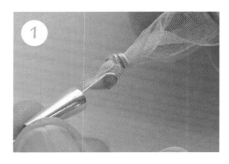

1 Tie a large overhand knot at the end of the cord or ribbon (see page 99). Wrap craft wire around the knot, leaving a tail at the top. Apply a few drops of jewellery glue over the knot before adding the end cone.

2 If necessary, add a small bead to reduce the hole size of the end cone. Use round-nosed pliers to make a plain or wrapped loop on the end of the wire (see page 105), then attach a clasp.

Ropes and Cords

Beaded ropes and cords are a versatile way to work with beads. Although often associated with bracelets, you can use long ropes to make necklaces or handbag handles (see Spiral Bag, page 70) and short lengths for earrings (see Herringbone Earrings, page 57).

Spiral twist

This is one of the easiest ropes to learn as you simply keep adding the same sequence of beads over and over again. This style of rope requires no additional finishing. There is a single thread at each end, which can be used to sew on a fastening or add a bead loop.

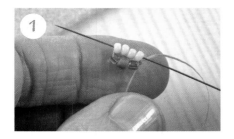

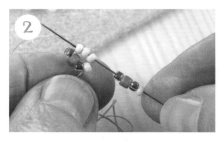

1 Pick up four size 11 opaque seed beads, then a three bead sequence of a size 11 transparent seed bead, a size 8 bead and a size 11 transparent seed bead and tie into a circle. Pass the needle through the four opaque seed beads again.

2 Pick up one opaque seed bead and the same three bead sequence. Take the needle through the last three opaque seed beads on the spiral. Pull the thread up and then take the needle through the last opaque seed bead added. Pull the thread taut.

3 Repeat step 2 to add a second loop of beads. Continue repeating step 2, making sure that the loops lie to the same side each time and right next to each other. After four or five repeats the spiral effect will be obvious.

Tubular herringbone stitch

Tubular herringbone stitch is easy to learn and quick to work as two beads are added at a time in a 'V' shape. The angle of the beads gives the stitch a wonderful texture that is enhanced by using triangle or hex beads.

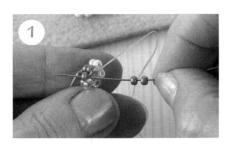

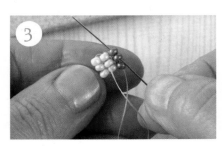

1 Work a double row ladder stitch tube (see page 94) by picking up four dark seed beads and tying in a circle. Pick up two light beads and take the needle through the last two dark beads and the two just added. Add two more light then two pairs of medium beads. Join the ends to make a tube by taking the thread through the first and last beads twice.

2 To work the herringbone stitch * pick up two beads the same colour as the bead you've just gone through and take the needle down through the next bead. Bring the needle up through the first bead in the next stack. Repeat from * until you reach the first stack again.

3 To 'step up' ready for the next round simply take the needle through the top two beads on the next stack. Repeat from * until the rope or tube is the required length.

Bead Knitting

Knitting with beads is easy as there are no fancy stitches to learn. You only need to know how to cast on and off and how to knit you will be able to make all sorts of wonderful beaded items.

Casting on

There are two methods of casting on, but the method shown here is the simplest and produces a nice firm edge to the knitting.

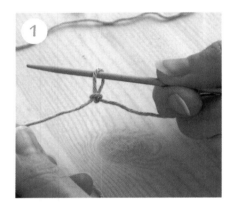

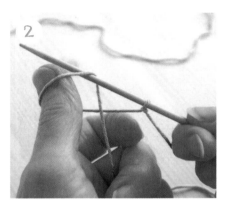

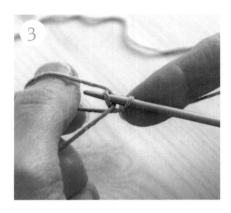

1 Make a slip knot part of the way down the yarn, leaving a tail. Leave 1–2.5cm (½–1in) per stitch, depending on the thickness of the yarn. Fit the slip knot on to the right-hand needle.

2 Wrap the yarn around your left thumb and slot the needle in the loop as shown.

3 Wrap the tail end of the yarn between thumb and needle and lift the loop over on to the needle to create the stitch. Repeat to make the required number of stitches.

Knitting a stitch

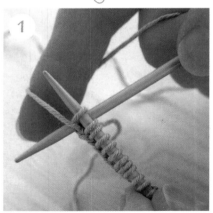

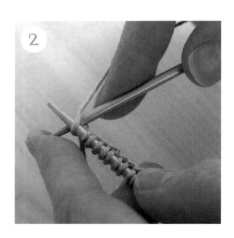

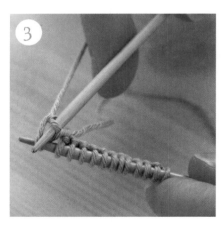

1 Put the spare needle into the first loop and take the yarn over the lower needle.

2 Holding the yarn taut, push the needle and bring the other needle through to form a stitch.

3 Lift the stitch off the lower needle. Begin at step 1 again and continue to the end of the row.

Making one stitch

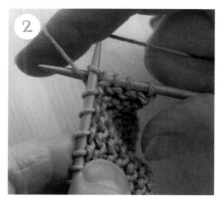

1 Knit a stitch as normal but keep the stitch on the left-hand needle.

2 Knit into the back of the stitch on the left needle before letting it slip off on to the right needle (thus creating two stitches where there was one).

Knitting two together

1 Insert the right-hand needle into the next two stitches from left to right.

2 Put the yarn over the needle and lift both stitches off together.

Adding beads into knitting

This quick and easy technique adds beads to the back of the knitting as you work, although this will be the right side of the knitting. The beads are added on every second row and lie more or less horizontally.

1 Pick up sufficient beads on the yarn. Cast on 14 stitches and knit two rows. Bring about 2.5cm (1in) of beads up near the right-hand needle and tension the yarn around your little finger. * Knit two stitches and bring a bead up to the right needle at the back of the knitting.

2 Knit the next stitch, making sure you don't pull the bead through the loop of yarn. Add beads on every stitch to the last stitch. Knit the last stitch. Keep the yarn fairly taut so that the bead is held firmly in position.

3 On the next row the beads will show on the front of the knitting. Knit a row without beads and then repeat from *. At the end of the piece of knitting knit two rows without beads and cast off (see page 118).

Casting off

1 Knit the first two stitches in the row. Insert the left-hand needle into the first stitch and lift it over the second stitch and carefully off the end of the needle.

2 Continue knitting one stitch at a time, lifting the previous stitch over the one just knitted until you have cast (bound) off the whole row.

3 To finish off a piece of knitting, cut the yarn and pull the last stitch until the tail comes through the stitch. Sew in the tail or use it for sewing pieces of knitting together.

Adding beads to fancy yarn

If the beads you want to work with have too small holes or the yarn is too thick, knobbly or fragile, you can string beads on to a fine yarn and then knit the two strands together as one, or string the bead yarn behind the knitting and only include it when you want to add a bead (see Beaded Scarf, page 47).

String the beads on to a thin yarn or thread. Hold the two yarns together and work as one thread. Cast on and knit until you are ready to add a bead. Bring the bead up the finer yarn to the needle ready to add the bead. If you knit with thicker yarn and only bring the thread into the stitch when adding a bead, make sure the finer thread isn't too tight across the back of the knitting.

Bead Embroidery

Bead embroidery transforms everyday objects into luxury items. It is used in several of the projects in this book including Flower Cluster Box (page 67), Trinket Box (page 68), and Beaded Tweed Bag (page 71).

Preparing to embroider

If the fabric is flimsy it needs to be supported in a hoop or frame while working so that the beadwork does not scrunch up. If possible use a backing fabric to anchor any threads on the reverse side. Use a double length of sewing thread in the needle or one strand of a beading thread such as Nymo.

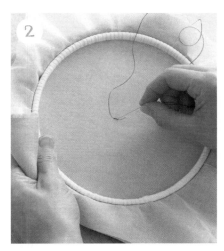

1 Cut the fabric and any backing fabric at least 5cm (2in) larger all round than the finished piece. Fit the fabric into an embroidery hoop or on to a rotary frame.

2 Take two tiny backstitches on the reverse side and bring the needle out on the right side where you want the beadwork to begin. You are now ready to start your bead embroidery.

Sewing beads on individually

When sewing beads individually it is essential to secure the thread carefully on the reverse side when beginning and finishing off.

1 It is advisable to go through each bead twice to secure it. This makes it less likely the bead will fall off and also prevents the thread pulling through if the beads are spaced out.

2 When stitching larger beads, space the two threads out in the hole so that the bead is held firmly in position. For extra security, take a tiny backstitch on the reverse side before sewing on the next bead.

Sewing on beads with backstitch

Backstitch can be used to add individual beads or several at a time. Only pick up one or two beads to follow a curved line but pick up more the straighter the line, taking the needle back through the last bead each time.

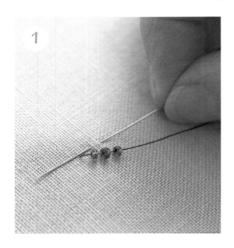

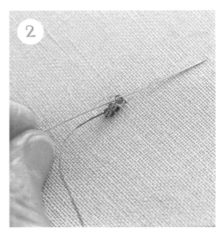

1 Pick up three beads and let them drop down to where the thread emerges. Put the needle back through the fabric at the end of the three beads. Take a small backstitch and bring the needle out between the last two beads.

2 Put the needle back through the last bead and then pick up another three beads ready to begin again. When a line of beads is complete, secure on the back of the work with a few tiny backstitches.

Stacking single beads

Add larger beads or lots of small beads one above the other to create a range of different textures (see Flower Cluster Box, page 67). Bugle beads also work well adding extra height and interest to a bead embroidery design. Vary the sizes of the beads in each stack to create a range of shapes and textures. Make a row of stacked beads along the edge of a piece of fabric to create a fringe.

1 Bring the thread out where you want to add a large bead. Pick up the large bead and a small seed bead. Take the needle back through the larger bead only and through to the reverse side.

2 To create a stack, pick up several small beads and a small pivot bead, which can be the same or a contrast to the other beads. Miss the pivot bead and take the needle back through the other beads and through to the reverse side of the fabric.

Couching

Couching is used to apply a string of beads to fabric in a straight line or curve. You need to use two needles on separate lengths of thread – one beading needle and one sewing needle.

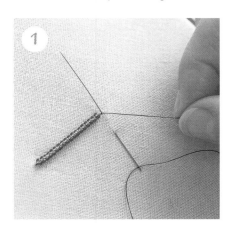

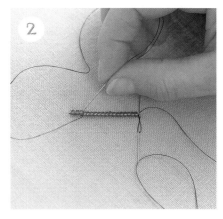

1 Bring the beading needle out where you want the beadwork to begin. Pick up sufficient beads to complete the line. If the beads are being couched in a straight line, put the beading needle in the fabric and wrap the thread around to hold the beads taut.

2 Bring the second thread out between the first and second beads. Take the thread over the bead string and back through the fabric. Work down the bead strand, stitching between every bead or in groups of three or four. At the end take both threads to the reverse side and secure them.

Attaching sequins

There are several ways to attach sequins to fabric. You can sew the sequins on individually or overlapping in a row. These techniques are also suitable for attaching washer-style beads.

To attach single sequins

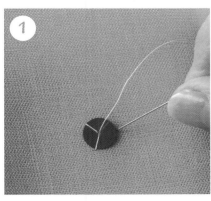

1 Secure the thread on the reverse side. Position the sequin where you want it and bring the needle up through the middle. Take the needle back down at the side. A second stitch secures the sequin and a third in a 'Y' shape will make it secure enough to wash.

2 Alternatively, secure the thread on the reverse side. Bring the needle up through the middle of the sequin. Pick up a seed bead and take the needle back down through the sequin only. Make a tiny backstitch on the reverse before attaching the next sequin.

To attach sequins in a row

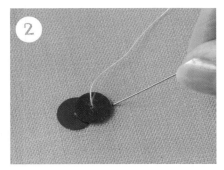

1 Position the first sequin and take a stitch from the centre hole and over the right hand edge. Bring the needle and thread back through to the right side.

2 Position the next sequin so that it covers the last stitch. Bring the thread up through the hole in the second sequin and over the right-hand edge. Repeat until the line is as long as required.

Templates and Charts

Trinket Box chart (page 68)

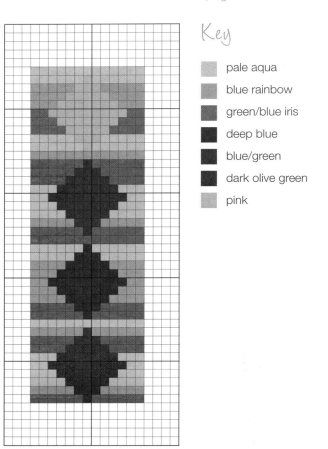

Key

- pale aqua
- blue rainbow
- green/blue iris
- deep blue
- blue/green
- dark olive green
- pink

Heart's Desire Key Ring template (page 80)

Friendship Bracelet chart (page 28)

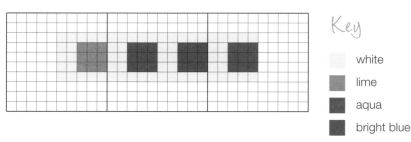

Key

- white
- lime
- aqua
- bright blue

Amulet Purse chart (page 62)

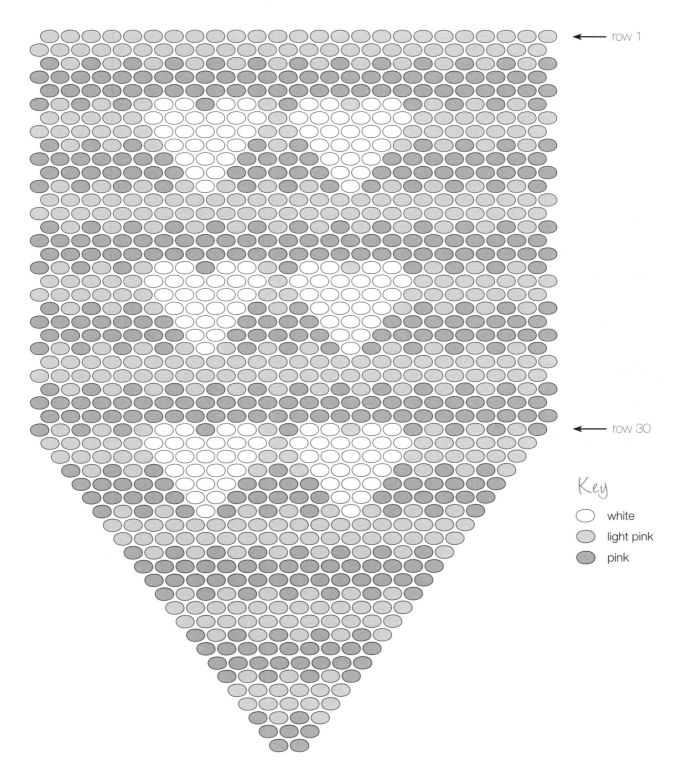

← row 1

← row 30

Key

⬭ white

⬭ light pink

⬭ pink

Bead Product Details

This list contains details of the various materials and products used in the projects (available at the date of original publication) – see Suppliers on pages 126–7 for contact details. Those beads without a shop reference or a specific reference in brackets are either fashion beads without precise details or basic beads generally available from your local bead shop.

Bracelets & Bangles

Charm Bracelet (page 22)
Silver-plated chain bracelet – local bead shop; beads and findings – The Spellbound Bead Company; Long crystal bugles – Creative Beadcraft

Ribbon Chain Bracelet (page 26)
Gold-plated chain with 5mm links, multicolour pebbles 15mm – Gütermann (616 494) colour (3665); metallic bead mix – The Viking Loom (BMB 16)

Hundreds and Thousands Bracelet (page 27)
Cracked horn round beads – Kars; antique silver beads – local bead shop; ceramic beads – Bead Crazy; size 11 triangle beads – Out On A Whim (hematite matte F451); silver-lined seed beads and cylinder beads – Rayher Hobby (14 120 22, moonstone 14 755 120, steel grey 14 751 568, anthracite 14 751 572)

Friendship Bracelet (page 28)
Cylinder beads – Spellbound Bead Company (white lustre DB201, limeaid DB237, aqua DB079, medium blue iris DB076)

Chain Maille Bracelet (page 29)
8mm cube and 10mm round crushed ice beads – John Lewis (5505)

Spiral Bracelets (page 30)
Bracelet in steps: size 8 seed beads (aqua green 335), size 11 seed beads (mint green 336 and grass green 547); other bracelet pictured: size 11 hex beads (bright green 257, green 452), size 11 seed beads (mint green 336) – all The London Bead Company

Waxed Cotton Bracelet (page 31)
Selection of beads from local bead shops

Bugle Bracelet (page 32)
3mm bugles – Beads Direct (size 1, in purple iris matt, lilac satin and white satin); 3mm hex beads – Beads Direct (silver-lined clear)

Square Stitch Bracelet (page 33)
Size 11 Toho seed beads (rainbow metal matte F463K and gold lustre green tea 457), 3mm cube (steel gold iris 462) – Out on a Whim; 12mm round glass beads – Bead Crazy (pale creamy yellow)

Chain Maille Watch (page 34)
All beads from a selection – Spellbound Bead Company

Necklaces & Scarves

Jadeite Pendant (page 36)
Jadeite bangle – The Mineral Warehouse; flower-shaped beads and resin leaf – Bead Time; other beads and charms – local bead shop

Luscious Links (page 40)
Bead selection, wire and findings – local bead shop

Love Heart (page 41)
Foil beads – The Bead Shop Edinburgh; other beads and charms – local bead shop

Sheer 'n' Swinging Scarf (page 42)
Bead fringing, silk and organza – John Lewis

Wood Works (page 43)
Dark wood beads – Gütermann (Craft Factory Natural World CF05/48A 42mm, 48B 50mm, 101 round); painted wood and coloured beads – Bead Crazy

Delightful Discs (page 44)
Jade donut pendant – Hobbycraft; size 11 seed beads – Out On A Whim (teal metal iris 459D)

Devoré Scarf (page 45)
4mm glass pearls (dark brown 3350, gold 2885), 9mm seed beads (apricot 1345, orange 1850, burnt orange 1970) – Gütermann

Rock 'n' Roll (page 46)
All beads from a selection – Bead Crazy

Beaded Scarf (page 47)
Size 8 seed beads – Stitch 'n' Craft Beads (light seafoam AB 263); 4mm faceted beads (smoke grey 6975), 6mm faceted beads (transparent AB and matt AB turquoise) – Gütermann

Netted Scarf (page 48)
4mm cube beads – Out on a Whim (hematite 451); mix of pewter glass seed beads – local bead shop

Rings & Earrings

Peyote Stitch Rings (page 50)
Size 11 seed beads (rainbow metal matte F463K, emerald raspberry gold lustre 318M), 3 x 4mm drop beads (multi iris 455) – Out on a Whim; 2mm bugle beads (pale pink 4805 and dark pink 5165), size 9 seed beads (silver-lined rose) – Gütermann

Pearl Drop Earrings (page 54)
White turquoise beads – Ilona Biggins; white glass pearls – Rayher Hobby (14 403 102)

Aztec Fringe Earrings (page 55)
Size 11 and 8 seed beads – Out on a Whim (SL red matt AB F638, SL gold matt AB F634)

Clustered Berries Ring (page 56)
Flower-shaped beads – Bead Time; other beads – local bead shop

Herringbone Earrings (page 57)
Cylinder beads – Spellbound Bead Company (rhodium plated 032); 3mm Toho bugles (nickel matt 451D), size 6 Toho (nickel matt 451D) – Out on a Whim; 7mm twisted bugles – Gütermann (gun metal)

Stardust Sparkle Earrings (page 58)
Beads from a selection – Bead Crazy

Pear Cluster Earrings (page 59)
Glass pearls – Bead Crazy; leaf beads – Bead Time

Ready-to-Wear Earrings (page 60)
12 and 15mm multicolour glass beads – Gütermann (7160); 3 x 7mm cylinder beads and decorative antique gold head pins – The Bead Shop Edinburgh

Bags & Boxes

Amulet Purse (page 62)
3mm bugles – Spellbound Bead Company (SL crystal clear RC031), size 11 cylinder beads (lined light pink DB082, pink DB106, white lustre DB201)

Starry Nights Jewellery Pouches (page 66)
Organza – John Lewis; star and round sequins – The London Bead Company

Flower Cluster Box (page 67)
Bead selection – The London Bead Company

Trinket Box (page 68)
Size 11 cylinder beads – Out on a Whim (Pale aqua DB083, green/blue iris, blue rainbow DB0111, pink 0106, blue lined aqua DB085, seafoam lustre DB0112, emerald gold lustre DB0125)

Spiral Bag (page 70)
Size 6 seed beads (teal matte AB), size 10 Miyuki triangle (sparkling aqua, blue-lined 1822), size 11 seed bead (dark brown); washer beads (turquoise), 8 x 6mm flat oval (brown) – The Bead Scene

Beaded Tweed Bag (page 71)
Size 6 seed beads (light amethyst colour-lined fuchsia matt F399D), size 11 seed beads (metallic rainbow transparent red AB 254, emerald raspberry gold lustre 318M) – Out on a Whim; size 9 and 11 seed beads (pink and white) size 12 seed beads (pinky-red), 6mm faceted glass beads (pink 5185) – Gütermann

Dolly Bag (page 72)
Silk dupion – John Lewis; sequin trims – Hobbycraft

Beaded Accessories

Wild Berry Tiara (page 76)
Size 11 seed beads (wild blueberry 03026, heather mauve 02024, matt lilac 02081, brilliant shamrock 02054, citron 02031 and autumn green 03029), bugle beads (willow 72045 and 82045, and rainbow 82045 and 92045) – Mill Hill Beads

Heart's Desire Key Ring (page 80)
Bead selection – The Viking Loom; wire, findings, swivel hook fastening and chain – local bead shop

Beaded Mules (page 81)
Petite beads – Mill Hill Beads (Crystal 40161, tapestry teal 42029, rainbow 40374, crystal aqua 42017, crystal pink 42018, heather mauve 42024)

Tasselled Key Rings (page 82)
Size 11 seed beads and 6mm bugles – The London Bead Company (Lime 239, fuchsia 255)

Brick Stitch Rosettes (page 83)
10mm round crushed glass bead – Gütermann (wine colour 5505); size 11 seed beads – Out on a Whim (raspberry bronze iris 460A); 4mm and 6mm Swarovski bicone crystals – The Bead Shop Edinburgh (rose 209)

Crystal Tiara (page 84)
6, 8 and 10mm Swarovski crystals (round, clear AB), 4mm Swarovski bicone crystals (clear AB), 4, 6 and 8mm pearls (round ivory) – The Bead Shop Edinburgh

Summery Sandals (page 86)
Bead selection – The Spellbound Bead Company; wire – local bead shop

Medallion Belt (page 87)
Oliver Twists one-off decorative yarn pack – Bangles and Tat; size 10 Miyuki triangle beads (lined lime green 1119, chartreuse AB 1153), 4mm cubes (matte transparent lime green AB 143) – The Bead Scene

Dragonfly Pin (page 88)
Size 11 seed beads (antique cranberry 03003, desert peach 03052, cherry sorbet 03057 and ice 02010), petite seed beads (ice 402010) – Mill Hill Beads; 6mm burgundy crystals – Gütermann

Suppliers

UK and Europe

Bangles and Tat
Pass Courtyard, Off Market Street
Ashby de la Zouch LE65 1AG
Tel: 01530 560930
Email: banglesandtat@btconnect.com
www.banglesandtat.gbr.cc
(For beads and findings)

Bead Crazy
55 George Street
Perth PH1 5LB
Tel: 01738 442288
Email: info@beadcrazy.co.uk
www.beadcrazy.co.uk
(For bead and jewellery supplies)

Beads Direct
Tel: 0870 086 9877
Email: service@beadsdirect.co.uk
www.beadsdirect.co.uk
(For beads and findings)

Bead Time
5 Church Road, Ashford
Middlesex T15 2UG
Tel: 01784 252438
www.beadtime.co.uk
(For beads, findings and voile bags)

Creative Beadcraft
1 Marshall Street, London W1F 9BA
Tel: 020 7734 1982
Mail order tel: 01494 778818
Email: beads@creativebeadcraft.co.uk
www.creativebeadcraft.co.uk
(For beads and beading supplies)

E-beads
5G1 The Leather Market
11/13 Weston Street
London SE1 3ER
Tel: 0207 367 6217
Email: info@e-beads.co.uk
www.e-beads.co.uk
(For beads and jewellery findings)

Hobbycraft Superstores
(stores throughout UK)
Help Desk, The Peel Centre, St Ann Way
Gloucester, Gloucestershire GL1 5SF
For nearest store tel: 0800 027 2387
Mail order tel: 01202 596100
www.hobbycraft.co.uk
(For a huge range of craft supplies and Mill Hill beads)

Ilona Biggins
PO Box 600
Rickmansworth WD3 5WR
Tel: 01923 282998
Email: info@ilonabiggins.co.uk
www.ilonabiggins.co.uk
(For semi-precious beads and pearls)

John Lewis (stores throughout UK)
Tel: 08456 049 049
www.johnlewis.com
(For fabric, bead trimmings, beads, haberdashery)

James Hare Silks
PO Box 72, Monarch House, Queen Street
Leeds LS1 1LX
Tel: 0113 243 1204
www.jamesharesilks.co.uk
(For silk dupion and organza)

Kars
PO Box 272, Aylesbury
Buckinghamshire HP18 9FH
Tel: 01844 238080
Email: info@kars.nl
www.kars.biz
(For craft and hobby products)

Rayher Hobby
Fockestrasse 15
88471 Laupeim, Germany
Tel: 07392 7005 0
Email: info@rayher-hobby.de
www.rayher-hobby.de
(For beads, jewellery accessories and other craft supplies)

Stitch 'n' Craft Beads
Swans Yard Craft Centre, High Street
Shaftesbury, Dorset SP7 8JQ
Tel: 01747 830666
Email: enquiries@stitchncraft.co.uk
www.stitchncraft.co.uk
(For bead and craft supplies)

The Bead Scene
Unit 4, Wakefield Country Courtyard
Wakefield Lodge Estate, Pottersbury
Northamptonshire NN12 7QX
Tel: 01327 810388
Email: stephanie@thebeadscene.com
www.thebeadscene.com
(For beads and beading supplies)

The Bead Shop Edinburgh
6 Dean Park Street, Stockbridge
Edinburgh EH4 1JW
Tel: 0131 343 3222
Email: info@beadshopedinburgh.co.uk
www.beadshopscotland.co.uk
(For beads, findings, tools and books)

The Bead Shop Nottingham
104–106 Upper Parliament Street
Nottingham NG1 6LF
Tel: 0115 9588899
Email: info@mailorder-beads.co.uk
www.mailorder-beads.co.uk
(For beads and findings)

The Mineral Warehouse
Tel: 01749 813342
Email: sales@minware.co.uk
www.minware.co.uk
(For semi-precious beads)

The London Bead Company
339 Kentish Town Road, London NW5 2TJ
Tel: 0870 203 2323
Email: londonbead@dial.pipex.com
www.londonbeadco.co.uk
(For beads and findings)

The Scientific Wire Company
18 Raven Road
London E18 1HW
Tel: 0208 505 0002
www.wires.co.uk
(For all kinds of wire)

The Spellbound Bead Company
45 Tamworth Street, Lichfield
Staffordshire WS13 6JW
Tel: 01543 417650
www.spellboundbead.co.uk
(For beads and findings)

The Viking Loom
22 High Petergate
York Y01 7EH
Tel: 01904 765599
Email: vikingloom@vikingloom.co.uk
www.vikingloom.co.uk
(For bead strings and bead mixes)

USA

Firemountain Gems
1 Firemountain Way, Grants Pass
OR 97526-2373
Tel: 1-800-355-2137
www.firemountaingems.com
(For beads and jewellery supplies)

Mill Hill Beads
Tel: (608) 788-4600
www.millhillbeads.com
(For Mill Hill beads)

Joann
2361 Rosecrans Ave, Suite 360
El Segundo, CA 90245
Tel: 1-800-525-4951
www.joann.com
(For beads and general craft supplies)

M & J Trimmings
1008 Sixth Avenue, New York, NY 10018
Tel: 212 204 9595
www.mjtrim.com
(For beads, buttons, ribbons and trimmings)

Out On A Whim
121 E Cotati Ave
Cotati CA 94931
Tel: 1-707-664-8343
www.whimbeads.com
(For beads, findings and tools)

Acknowledgments

Many thanks to all the companies who so generously supplied materials for this book. Thanks to the whole team at D&C: Fiona, Cheryl, Jane, Ali, Jennifer, Lin, Ame, Jean, Lisa, Sarah, Sue and Prudence. Thanks also to photographers Ginette Chapman, Kim Sayer and Simon Whitmore, and to Ali Sharland, Rosemary Vernon and my sister Linda who allowed us to take over their homes for photography. Finally, thanks to Louise Smythson and my daughter Barley, who worked with me and assisted on several of the projects.

About the Author

Dorothy Wood is a talented and prolific beader, craft maker and author. Since completing a course in Advanced Embroidery and Textiles at Goldsmith's College, London, she has written over 20 craft books, and contributed to many others, on all kinds of subjects. This is Dorothy's eighth book for David & Charles, her previous books including the best-selling *Simple Glass Beading*, *Ultimate Necklace Maker* and *The Beader's Bible*. She also contributes to several well-known craft magazines, including *Make Jewellery*, *Knit Today*, *Beautiful Cards*, and *Cardmaking & Papercrafts*. Dorothy can be contacted via her website **www.dorothywood.co.uk**

Index